The Poetry of W. H. Auden

EDITED BY PAUL HENDO

Consultant editor: Nicolas Tredell

palgrave
macmillan

Published by
PALGRAVE MACMILLAN
Houndmills, Basingstoke, Hampshire RG21 6XS and
175 Fifth Avenue, New York, N. Y. 10010
Companies and representatives throughout the world

PALGRAVE MACMILLAN is the global academic imprint of the Palgrave
Macmillan division of St. Martin's Press, LLC and of Palgrave Macmillan Ltd.
Macmillan® is a registered trademark in the United States, United Kingdom
and other countries. Palgrave is a registered trademark in the European
Union and other countries.

First published 2000 by Icon Books Ltd

ISBN-13: 978-1-84046-046-9
ISBN-10: 1-84046-046-6

This book is printed on paper suitable for recycling and made from fully
managed and sustained forest sources. Logging, pulping and
manufacturing processes are expected to conform to the environmental
regulations of the country of origin.

A catalogue record for this book is available from the British Library.

Printed and bound in Great Britain by
CPI Antony Rowe, Chippenham and Eastbourne

CONTENTS

The Longer Poems

In this chapter Auden's return to the Christian faith is placed in the foreground through discussions of the longer 'religious' works of the 1940s. The relation of the poet to history, art and politics have undergone revision, and these shifts are discussed here.

CHAPTER SIX

The Later Collections

Here, the later collections are discussed through selected close readings, primarily those of Stan Smith and Lucy McDiarmid. Attention is focused on 'The Shield of Achilles' and 'In Praise of Limestone', while the later collection *About the House* is examined by Edward Callan.

Summary of Critical Texts

A map of the main Auden texts is laid out in chronological sequence.

Conclusion

Chronology of Auden's main works discussed in this text.

A NOTE ON REFERENCES AND QUOTATIONS

All references to Auden's poems will automatically refer to the 1991 or later revised editions of *W.H. Auden: Collected Poems*, edited by Edward Mendelson. This is the only collection that gathers together the long and the short poems in one volume. Pending the publication of the poems as part of Mendelson's authoritative series *The Collected Works of W.H. Auden*, the *Collected Poems* are the nearest we have to a complete set of the poems. References will be given in the body of the text as (*C.P.*, p.x). However, this work has significant omissions that are addressed by the important collection *The English Auden: Poems, Essays and Dramatic Writings 1927–1939*, also edited by Mendelson. This will appear in the body of the text as (*The English Auden*, p.x).

When the author of a cited extract simply gives a reference to a text, I have incorporated their end/footnote style into my scheme. I will announce notes as those of the author's at the beginning of the note.

In any quotation, a row of three dots indicates an editorial ellipsis within a single sentence or paragraph, and a row of six dots (that is, two ellipses) indicates an editorial omission of a paragraph break. I have marked editorial omissions in cited quotations by placing the ellipses in brackets thus [. . .].

INTRODUCTION

AUDEN'S CAREER flourished in spite of a series of transgressive and controversial problems. At first his work was too obscure and dense. This was compounded by his tendency to use personal references in his poetry which his audience could not place: 'it is evident that he has not taken enough trouble to make his private counters effective currency'.[1] Then there was the problem of Auden's left-wing politics, especially evident in the plays of the thirties written with Isherwood. Was he a fellow traveller? Was he simply *pretending* to be committed to Marxism while secretly laughing up his bourgeois sleeve? And speaking of travelling, what did he think he was doing in Iceland, Spain and China? Then there was the 'defection' to America at a sensitive time, just before the outbreak of World War Two. Then there was the problem of Auden's return to the Christian faith – disappointing to all those who expected great things from the politically explosive young turk of the thirties. Then there was the problem of the long poems. What was he up to in *New Year Letter*? What was this ostentatious display of erudition all about? And if his critics did not find it daunting they found it wanting, a case of Auden spreading himself too thinly: '*New Year Letter* shows Auden's final abdication as a poet. . . . Written in slapdash octosyllabic couplets, the work is entirely general and abstract, the poverty of imagery expressing the paucity of its experiential background.'[2] Then, as Auden aged, his once spectacular ability to discuss vast areas of human experience through his own brand of psycho-politics dwindled, as did his output, until we see a poet celebrating the mundane qualities of his home in Austria in *About the House*. Then there was the problem of his language. Once so contemporary and exciting, the later Auden rifled the OED for outré words that he knew would make his readers blanch. And the biographical story of Auden's life doesn't help. His later years show a man bound into a decreasing circle of repetition, absurdly rigid in his habits, slovenly in dress and manners, and never seen without his shuffling carpet slippers, even at the opera.

But these are only stories.

'We never step twice into the same Auden', said Randall Jarrell, and the criticism gathered in this collection has confirmed Jarrell's statement over and again as we see Auden praised and blamed for his poetry. Much of the criticism used in this Guide will represent *indirect* readings of Auden's poetry. There are two main reasons for this: first that the sheer bulk of Auden's collected works forbids a comprehensive representation of specific poems, and secondly, that while the Guide is aimed at presenting a broad selection of Auden criticism, it is also attempting to produce a sense of what Auden is like as a poet, and this requires material that speaks *across* Auden's work in order to get a sense of its major themes and issues.

Auden's life and work are most conveniently presented in chronological narrative form, mainly because one of the key issues of his work has been about the supposed 'falling off' of his creative power as he aged, the focus of that change being the move to America in 1939. In order to assess the validity of such a claim, indeed, to assess the validity of a chronological narrative itself, I have chosen to discuss the work in sequence from the juvenilia to the last poems using critical material that is sometimes contemporary but mainly not.

Auden's life and work does not fit into tidy categories, and there are obvious overlaps and shortfalls when trying to create compartments in which to fit him. However, I have weighted the critical material toward Auden's early period (1928–1940), as this covers the poet from the formative stage to when his poetic profile is most jaggedly visible.

There is a distinction between the immediate critical reaction to Auden's works as they were published – such as those represented in John Haffenden's excellent *W.H. Auden: The Critical Heritage* (1983) – and those critical works which are drawn from a considered and perspectival view. In order to provide elements of both types of response, I have written an introductory chapter which lays out some key biographical details while providing description and examples of contemporary responses to Auden's works. This is a chronological section moving from the early *Poems* (1928) to the posthumous *Thank You Fog* (1973). In the main chapters, however, I select extracts from books and articles on Auden drawn from the whole range of critical material according to its subject rather than its date. For example, discussion of Auden's very early poems is given to Katherine Bucknell, whose comparatively recent editing of the *Juvenilia* provides an introduction to the earliest work.

CHAPTER ONE

Biographical Summary and Guide through Auden's Works

A T THE outset, it may be useful to follow a discursive chronological description of Auden's works in order to appreciate how they relate to one another, and to understand their relative importance for the critical discourses that have grown over them since they were written.

Wystan Hugh Auden was born at York on 21st February 1907. He spent his schooldays at boarding schools in Hindhead in Surrey and Gresham's School, Holt. It was in 1922, the year that *The Waste Land* was published, that Auden, then aged fifteen, decided that he wanted to be a poet – it was the same year that he discovered that he had lost his faith, and it was also around this time that he began to understand and explore his homosexual identity. Auden's poetic career began in 1924 when the poem 'Woods in Rain' appeared in an anthology of Public School Verse with his name misspelt 'W. H. Arden'. The next year he went to Oxford, surprising himself and his friends by achieving a third-class degree.[1]

Auden's early attempts at poetry were, as is often the case, derivative: Thomas Hardy, Edward Thomas and Robert Frost being considerable influences. (See Bucknell's piece in chapter three.) At Oxford Auden was exposed to the immense aura of Eliot's work, first reading *The Waste Land* in 1926. As joint editor and contributor to *Oxford Poetry* between 1926 and 1928, Auden showed in both his poetry and editorial remarks an Eliot-like drive toward austerity. He very quickly imitated, parodied and subsumed Eliot into his own work, and by 1928 when his friend Stephen Spender had the bright idea of publishing a collection of Auden's poems on a chemists' press, Auden had developed a style and a voice recognisably his own. Only about 45 copies of this privately published *Poems* (1928) were made, and it says much about the power of the young Auden's writing that a poem such as 'The Watershed' remained in all his major collections throughout his life, the sureness of touch already in place:[2]

■ Beams from your car may cross a bedroom wall,
They wake no sleeper[3] (*C.P.*, p. 33) □

It was through his correspondence with Eliot that the Charade, *Paid on Both Sides*, was published in *The Criterion* in January 1930. Humphrey Carpenter reports that Eliot found Auden's Charade 'quite a brilliant piece of work' and adds comfortingly that

■ Eliot no doubt found the play difficult to understand . . . and even today much of the detail of its imagery cannot be elucidated by the most patient critics. But its richness of language and sudden surprising shifts of diction are so remarkable as to override the obscurity; and Eliot recognised this.[4] □

Paid on Both Sides was written in a peculiar idiom somewhere between an Icelandic saga and a Scout's jamboree, where two opposing teams in rugger strips feud in a remote and rugged northern landscape and speak a clipped Anglo-Saxon verse.

■ Could I have been some simpleton that lived
Before disaster sent his runners here
Younger than worms, worms have too much to bear. (*C.P.*, p. 11) □

Further disorientation arises when the action is interrupted by the comedy antics of the Mummers' Play where a doctor and Father Christmas appear in a hallucinatory dream sequence and extract a giant tooth.

It was Eliot who at first rejected, but later accepted the poems that make up the important *Poems* (1930), a two and sixpenny paperback published by Faber and Faber. The collection is made up of the Charade *Paid on Both Sides* followed by thirty poems, austerely titled with Roman numerals. These muscular, clipped poems make few concessions to common expectations of sense and context, but what *is* clear is that things are about to change, and Auden's insinuating voice is perfectly suited to deliver the news of that change. He speaks of a powerful, healing and restorative 'love' that

■ Needs death, death of the grain, our death,
Death of the old gang; would leave them
In sullen valley where is made no friend (*C.P.*, p. 49) □

These poems, as well as *Paid on Both Sides*, radiated the 'sort of completeness that makes a work seem to define the attitude of a generation'[5] and exuded a much needed confidence in an age that, following the reign of Eliot, could easily represent itself as lost and rootless, aimless and tired.

Orwell claimed that in 'Sweeney Agonistes', for example, Eliot achieved 'the difficult feat of making modern life out to be worse than it is'.[6] Here, on the other hand, was a voice that demanded action, asking for recognition that things had to change. Here was the sound 'Of new men making another love' (*C.P.*, p.63).

The importance of a work can usually be assessed by the critical confusion that greets it; *Poems* (1930) was such a text. The critical reception of this collection can be sampled in Haffenden's *Critical Heritage*, with some reviewers being fundamentally baffled, and others, more perceptive and prophetic, seeing something new emerging into view. The question of Auden's obscurity, however, permeated much of this criticism. Dudley Fitts, for example, claimed that 'Mr Auden, too, knows how to be direct, but he elects more often to be oblique'.[7]

Eliot again oversaw the publication of Auden's most notorious work, *The Orators* of 1932. This was a fragmented and sporadic piece made up of material invested with coherence by the overall theme of hero worship. It was to be a kind of 'memorial to T. E. Lawrence' and contains both poetry and prose ranging from the slapstick to the surreal. Here the problem of obscurity was always going to be an integral element of the work. Auden, already disappointed that *Poems* (1930) had seemed obscure to some readers, now approached Eliot and asked if he might insert an explanatory preface into the work to forestall charges of incomprehensibility. To Naomi Mitchison he wrote 'Am I really so obscure? Obscurity's a bad fault'.[8] Eliot, a poet with experience in these matters, advised against Auden explaining himself in this way, and consequently *The Orators* had to be read without the dubious benefit of an explanatory scheme. The resulting critical response proved Eliot right, as it was the very ambiguity of the work that constituted a good deal of its meaning, political as well as sexual (see Spender on the Airman in chapter three). Alan Pryce-Jones, for example, laments that

■ before *The Orators*, I find myself nearly as blank as the old gentleman – vaguely aware that something is going on, vaguely catching a glimpse of light, and quite unable to decide in the end what it is all about.[9] □

When the collection of diverse writers *New Signatures* appeared in 1932 it was no surprise that Auden's voice was selected as that which could speak for them all; the mythical 'Auden Generation' was born.[10] Michael Roberts, the editor of *New Signatures*, makes the important point that Auden and his fellow poets were able to speak of contemporary life in a language of images drawn not from some distant or archaic past, but from the immediate present:

■ Mr Auden's *Poems* and Mr Day-Lewis's *From Feathers to Iron* were, I think, the first books in which imagery taken from contemporary life consistently appeared as the natural and spontaneous expression of the poet's thought and feeling.[11] □

The ease with which he incorporated the contemporary world into his poetry was a key factor in the construction of Auden as a political poet, the time being one of communist sympathy and left alignment in the arts. Auden, however, always took care to remain *un*committed to communism, despite his obvious sympathy with its broad aims. This political ambiguity is exemplified in the poem 'A Communist to Others' published in the *Twentieth Century* in September 1932. The poem was reprinted in March 1933 in *New Country*, the companion collection to *New Signatures*, and fed the critical perception of Auden's left alignment, although today, the poem tends to be read as satirical of its apparently 'committed' stance. An interesting analysis of this poem can be read in *Auden Studies 1*, in the form of a 'Symposium'.[12]

The two collections *New Signatures* and *New Country* helped to collect the poets together into a group, as well as ascribe a political character to them all: young committed near-communists (with the 'near' remaining the essential aspect of this description). The idea of a group of poets and writers with Auden at the centre of its field of force was almost inevitably based on a myth, as the four poets that made up the 'MacSpaunday' group (MacSpaunday was a concatenation of the names MacNeice, Spender, Auden and Day-Lewis) were never together in the same room during the thirties.

Look, Stranger! (1936)

Auden worked as a schoolmaster for five years between 1930 and 1935 and then for the GPO Film Unit with painters such as William Coldstream and composers such as Benjamin Britten. His next collection *Look, Stranger!* appeared in 1936. Here the poetry is clearer, has a more lyrical cast than the earlier starkness of *Poems* (1930) and delivers Auden into the centre of the 1930s as an established and respected writer. In this collection appeared the much praised poem 'Our Hunting Fathers' with its succinct and powerful political assessment of the times.[13] Politically oriented poems sit alongside works of great lyrical beauty such as 'Look, stranger at this island now' and the two songs for Benjamin Britten. The record of Auden's experience of selfless Christian brotherly love, Agape, is here too, in the poem later called 'A Summer Night'. It was this collection that earned him the King's Gold Medal for Poetry, as well as jeering disbelief on account of this award from some of his former admirers.

Reviewers recognised echoes of Wilfred Owen in *Look, Stranger!* and the parallel is worth drawing. The effect of being a boy too young to fight in the Great War was pervasive in Auden and his contemporaries. Janet Adam Smith, for example, thought that a 'difficult doctrine' emerged from these poems (discussing 'Here on the narrow ridge I stand'), claiming that

■ it may mean accepting, for a time, an order of things which is felt to be wrong (as, for instance, Wilfred Owen was against war, but he knew that his place was with his company), it lays down no precise rules for behaviour, and it demands not a surrender of the intelligence, but a sharper use of it.[14] □

Auden's position is more comprehensible if we understand how he was the product both of Eliot's post-war 'Waste Land' as well as the more decadent and romantic outlook of Owen – a hybrid modernist-Georgian.

It was significant that the writer and editor Geoffrey Grigson promoted Auden as a good poet (not a political poet). His 'Special Double Number' of the journal *New Verse* was solely dedicated to Auden. Grigson carried a lot of critical weight, and readers would be sure that Auden had been taken up because of the quality of his poetry, rather than the fashionable nature of his politics. (See chapter two.)

Drama

Auden began his theatrical collaboration with the novelist Christopher Isherwood in 1928 in their knockabout romp *The Enemies of a Bishop*, an unperformed farce which remained unpublished until posthumous collection by Edward Mendelson in the *Complete Works* collection *Plays 1928-1938*.[15] Auden worked alone on *Paid on Both Sides*, which was originally written to be performed at a friend's country house, and in 1932 he ventured alone again on a play, *The Dance of Death*, written for the Group Theatre, led by the choreographer and dancer Rupert Doone. In *The Dance of Death* a Marxist prophecy of the end of bourgeois society is overlaid by Auden's psychological analyses in which the bourgeoisie play out their death wishes in a futile striving for novelties that are revealed as repetitions. (See Michael Sidnell's piece on *The Dance of Death* in chapter four.)

Later, the team of Auden and Isherwood produced *The Dog Beneath the Skin* (1935), *The Ascent of F6* (1936) and *On the Frontier* (1938). Formally, these works hovered between the revue and the farce, with unmistakable elements of surrealism and expressionist symbolism. Whether exploring the damaging restrictions of village life (*The Dog Beneath the Skin*), the hidden Oedipal dramas of bourgeois heroism (*The Ascent of*

F6) or the Machiavellian intricacies of political expediency (*On the Frontier*), the mixture of poetry, humour and satire welded onto a fundamentally serious social critique made the plays varied and patchy and they were unevenly reviewed. Louis MacNeice, for example, recalls some scenes from *On the Frontier* which made him 'long for a sack to put one's head in'.[16]

The main references here are Mendelson (ed.), *Plays 1928–1938* and Michael Sidnell's excellent survey of Auden's plays and the Group Theatre that produced them: *Dances of Death: The Group Theatre of London in the Thirties*.[17] The plays are also important as public and more explicit statements of themes and anxieties that circulate in the more private poems. Many verses were lifted from the plays and placed in collections, where they appear shorn of context, and so it can help to judge the mood of a piece to discover that it was originally delivered in a particular (sometimes farcical) dramatic context.

Travel

The geographical locations of his teaching posts (Helensburgh in Scotland, The Downs' School in the Malverns) feature strongly in Auden's poetry, and are especially prominent in *Look, Stranger!* There we see a stubborn sense of place commingled with an alienation recorded as early as 1929 when the young poet, returning from a season in a sexually liberated Berlin, found that this country was always going to hold something back from him, would always refuse him a full expression of his sexual identity:

■ Being alone, the frightened soul
   Returns to this life of sheep and hay
   No longer his. . . (*C.P.*, p.48) □

The opportunity of going to Iceland in 1936 to write a travel book with fellow poet Louis MacNeice was not to be refused, offering as it did a chance to look once more at England from a distance. As MacNeice observes:

■ We are not changing ground to escape from facts
   But rather to find them. This complex world exacts
   Hard work of simplifying; to get its focus
   You have to stand outside the crowd and caucus.[18] □

The resulting book, *Letters from Iceland* (1937), is a magnificent mélange of miscellaneous facts and personal dramas, of which one of the most entertaining is the acting out of a camp relationship between the straight

MacNeice ('Hetty') and the homosexual Auden ('Nancy'). The book contains some fine poetry by MacNeice, but the centrepiece is the inexhaustible 'Letter to Lord Byron' which takes full advantage of the holiday spirit, as well as the distance from home, to create a picture of England in the mid-thirties at once whimsical and penetrating. This is a text that repays attention, as it was while Auden and MacNeice were in Iceland that the Spanish Civil War broke out – and all the implied criticisms of contemporary Britain are placed under the severe gaze of this event which was soon to absorb both Auden and MacNeice in different ways as well as many other writers and artists of the period.

'Letter to Lord Byron' was a long, satirical piece that exemplified the poet's growing interest in the power and the possibility of light verse. His Introduction to the *Oxford Book of Light Verse* (1938) which he edited contains some interesting parallel material on the role of the poet and the possibility of making useful and lasting contributions to the society in which he or she lived. John Blair discusses the importance of the unserious in Auden's poetry in the extract in chapter two, while Tom Paulin looks at the politics of 'Letter to Lord Byron' in chapter four.

The Spanish Civil War (1936–9) is in many ways one of the most critical events in Auden's career, yet its significance is completely out of scale with the facts of what Auden actually did during his brief visit. Ostensibly in search of a job driving ambulances, Auden made propaganda broadcasts on behalf of the Republican Government, and returned to England shortly after, unusually reticent about his experiences. His main contribution was, though, *Spain*, a poem that was published as a little pamphlet which sold for a shilling (5p.), proceeds from the sales going to 'Medical Aid for Spain'. Critical opinion, as always with Auden, was divided over the importance and value of *Spain*. Depending on the political requirements of the critics, the poem was seen as more or less successful in persuading its readers to take a stand. Auden's position in the poem is certainly not propagandist in a crude sense – the fact that the poem has been treated seriously by such a wide array of critical voices stands as testimony to its careful and intelligent depiction of a situation that was as packed with contradictions as with tragedy.

Later, Auden revealed that it was the sight of bombed and burned out churches that had a profound effect on him, such that it began the slow, winding path back to the religious faith that he had ostensibly rejected as a teenager. *Spain*, a poem branded into the literary history of the 1930s, became a source of trouble to the later Auden who wanted to erase it from consideration. But it remains as a site of stark and passionate controversy as well as a poem that spoke through the political expediencies of the time to the very marrow of men such as Arnold Kettle (see chapter four) who could appreciate the difficulty of its refusal to compromise the *human* element of the struggle, which a more fashion-conscious poet may have inevitably had to do. Orwell's famous criticism of the poem in 'Inside the Whale' sits at the heart of the controversy. Speaking of the line 'The conscious acceptance of guilt in the necessary murder', he says that this is part of a 'thumbnail sketch' of a 'good party man':

■ In the morning a couple of political murders, a ten minutes' interlude to stifle 'bourgeois' remorse, and then a hurried luncheon and a busy afternoon and evening chalking walls and distributing leaflets. All very edifying. But notice the phrase 'necessary murder'. It could only be written by a person to whom murder is at most a *word*. . . . Mr Auden's brand of amoralism is only possible if you are the kind of person who is always somewhere else when the trigger is pulled. So much of left-wing thought is a kind of playing with fire by people who don't even know that fire is hot.[19] □

Auden's response to Orwell's criticism was indirect – Mendelson shows how he changed the line on his own account.[20] But this is only a fragment of a much larger unease that surrounds this poem as Auden's political and religious future is bound up in its ambiguous and uncertain tone. Orwell's excellent book on the Spanish Civil War, *Homage to Catalonia* (1938), is invaluable for filling in the inter-party rivalries and complicated allegiances of Spain, and to portray what was going on 'when the trigger is pulled'. Valentine Cunningham's *Spanish Front* (1986) is a useful text which brings together extracts from many sources to build up a picture of the Spanish War and its literary ramifications.[21]

The war in Spain made the question of commitment pressing, and it is in the memories of writers such as Stephen Spender that we read of the pressure to make public statements that firmly indicated on which side of the border you stood.[22]

A brief stay in Brussels in 1938 where he saw some Brueghel paintings inspired one of Auden's most famous poems: 'Musée des Beaux Arts'. Initially dwelling on the relation between important historical events in the foreground and the mundane existence that really constitutes our 'human position', Auden affirms the power of the 'Old Masters' to notice and contextualise the importance of the background:

■ Where the dogs go on with their doggy life and the torturer's horse Scratches its innocent behind on a tree. (*C.P.*, p. 179) □

In Breughel's *Icarus*, the ploughman is placed in the foreground and remains apparently oblivious to the minute splash and faintly ridiculous legs of Icarus who disappears into the sea in the background.[23] Auden tells us that to the ploughman, the great mythical disaster 'was not an important failure', and immediately puts into question the importance of historical narratives. (Auden's relation to history is addressed by Stan Smith in chapter six.) This poem also has a biographical element, and can be read as Auden's attempt to digest his experiences in Spain while thinking ahead to his imminent move to America. 'Musée' is a poem which affirms and explores this decision – the mythical Auden/Icarus figure of the political thirties plunging into the water while the ship 'Had somewhere to get to and sailed calmly on'. (*C.P.*, p. 179)

Later, this time with Isherwood, Auden went to China to experience and gather material for a book on the Sino-Japanese War. The prose that makes up *Journey to a War* (1939), although predominantly Isherwood's work, had significant input from Auden, who also wrote the introductory sonnets as well as the final 'Commentary'. The distance of China (not this time for him the Aryan homeliness of Iceland) along with a very real danger ('Here, though the bombs are real and dangerous' (*The English Auden*, p. 249)) shook the two writers out of the world of 1930s Britain, and directed them to the America of the next decade. Returning from China via America, the experience of their visit to New York convinced both writers that their time in England was up. Even as they lectured in America about their experiences in China, the glamour of being political spokesmen was gone. Auden remembered a speech he made which roused the audience to belligerent cheers – he never forgot the power of this oratory, for the experience sickened him, and made him feel dirty.[24]

The major journey of the decade was made by Auden and Isherwood as they left England for a new life in America early in 1939. They leaned together on the rail of the ship and confided to one another that they could no longer swallow any more popular front politics. The pattern of their lives had irrevocably changed.

After moving to America, Auden wrote a private unpublished journal, *The Prolific and the Devourer*, in which he assessed his relation to politics in the thirties (extracts from this journal appear in *The English Auden*).[25] His mood, like that of Orwell, was one of resigned withdrawal from the 'activist' position that he had been wrongly assumed to inhabit. Often in Auden's life, one particular vivid event stands in for a change of heart or direction in his life. It was in New York, at a cinema in a mainly German-speaking area, that the hatred that had built up around the war in Europe became real to him:

■ the film he saw was *Sieg im Poland,* an account by the Nazis of their conquest of Poland. When Poles appeared on the screen he was startled to hear a number of people in the audience scream 'Kill them!' He later said of this: 'I wondered then, why I reacted as I did against this denial of every humanistic value. The answer brought me back to the church'.[26] □

Another Time (1940)

Although Auden decided that he would move to America as early as 1938, he was nevertheless criticised for abandoning his country in time of need. There are obvious ironies abounding in the position of these critics which, if they had taken heed of Auden's observations of England from *Poems* (1930) onwards, would need to 'think about England, this country of ours where nobody is well' and realise that 'No doctor in England can cure all that'.[27] The abandonment of British nationality meant that Auden could begin again with a clean slate in a country with 'no past'.[28] These were difficult times for Auden and Isherwood. The defections were seen as the end of their political posing and carping, the two writers showing their true colours as they fled the country that had tolerated their antics for so long. In fact the reaction to Auden's so-called 'defection' precisely summed up everything about the parochial, family atmosphere that England represented for Auden; but he had left the myth of the Auden group behind him, he was now on his own.[29]

In a letter to Spender, sent as a rebuke for a backstabbing review, Auden made a defence of his move to America. 'If I thought I should be a competent soldier or air-warden,' he said, 'I should come back tomorrow.' His second reason was spoken from the position of the writer and pedagogue: 'for the intellectual' he claims, 'warfare goes on always and everywhere, and no one has the right to say that this place or that time is where all intellectuals ought to be'.[30]

The collection that Spender reviewed so slightingly was *Another Time* (1940) which contains poems written on both sides of the 'defection', including (on the English side) the justly famous 'Musée des Beaux Arts' and 'Spain, 1937' and (on the American side) the elegy 'In Memory of W. B. Yeats' and the controversial 'September 1, 1939'. This latter poem took on the role, perhaps unreasonably, of encapsulating Auden's move to America. It is the poem that labelled the 1930s a 'low, dishonest decade', dangerous words that critics were quick to pounce on in their attempts to discredit a poet who had the audacity to sit 'in one of the dives/On Fifty-Second Street/Uncertain and afraid' while his country fell headlong into war on the other side of the Atlantic. But of course, the controversy simplified a situation that was far from clear, and the defection can be seen gestating as early as the very first *Poems* (1930):

■ A neutralising peace
And an average disgrace
Are honour to discover
For later other. (*C.P.*, p. 43) □

The close attention given to 'September 1, 1939' by Joseph Brodsky teases out the nuances of language that encapsulate Auden's anxieties about his new role in America (a sample appears in chapter four), while the material by Mendelson on revision (chapter five) demonstrates Auden's sensitivity to the ways that a poet's voice is put to other uses after he has ceased to inhabit his poems. This is why the thrust of the elegy to Yeats is such an important part of the second major section of Auden's career. 'He became his admirers.' No poet knew as well as Auden the fine appropriations of voice and text made in that conjunction of history, discourse and poetry that we call 'literary criticism', and if anything is a defence of his move to America, then 'In Memory of W.B. Yeats' is that. This was one of several poems about other artists that Auden wrote at this time.[31]

The publication of *Another Time* gave critics the chance to assess the 'new' Auden and to ascertain whether his 'defection' had been a positive or a negative move. Haffenden suggests that 'Virtually all critics accordingly concurred in the view that Auden had obviously reached a divide in his career and was taking new bearings'.[32] Certainly this was the case in his personal life. In April, 1939, shortly after arriving in America, Auden began a relationship with a young student, Chester Kallman. Carpenter claims that Auden regarded his relationship with Kallman as a marriage, wearing a ring, and discussing 'honeymoon' holidays after only a month together.[33] The intensity of Auden's feelings for Kallman underwrote the crisis he experienced as a result of Kallman's infidelities, which he discovered after more than two years of a happy, stable relationship. When the crisis abated two significant decisions had been taken: first, that Auden was prepared to spend the rest of his life with Kallman despite his 'extra-marital' affairs, and second, that Auden had permanently returned to the Christian faith.

America

As part of his self-induction into American life and culture, Auden, in partnership with Benjamin Britten (the British composer, then also an exile) took up the task of writing an operetta about Paul Bunyan, the mythical giant lumberjack who symbolises the spread and settlement of America. Often criticised for its temerity in telling the Americans their own history and for its ambiguous, potentially satirical tone, the operetta should be recognised as an important moment in both the relation between Britten and Auden, and between Auden and America. Although critics were none too pleased with these British upstarts who presumed to present the American people with their own legends, Auden's immersion in American culture and language can be seen here as warm hearted and enthusiastic. Revived later with some success, this interesting operetta was soon forgotten.[34]

As if to begin his poetic life from scratch, Auden's first published fully 'American' work was *The Double Man* of 1941 (or *New Year Letter* as it appeared in England). The Auden that had spoken for a 'generation' was now speaking for the individual, and the moral here is to set one's house in order before presuming to preach to the many. Here, then, it is the moral and ethical life that comes under scrutiny in this long, three part epistle to Elizabeth Mayer, his patroness and friend. Edward Callan notes that the three parts of this letter correspond to Kierkegaard's categories of the *aesthetic,* the *ethical* and the *religious,* and Callan's analysis of these categories appears in the chapter on the longer poems. This work is generally acknowledged to represent Auden's tentative return to faith, trying out the sound of his beliefs in a sustained poem. The critical reception of this work was mixed, ranging from the positive support of Marianne Moore to the dismissive curmudgeonly D.S. Savage who saw it as a flawed venture undertaken by a poet who wasn't up to it.[35]

What was starting to become obvious was that the withdrawal from overt political posturing was being slowly replaced by a meditative, theological interest which manifested itself in ethical and moral questions being posed in Auden's poetry: the form, as well as the relation to other works of art or religious events, were as important as the content. *The Double Man* was no exception, and critics saw Auden perched precariously on the edge of religious commitment while he examined the state of modern secular knowledge.

For the Time Being (1944)

In 1944 Auden published two long works together under the collective title *For the Time Being.* The 'Christmas Oratorio' that gave the collection its name was 'For the Time Being', a remarkable work that recasts the Christmas story in a modern setting. At the same time as it dealt with the death of his mother Constance Rosalie Auden, it also acknowledged that his relationship with Chester Kallmann was going to be a lifetime of unequal affection and modern 'convenience' instead of the marriage that he had mistakenly imagined to be firmly in place. Carpenter tells us that Auden identified with Joseph, telling a friend that 'Joseph is me'.[36]

Written at a convergence of crises in Auden's life, *For the Time Being* was generally well received, with critics admiring the virtuosity of the language while remaining unsure about the nature of the religious statement being made.[37] Some believed that Auden had arrived logically at a point of belief, but had failed to make the important spiritual leap. Again, with all discussion of Auden's religious belief, we must listen to what he said himself about the possibility of a 'Christian' art in 'Making, Knowing and Judging':

■ The impulse to create a work of art is felt when, in certain persons, the passive awe provoked by sacred beings or events is transformed into a desire to express that awe in a rite of worship or homage, and to be fit homage, this rite must be beautiful. This rite has no magical or idolatrous intention; nothing is expected in return. Nor is it, in a Christian sense, an act of devotion. If it praises the Creator, it does so indirectly by praising His creatures – among which may be human notions of the Divine Nature. With God as Redeemer, it has, so far as I can see, little if anything to do.[38] □

What starts to become apparent in the criticism of Auden's theologically orientated works is that those who championed his earlier political stance now had difficulty in seeing the good in the new material, so obviously giving up, as it did, the easy pose of the fellow traveller and replacing it with the difficult and friendless role of the spiritual quester. This problem is exemplified in *The Sea and the Mirror* (1944), Auden's commentary on *The Tempest*, where the character of Prospero is troubled by the choice between the artist's frivolous control of the magic of his art and the ordinary, but spiritually valuable life that he decides to accept in its place.

The Sea and the Mirror remains a fascinating and enigmatic work. The poetry contains moments of deft and sudden beauty, while the long prose section spoken by Caliban on the nature of art (in the style of Henry James) is full of ideas that challenge our conception of the nature of the relationship between artist and work, artist and audience, and work and audience. Intensely aware of the implicated and implicating nature of these relationships, Auden's interest in the status of the artist and his relation to spectacular magic on the one hand, and a hidden, mundane ordinariness on the other, is shot through with his reading of Kierkegaard, and makes fascinating analysis when considering, for example, the decision of Prospero to 'renounce' his magic books even as he is aware that his faith, his suspension over 'seventy thousand fathoms'[39] is not accessible to any reader or indeed, any other person at all. This existential sense of self pervades the work of the 1940s and produces occasional startling insights into the often glib nature of a critical commentary that demands things of a writer that it cannot in fairness expect from anyone. (See chapter five on the longer poems for further discussion of Kierkegaard.)

Revisions in *The Collected Poetry of W.H. Auden* (1945)

In 1945, Auden published *The Collected Poetry of W.H. Auden* and the collection was well received. Here was a chance for critics to evaluate Auden's writings thus far, and the overall impression was favourable.

However, this was the start of Auden's notorious revisions of his work, and there is considerable critical controversy over the status of these later revisions. A relationship of contestation is set up between Auden and his critics as he visibly and publicly takes control over his *oeuvre*, removing poems that he knew were critically respected and had come to represent certain elements of his career. This is an aspect of Auden's work that will be dealt with when critics such as Jarrell (chapter two) and Mendelson (chapter five) consider what can be inferred from these changes, and indeed what such changes actually tell us about the work and the man.

The problem of his talent falling off was keenly felt by Auden himself. Carpenter cites a letter to Spender in which Auden justifies his alphabetical organisation of the *Collected Poetry* of 1945: 'I wanted to test the reader who believes that my earliest poems are my best.'[40]

The Age of Anxiety (1948)

In 1948 Auden produced *The Age of Anxiety*, another long poem that he described as a 'Baroque Eclogue'. Along with moderate critical praise for the poem was a repetition of the criticism that the piece showed Auden's 'failure to assimilate or even come to terms with the American experience'.[41] Patric Dickinson writing in *Horizon* in 1949 exemplifies this strand of criticism:

■ Purely as a work of art it seems utterly remote from living experience; quite emotionless; full of carefully written words and carefully contrived ideas, but all *in vacuo* – and it is difficult not to conceive that this vacuum has been created by the poet's life. When he really has become American, inside as well as out, in diction, in rhythm, in feeling, in thought (as Mr. Eliot has become English) surely he will again produce living work?[42] □

Dickinson's remarks contain all the assumptions, misrecognitions, prejudices and historical mispredictions that run through criticism of Auden's poetry, but he usefully points to the key areas that this Guide will focus. The question of identity is here. Auden's American identity, like his homosexuality, returns as an element that is not easy to dismiss. The 'real' Auden is often cited as a benchmark for his poetry, but throughout his career Auden rarely presented a stable sense of the 'I' in his poems. Even the later, crusty poet, can be seen as one more role played in language. The problem of 'contrivance' is the other main thread. The relation of art and life was an important and dominant theme in Auden's poetry, and Dickinson falls directly into Auden's trap by complaining that 'living work' must be produced by uncontrived poetry.[43] Auden is two steps ahead here: aware that contrivance is the artist's mode of being, he stresses that only through formal technique can life be approached, and even then, we should be aware that we are dealing with art and *not* life.

Nones (1951)

Nones (1951) introduces an older poet (*Another Time* was some ten years earlier) whose tone had become more relaxed even as his verbal and formal virtuosity had increased. This collection produced another interesting set of responses from contemporary critics. While some appreciated the verbal brilliance of the poetry, others were concerned at the apparent detachment and impersonality of the material. As Haffenden notes, it was Auden's 'wry, ironic, meditative tone' which some critics found complacent or detached from 'deep personal engagement'.[44] Interestingly for a reader used to the claims of post-structuralist criticism, Spender's accusation that the poet seems to inhabit 'an entirely verbal world' only makes Auden more intriguing as a poet who realised just how much experience is modified and mediated by language (see Auden on the power of words in chapter two). *Nones* contains one of Auden's most famous poems, 'In Praise of Limestone', in which the psychological, geographic and social realms are brought together to look self-reflexively at his art. There is specific discussion of this poem in chapter six.

The Shield of Achilles (1955)

Once more, at the publication of *The Shield of Achilles* (1955), the problem of tone was aired in reviews, for critics were always uncomfortable with Auden's flip remarks and apparently throwaway lines – uneasy perhaps that Auden was not taking them as seriously as he ought. Opinion gathered around the idea that Auden's technical virtuosity was not being met by an equal authenticity of feeling – that the poet was some distance from the emotional heart of his work. Readers today, however, will seize the chance to exploit these aspects of the poet, a poet who enjoyed playing on the contradictions and difficulties of rhetorical speech. Although Auden's 'misplaced frivolity' and 'irresponsible smartness' was obviously too much for some critics,[45] this is what makes Auden such a challenging and rewarding subject of study – his very tone prevents critical neutrality while raising many questions about the relation between authenticity and surface, suffering and laughter, mask and identity. The problem with the later poetry is that its voices sound convincingly enough like an authentic Auden (being full of his references, his reading, his worries) to appear autobiographical. Even though the poetry can seem overfull of the poet's fusty ego, Auden's ability to purge and transform those carpet-slippered complaints about the modern world is one of his brilliant techniques. As the later poems unfold, we see an apparent repetition of

Prospero abjuring his art in favour of the commonplace, and witness the intrusion of the homely, the cosy, the local, and see the trifling and insignificant being effortlessly transformed into art.

The Shield of Achilles is divided into three sections. The first, 'Bucolics', contains the animated sequence of poems based on the natural world: 'Winds', 'Woods', 'Mountains', 'Lakes', 'Islands', 'Plains' and 'Streams'. The second part, 'In Sunshine and in Shade', presents the important poem, 'The Shield of Achilles', which is discussed in some detail in chapter six, and which continues Auden's long involvement with the importance and limits of art. Poems such as 'Hunting Season' with its light-hearted reference to the author at work interrupted for his meal of 'suffocated fish' and 'The Truest Poetry is the Most Feigning' serve to complicate Auden's relationship to his readers and his work. The final section, 'Horae Canonicae', charts the hours of the Christian day (apologetically reprinting two poems that first appeared in *Nones* so that they could find their proper context) and shows Auden treating his art to a rare Christian outing, boldly, but seriously, bringing together the aesthetic and the religious in a successful alliance.

Homage to Clio (1960)

With the collection *Homage to Clio* (1960) the unease of certain critics about Auden's levity increased. Haffenden notes that two poets, Thom Gunn and Philip Larkin, were outspoken about what they saw as Auden's later lapse into 'unserious' work, reading this as a sign that he had little to say, and that he had lost his edge. While Philip Larkin accused Auden of no longer being a serious poet (see Larkin's criticism of Auden in chapter four), John Bayley neatly turns this criticism around by suggesting that Auden has *never* been a serious poet, nor should he be:

■ Attacks on Auden are invariably based on his irresponsibility, his unfounded pretensions to intellectual power and weight, and his enjoyment of the private joke or absurdity for its own sake, etc., and all these strictures lose their force if his poetry is read for what it is, and not for what his critics – misled by the poet's ambiguous attitude – have supposed it is attempting to be.[46] □

Bayley explores this ambiguous attitude in the extract cited in chapter two. But it is the relation to history that becomes the centre of attention in Stan Smith's discussion of *Homage to Clio* in chapter six, where he claims that Auden still had a lot to say, and that his work still retained a political edge, despite the critical scepticism aroused by his apparent lack of seriousness.

About the House (1965)

These criticisms were fuelled by *About the House* (1965), a consciously domestic collection that focused its attention on Auden's house in Kirchstetten and the parabolic meanings that arise through a poetic exploration of home life. Critics found the work frustrating, in that whatever direction their criticism may have taken, there was the possibility that Auden was aware of it in advance. When Auden writes

■ At lucky moments we seem on the brink
   Of really saying what we think we think:
   But, even then, an honest eye should wink
                    (*C.P.*, p.695) □

Christopher Ricks complains that it 'too much resembles the nervous tic of "I know you know I know you know I know"',[47] but this is precisely the difficulty that Auden wants to present to his readers, and it ties up with his poetic projects from *The Sea and the Mirror* onwards. Edward Callan gives a sympathetic and perceptive reading of *About the House* in chapter six. Callan trusts Auden's judgement and finds in these poems a good deal more than a parochial and grumpy self-obsession. Still the dictionary is being raided for the word that can shock the reader from his or her complacency, still the camp, personal tone is to the fore with its delicate treatment of exclamations, and still the reader is unsure of whether this poet is taking his job as seriously as he should.

■ Lifted off the potty,
   Infants from their mothers
   Hear their first impartial
   Words of worldly praise:
   Hence to start the morning
   With a satisfactory
   Dump is a good omen
   All our adult days.
                    (*C.P.*, p.698) □

But to the modern reader, Auden's camp frivolity is full of potential for examining the anxieties of critical language itself, and can be a fruitful route to follow through Auden's later poetry.

The Dyer's Hand, a collection of critical essays by Auden, appeared in 1962, and demonstrated that Auden was an entertaining and idiosyncratic critic, as well as an original and illuminating reader.

Collected Shorter Poems (1966) and Collected Longer Poems (1968)

Auden made the concession in *Collected Shorter Poems* (1966) of grouping the poems in a rough chronological sequence, giving as his reason that he felt that he was now in a position (unlike 1945) to bear the scrutiny of a historically minded criticism looking for patterns of development. He adds that

■ A good many of the poems have been revised. Critics, I have observed, are apt to find revisions ideologically significant. One, even, made a great to-do about what was in fact a typographical error. I can only say that I have never, consciously at any rate, attempted to revise my former thoughts and feelings, only the language in which they were first expressed when, on further consideration, it seemed to me inaccurate, lifeless, prolix or painful to the ear.[48] □

Here, with the revision of the shorter works, the problem hinged on Auden's defence that he was only modifying the *surface* of the poetry, leaving the sense untouched. This was, of course, a contentious statement – for how can you separate language and sense, language and thought? Haffenden cites Francis Berry who claimed that some shorter poems which had retained a 'vague suggestive imagery' in their original state had now been endowed with an 'allegorical explicitness' which belonged to the 'post-1948 writing' and had therefore changed the sense altogether.[49]

We need, I think, to take a practical view of these modifications and revisions. To the student of Auden, rather than the disappointed critic who had followed his career through three decades, these changes and revisions, these arguments and judgements only serve to make the field richer and more unpredictable. Instead of dealing with one poem such as *Spain*, we now can explore a poem that speaks to the world of 1937, as well as a poem that contains the discomfort of the poet at a later time. The revisions have not made the original poem disappear, but have only served to *focus* our attention on the form and effect of the earlier poem, to witness and experience the *transformation* of that poem through a particular historical intervention. The student need not be pious about these changes – rather they provide the very soil from which new and interesting scholarship can grow.

Collected Shorter Poems revealed how much Auden was prepared to excise and transform the memory of his thirties poetry. Not only did he completely remove poems that he considered to be 'dishonest or bad-mannered or boring'[50] (including 'Spain', 'September 1, 1939', and 'A Communist to Others') but he gave irreverent and ironic names to poems that had previously been graced with only an austere number. It is in relation to these revisions that Joseph Warren Beach's book *The Making of the Auden Canon* (1957) is relevant:

■ It is true that, by discreet revisions and eliminations in the poems of the thirties, and by throwing the poems of all periods together in a heap without regard to their temporal sequence, the author does his best to iron out the contradictions and incongruities. And here perhaps the ordinary reader, who does his reading perforce in one of the later collections, will do well to settle down cozily in his deck chair, give up trying to take his bearings, and submit to the sleepy charm, as distinct outlines are blurred in the general haziness that envelopes the landscape. But for anyone with access to the earlier volumes, the uneasiness becomes still more acute as he compares the original texts with those of 1945 and 1950, where so many relatively unambiguous poems are translated into the terms of Auden's later thinking, only to find themselves rather shockingly out of place. And at this point we are obliged to conclude that the poet, with the best of intentions, is virtually misrepresenting the thought which actually informed the earlier writing.[51] □

As an answer to this kind of complaint, Mendelson's meditation on the nature of Auden's amendments – 'Revision and Power' – appears in chapter five.

The Collected Longer Poems (1968) enabled Auden to gather together his longer works including the early *Paid on Both Sides*, the important 'Letter to Lord Byron', and the long American works *New Year Letter, For the Time Being, The Sea and the Mirror*, and *The Age of Anxiety*. These poems appeared with the minimum of revision (although *New Year Letter* is shorn of its notes), being later works in the main, and escaped the censure laid against the revision of the shorter works.

These two volumes created the opportunity for critics to assess, in Larkin's words, 'What's become of Wystan'. As Haffenden notes, the appearance of these collections produced yet another revaluation of Auden's life and career, and while the overall achievement of the poet was undeniable, there was always a quiet sense of a falling away of the later work when read against the gusto and engagement of the earlier.

City Without Walls (1969)

The collection *City Without Walls* (1969) begins with the title poem surveying the state of the modern 'Megalopolis'. The poem interrupts itself with a 'sharp' counter voice, only to be overlaid again with a 'bored' third voice that commands the others to 'Go to sleep now for God's sake'.

This self-conscious dialogue between the poet's varied personae sets the tone of this collection.

The demotic, cosy strains accumulate while the poet pushes ahead with his craft while looking back over his life. The domestic net appears to be closing in: elegies to friends, housekeepers, former tutors, a self-examining 'Profile', commissioned works and some songs from Brecht as well as another dose of words that send one running to the OED. In the poem for Nevill Coghill he writes

■ Now of the body
I brashly came to my first
tutorial in
not a molecule remains,
but to its mind's eye
optically definite
is our meeting still. (*C.P.*, p. 764) □

Here Auden tells his audience that he is not the same poet as that boy Icarus that fell from the sky in 1938, and yet the critics' (as well as his own) memory of the early Auden is still sharp. But Auden's lines remind us that the early Auden is now only an object of fantasy, long since transformed. Auden writes in the space between a disintegrated past and a fantasy present, and what he writes, perhaps unsurprisingly considering his temperament, does not please critics who prefer poets to remain stable entities in their history and their writing. Auden's poetry questions the stability of the relationship between writer and critic, while remaining sensitive to his meeting with posterity that loomed in the not far off future.

John Fletcher commented that it may not be *fashionable* to speak in the registers Auden used, but nevertheless, his poetry retains a 'simplicity and directness' which 'may no longer be able to get through to posterity's punch-drunk sensibilities'.[52]

Epistle to a Godson (1972)

Frank Kermode says of *Epistle to a Godson* (1972) that it is the work of a

■ man concerned with a purely human and un-tragic situation: moving towards death, owning a past, possessing 'a sense of real occasion, of beginnings and endings', aware of his moment in history.[53] □

and it is this heightened awareness of his position in history that makes the work of Auden so vibrant and so difficult to pronounce upon definitively. Clive James, in a penetrating and concise summary of Auden's career inspired by the occasion of his review of *Epistle to a Godson*, sees the mode of the later Auden as 'a movement away from excitement and towards satisfaction', describing the poet as a man so full of his creative gift that he needed to control its facility even before he published his first public collection. (See chapter six.)

The continued domestic element of the poetry, the interest in the natural world, the crusty, almost cranky tone, combine to form a substantial collection which looks back – perhaps unwittingly – over a life in language and pays tribute to the fact that even now he is still writing, still performing his craft. Haffenden reports that *Epistle to a Godson* was received by an amused audience who 'seemed quite content to accept him as an ageing entertainer, part jester and part valedictory sage . . .'.[54] By now the use of outrageous words was suffused in a camp glow as he stubbornly refused to return to his old ways.

Thank You Fog (1974) Posthumous

Auden died in his sleep in 1973. The posthumous collection *Thank You Fog* (1974) presents us with Auden's final poems, and appropriately the title refers to the poem written in praise of foggy weather that prevented Christmas visiting and allowed him to relax back into the Wiltshire household of James and Tania Stern with whom he was staying. Auden praised a natural event for allowing an ageing poet to have his own way, what he really secretly wanted, but which etiquette prevented. Haffenden remarks that two 'strong voices' at the time (Edna Longley and Terry Eagleton) both took this occasion to bemoan Auden's loss of power, Eagleton referring to Auden's 'historically obsolescent postures'.[55]

When Philip Toynbee assessed this final collection he pointed to what he described as a 'dissociation' between the reality of the poet's life and the artificial mask worn by the later poetry. Toynbee suggests that the 'tormented private reality' of Auden's life was never allowed to filter into the poetry, thus rendering it in some ways unfit for greatness:

■ I doubt whether compensatory verse is ever very good poetry; and if it is true, as I cannot help suspecting, that in too many of Auden's later volumes he was clinging to a part rather than expressing the truth of his distress, then this may well account for the dismay so many of the oldest admirers of this marvellous poet have felt at the note of unreality which had crept into too much of his later verse.[56] □

But this 'note of unreality' is the very space that critical work on Auden can now explore. This is precisely where the arguments made so long before in *The Sea and the Mirror* begin to chime in with their cold warnings. Prospero, magician, prepared to give up his magic and replace it for something mundane yet terrifying:

■ ... When the servants settle me into a chair
    In some well-sheltered corner of the garden,
  And arrange my muffler and rugs, shall I ever be able
    To stop myself from telling them what I am doing, –
Sailing alone, out over seventy thousand fathoms – ?
    Yet if I speak, I shall sink without a sound
Into unmeaning abysses. Can I learn to suffer
    Without saying something ironic or funny
On suffering? I never suspected the way of truth
    Was a way of silence ... (*C.P.*, p.409) □

These, I think, are the considerations we need to bring to bear on the later work of Auden – not a request that he should put aside his mask and show us his real face, but to sense the power of that reticence. In a way that makes comprehensible Auden's refusal to defend himself publicly for 'deserting' England in 1939, the later works and the status of the mask are essentially bound together in a compact whereby the truth of Auden's poetic or religious identity can never, by definition, be found. But in the process, we have to step out for a moment onto that unsteady and unstable platform of the later poetry, and get a sense of what was being woven into that vast unspoken and unspeakable reticence concealed within the anecdotes and the poetry of that garrulous and repetitive old man.

It is quite clear, then, that Auden's career can be crudely displayed as a downward curve, a trajectory that begins in a blaze of praise, energy and vitality, able to speak in the voice of a generation, and which ends with the unearthing of obsolete and dying words from the OED, and a narrowing of vision from the vibrant world of politics and art, to the domestic security of the house.

But this is only a story, and I hope that the material here will make that story less credible.

CHAPTER TWO

What Kind of Poet is Auden?

A UDEN'S LIFE and work are, to some extent, critical constructions. When a reader of Auden's poetry takes their bearings from the contemporary critical field, they are confronted by layers of narrative and analysis, anecdote and prejudice. We should remain aware that at a fundamental level the life and work are *stories* to be retold and modified by subsequent generations. Auden was particularly sensitive to the way his work was destined to undergo transformations beyond his control, and his resistance to having a biography written about him was part of this sensitivity to his future literary construction. It is that construction that we are helping to build now.

In this extract from Stan Smith's useful book *W.H. Auden* (1985) from Blackwell's 'Rereading Literature' series, Smith amplifies the importance of *narrative* and *discourse* when considering Auden's work. Smith's approach is immensely enabling, considering the biography as one more narrative, not to be dismissed, that makes up the 'constructed "I"' that inhabits the poems, reminding us that 'Strictly speaking . . . a poet is simply a bundle of texts':

■ There is a story, a moral fable called 'W.H. Auden' which goes something like this. Once upon a time there was a good little boy from a solid middle-class background, who went to public school and Oxford, fell into bad company, and became a Marxist and a Freudian. Then he went to Spain during a civil war and saw that Marxists were a bad thing because they closed down all the churches. So he ran away to America and became a Christian. After this he was a lot happier and became a grand old man of letters. Then in his old age he came home to Europe and Oxford, and died peacefully in his bed. He lived happily ever after in his poems.

There is another story, which bears a superficial resemblance to this, and is also a moral tale. It says: once upon a time there was a petty-bourgeois intellectual born into the dying culture of a declining empire. The after-shock of a world war caused by inter-imperialist rivalries, the rise of Fascism and the growing threat of a second world war, brought about by social and economic collapse, drove many from his background briefly to identify with the international working-class struggle. Having discovered that you can't make an omelette without cracking eggs, however, this sensitive young man soon defected, returning to the Christian pietism of his origins, emigrating to an America which was now the ascendant imperialist power. As the Cold War brought a shift into global confrontation between capitalism and socialism, he became increasingly strident in his denunciations of the creed he had once espoused. Elements of this kind are always politically unreliable and such renegade activity is to be expected. During his brief flirtation with Marxism he wrote some powerful political poems, most of which he subsequently disowned. Thereafter he wrote much insipid verse which was lauded for the wrong reasons. Though this poetry proclaimed his reconciliation with the status quo it could not conceal the great unhappiness of his wasted talent. Such is the fate of all who turn their back on the movement of history.

There are many different versions of these stories, and not all are told with such partisan fervour. Some emphasize the superficiality of one or the other belief. Some affirm the superficiality of both, seeing them simply as ways of providing metaphors for his poetry. A few even presume the equal seriousness of both. Each version has a comic or tragic inflection, or the two modes can be reconciled by the device of irony. A fable of redemption can be rewritten as a saga of betrayal, a journey of self-discovery represented as a flight into self-delusion. We can read Auden's life as a chronicle of ignorance overcome or truth denied, as warning or example, poetry or pity. What all the accounts share, however, is the structure of the traditional Aristotelian narrative, with a beginning, a middle and an end. A character who knows but does not know himself progresses to a crisis of recognition which is also a reversal of fortune. This reversal both makes and breaks him; thereafter he will never be the same.

Strictly speaking, of course, a poet is simply a bundle of texts. Unfortunately for the purists, at least one of those texts is a biography, whether written or inferred. Auden himself made it clear on many occasions that he thought 'most genuine artists would prefer that no biography be written', and that 'The one thing a writer . . . hopes for, is attentive readers of his writings . . . And he hopes they will read with patience and intelligence so as to extract as much meaning from the text as possible'.[1] His elegy for Yeats spoke of how, at his death, the poet 'became his admirers' and of how 'The words of a dead man/Are modified in the guts of the living'. In the essay just quoted he speaks of the ghost of Shakespeare possibly puzzled by William Empson's famous reading of Sonnet 94, but none the less grateful for his 'loving care'. In 'Making, Knowing and Judging', he goes as far as to nominate his own ideal reader, and also outlines the two questions he would ask of any poem.

> The first is technical: 'Here is a verbal contraption. How does it work?' The second is, in the broadest sense, moral: 'What kind of guy inhabits this poem? What is his notion of the good life or the good place? His notion of the Evil One? What does he conceal from the reader? What does he conceal even from himself?'[2]

The play between 'technical' and 'moral' places the emphasis on the constructed 'I' of the poem, which in turn constructs a reader to decipher this 'I' from the workings of what, after all, is no more than a 'verbal contraption'. Both 'guy' and 'reader' are effects of the text. . . . .

The Auden we perceive as a historical figure is also the product of discourses which run through and beyond him. There was (no doubt about it) a poet called W. H. Auden. There is a general consensus that he did certain things, lived in certain places, and wrote certain texts. But the meaning of those events, like the meanings of those texts, is not perpetually fixed in history, unchangeably inscribed in the record. When we come to read Auden, we must be alert to the fact that we can, in reality, only reread him. The poems he produced have been rewritten by the historical process, as he himself acknowledged when he sought, with hindsight, to modify, censor and repress some of them. But Auden the historical subject has been rewritten too. 'We shan't, not since Stalin and Hitler,/trust ourselves ever again: we know that, subjectively,/all is possible', he wrote in 'The Cave of Making' (*C.P.*, p. 692). There is no original meaning that we can recover, only the play of language in our own moment of history, interlocking with the play of language of texts which have a certain antiquity, but are nevertheless our contemporaries, waiting for their ideal reader – a perpetually deferred and imaginary subject.[3] □

The contradictory arguments and conflicting opinions that run through the extracts reproduced in this Guide make it clear, as Smith suggests, that Auden is a collection of fragmentary texts *which do not cohere into a whole*. Smith is an important reader as his book opens up a whole new Auden to explore, an Auden whose poetry willingly and effortlessly meshes with a post-structuralist treatment. (See his analysis of some of the later poems in chapter six.)

Earlier criticism tended to keep an image of a real, authentic, consistent Auden in view, whereas the later criticism affirms the 'bundle of texts' theory, and revels in the play that Auden's poetry allows. An example of the earlier attitude can be seen in Stephen Spender's complaint in 1945 that

■ Auden is a dazzling observer and enormously clever but one relates the conclusions of his poetic arguments to some rational argument or to some book, nearly always, hardly ever to the poet's deepest experience. For this reason . . . his books themselves are almost entirely lacking in form, they are ideas of a brilliant mind strung together, because they lack that wholeness and depth of form which comes from an inner and complete experience which moulds a work of art into an organic unity.[4] □

Spender suggests that Auden has more affinity with the 'book' than with an 'inner and complete experience' and this is precisely the element of Auden's work that allows post-structuralist, intertextual readings their scope. There is no need to reconcile the grumpy old conservative in his carpet slippers with the poet who revels in the fact that his language is constitutive of all he does and desires. Auden's playful baiting of the critical discourses that surrounded him (such as in the essay 'Reading' in *The Dyer's Hand*[5]) show us a poet who carefully anticipated his literary and historical construction, and who sometimes mischievously played roles which either confirmed or refuted their claims.

There are many stories to be made of Auden, and I begin with one of his own. Auden began writing poetry seriously at the age of fifteen after a famous encounter with his friend Robert Medley,[6] who asked him a casual and fateful question: 'Do you write poetry?' Auden claimed that from that moment he knew his vocation. It was an interesting and unusual call from his 'muse' and it is worth taking a little time to think about Auden's retelling of these events, as they help to place the peculiar and compelling tone of the early poetry in a context of personal obsession and anxiety:

■ As a child I had no interest in poetry, but a passion for words, the longer the better, and appalled my aunts by talking like a professor of geology. To-day words so affect me that a pornographic story, for example, excites me sexually more than a living person can do.

Besides words, I was interested almost exclusively in mines and their machinery. An interest in people did not begin till adolescence.

My interest and knowledge were such that I deceived not only myself but my parents into thinking that it was a genuine scientific interest and that I was gifted to become, what I said I was going to become, a mining engineer. A psychologist, noticing that I had no practical mechanical gift whatsoever, would have realised that the interest was a symbolic one. From the age of four to thirteen I had a series of passionate love-affairs with pictures of, to me, particularly attractive water-turbines, winding-engines, roller-crushers, etc., and I was never so emotionally happy as when I was underground.

The same psychologist would have also detected easily enough the complexes which were the cause of these affairs, but what was important for the future was not the neurotic cause but the fact that I should have chosen to express my conflicts in symbolic phantasy rather than in action or any other way. I cannot now look at anything without looking for its symbolic relation to something else.

I doubt if a person with both these passions, for the word and for the symbol, could become anything but a poet. At any rate, when at the age of sixteen a schoolfriend casually asked me one day if I wrote poetry, I, who had never written a line or even read one with pleasure, decided at that moment that poetry was my vocation, and though, when I look at my work, I am often filled with shame and disgust, I know that, however badly I may write, I should do anything else even worse, and that the only way in which I shall ever see anything clearly is through the word and the symbol. (*The English Auden*, pp. 397–8) □

The fact that his poetry sometimes filled him with 'shame and disgust' is a point to remember when considering the controversial revisions of his work that Auden made from the mid-forties onwards.

Written when he was thirty-two in an 'unpublished book' called *The Prolific and the Devourer* (1939),[7] Auden's remarks reveal a poet who not only had the ability to analyse himself in honest detail, but who also had the desire to *narrate* his early life in such a way as to confirm his present beliefs. Even here, Auden participated in the construction of the historical and literary narrative of himself. Written at an important time (on his 'honeymoon' with Chester Kallman) Auden's remarks on the beauty of mining machinery are worked through in a key poem, 'Perhaps I always knew what they were saying' (1939), in which he acknowledges the importance of his early infatuations and how they had led him finally to the true love of his life:

■ Those beautiful machines that never talked
But let the small boy worship them and learn
All their long names whose hardness made him proud
(*C.P.*, p. 255) □

The sexual ambivalence is rife in these lines as Auden describes his sexual path to Kallman through a succession of hired boys who appear here as 'beautiful machines'. Note the sexual link being made between words and the machines they describe.

Auden's reputation as a poet spread in the early 1930s until his style and his vision was recognisable, and widely considered to be important – a poet speaking in the voice of his time. The recognition of Auden as an important poet is summed up in the tribute mounted by Geoffrey Grigson in November 1937, when as editor of the poetry journal *New Verse* he dedicated a double issue solely to Auden, inviting an impressive range of artists and writers to make a statement about the poet. Besides sixteen short assessments from writers such as Dylan Thomas and Graham Greene, there is a piece on Auden's politics by Edgell Rickword and an abrasive attack on Auden as playwright by Kenneth Allott. Here is Grigson's opening editorial comment:

■ We salute in Auden (though we do not forget all that can be said against him) the first English poet for many years who is a poet all the way round. There are angles from which Mr. Eliot seems a ghost and even Mr. Yeats a gleam. Most authors still belong to the 1900 in which Mr. Sturge Moore, one of the spectres attendant on Mr. Yeats, said that 'art seeks to reveal beauty, and that contemplation of beauty exhilarates, refines and elevates'. Some others stick in those curious years when the limitations of Eliot and Pound were made into a system because their virtues were considerable and rare. But Auden does live in a new day. He is solid enough, poke him where you will, not crumbling like fudge. He is traditional, revolutionary, energetic, inquisitive, critical, and intelligent. Some of the older living writers, Yeats, Wyndham Lewis and Eliot among them, have recognised this and committed themselves publicly (Lewis in 'Blasting and Bombardiering') in Auden's praise. Others are peevish, petty, jealous and silent. But, as this number shows, there are plenty of writers who do recognise Auden's broad power of raising ordinary speech into strong and strange incantation, and do see no reason for waiting to praise and criticise Auden until he has been dead a hundred years.[8] □

Grigson confirms that Auden was a poet writing of his time, and who deserved to be praised in his time. ('Let us honour if we can/The vertical man/Though we value none/But the horizontal one'.[9]) Dylan Thomas marked this unusually premature tribute by signing off his contribution with: 'P.S. – Congratulations on Auden's seventieth birthday'.[10] Auden was actually just thirty. In 1975, after Auden died, Stephen Spender edited *W.H. Auden: A Tribute* in which friends paid their respects; one of whom was, appropriately, Grigson.[11]

One of the important and revealing contributions to this Auden 'Double Number' was that of Auden's close friend Christopher Isherwood who provided a comical yet useful analysis of his friend's work. Isherwood knew Auden in the early formative years and he makes light of the 'celebrated' obscurity of Auden's verse, but he also gives us some important bearings from which we can begin to engage with the poems.

■ If I were told to introduce a reader to the poetry of W.H. Auden, I should begin by asking him to remember three things:

First, that Auden is essentially a scientist: perhaps I should add, a schoolboy scientist. He has, that is to say, the scientific training and the scientific interests of a very intelligent schoolboy. He has covered the groundwork, but doesn't propose to go any further: he has no intention of specialising. Nevertheless, he has acquired the scientific outlook and technique of approach; and this is really all he needs for his writing.

Second, that Auden is a musician and a ritualist. As a child, he enjoyed a high Anglican upbringing, coupled with a sound musical education. The Anglicanism has evaporated, leaving only the height: he is still much preoccupied with ritual, in all its forms. When we collaborate, I have to keep a sharp eye on him – or down flop the characters on their knees (see 'F.6.' passim): another constant danger is that of choral interruptions by angel-voices. If Auden had his way, he would turn every play into a cross between grand opera and high mass.

Third, that Auden is a Scandinavian. The Auden family came originally from Iceland. Auden himself was brought up on the sagas, and their influence upon his work has been profound. . . . . . .

The saga-world is a schoolboy world, with its feuds, its practical jokes, its dark threats conveyed in puns and riddles and understatements: 'I think this day will end unluckily for some; but chiefly for those who least expect harm.' I once remarked to Auden that the atmosphere of *Gisli the Outlaw* very much reminded me of our schooldays. He was pleased with the idea: and, soon after this, he produced his first play: *Paid on Both Sides* in which the two worlds are so inextricably confused that it is impossible to say whether the characters are really epic heroes or only members of a school O.T.C.

Auden is, and always has been, a most prolific writer. Problems of form and technique seem to bother him very little. You could say to him: 'Please write me a double ballade on the virtues of a certain brand of toothpaste, which also contains at least ten anagrams on the names of well-known politicians, and of which the refrain is as follows. . . .' Within twenty-four hours, your ballade would be ready – and it would be good.

When Auden was younger, he was very lazy. He hated polishing and making corrections. If I didn't like a poem, he threw it away and wrote another. If I liked one line, he would keep it and work it into a new poem. In this way, whole poems were constructed which were simply anthologies of my favourite lines, entirely regardless of grammar or sense. This is the simple explanation of much of Auden's celebrated obscurity.[12] □

Isherwood claimed that Auden 'is still much preoccupied with ritual, in all its forms' and at the end of Auden's life this trait is still prominent, as he writes in the poem 'Profile' in *City Without Walls* (1969):

■ So obsessive a ritualist
a pleasant surprise
makes him cross. (*C.P.*, p.775) □

But even without the benefit of close personal knowledge of the poet, some of his early critics noted that Auden's voice contained something essentially novel that spoke of the economic, political and spiritual problems of the time in heretofore unexpressed ways. Naomi Mitchison, for example, sensed that Auden was onto something, tapping into the past in ways that recall Eliot's interest in tradition, but in a more up to date, contemporary context. She says of the poems:

■ They may be romantic, they may be obscure, but they have the curious, archaic maleness which seems to me to fit in with three things: the fifth century before Plato came and muddled it, the heroic age in Iceland and the modern youth movement in Germany.[13] □

Given that Auden's poetry was being fed from the varied sources described so well by Isherwood and Mitchison, how did Auden's style manifest itself in the poetry?

In his book *Reading the Thirties* Bernard Bergonzi isolates and discusses what he calls the 'Audenesque' – that is, the essence of the Auden style. His entertaining piece discusses the use of the definite article in Auden's poetry, and makes some useful links to Eliot's work, suggesting an interplay between the two poets. Bergonzi notes Rostrevor-Hamilton's disapproving remark that Auden's use of the definite article gives to his poetry the sense that 'an entire stranger were claiming our acquaintance'[14] and this is fundamental to the way that Auden addressed his audience in that close, personal way that recruited his readers into the group.

William Logan's piece 'Auden's Images' from an interesting collection of essays gathered by Alan Bold, *W.H. Auden: The Far Interior* (1985), helps us explore the raw material of Auden's poetic world, introducing the significance and relatedness of images such as the spy, the border, maps and industrial ruins. Discussing Auden's psychological landscapes, he suggests that 'Auden's imagination worked from the literature toward the world, rather than vice versa', confirming Smith's sense of Auden as a poet aware that he is made of texts.[15] Logan mentions the importance of the fairy tale, and this is the subject of Janet Montefiore's interesting piece 'Goebbels and Goblins: Politics and the Fairy-Tale in Auden's Poems' which is also in Bold's collection.[16] Cleanth Brooks has also written on 'Auden's Imagery', claiming that 'his attitude is one which accommodates in a dramatic unity the various elements which in our practical oversimplification are divided and at war with one another'.[17]

Randall Jarrell was one of the first critics to provide an extensive overview of Auden and his work. In the following extract from his excellent long essay, 'Changes of Attitude and Rhetoric in Auden's Poetry' (1945), Jarrell writes critically and perceptively of Auden's work, and while he castigates the poet for holding untenable and brittle beliefs, his overall tone is one of frustration with the way that the later Auden turned his attention from his earlier brilliant diagnoses of a society in decay to the spiritual exploration of the social self.

Ian Samson's essay '"Flouting Papa": Randall Jarrell and W.H. Auden' in *Auden Studies 3* describes Jarrell's intense interest and love for Auden's work and notes how it took Jarrell six years to write 'Changes of Attitude. . .'.[18] Of Jarrell's harsh criticism, Auden typically rejoined to Stephen Spender: 'Jarrell is in love with me!', and Samson thinks that: 'Auden got it right – Jarrell did regard him as a father figure and both loved and hated him.'[19]

In this extract Jarrell lays out the fundamental oppositions and tensions of the early poetry, particularly in *Poems* (1930) and *The Orators* (1932). While his ironic, dry humour has the benefit of hindsight (looking back on the decade from 1941) there is an undeniable perceptiveness in his remarks, even if they do verge, at times, on parody.

Jarrell demonstrates Auden's special ability to *position* his audience by either explicitly or implicitly setting up a division between 'us' and 'them'. The reader is asked to recognise what side they are on and whether they should begin to rethink the fundamental questions of identity which bind them to their class and their time. As Jarrell remarks, Auden extended Eliot's literary based allusions, drawing upon obscure and forgotten knowledge and rituals which had been either 'rejected, neglected, or misinterpreted' by the present generation. It is here, in an often stridently 'lowbrow' sense of tradition, that the significance and power of his first collection resided. Naomi Mitchison (whom Jarrell mentions) suggested that Auden's early poetry exuded an 'archaic maleness', and the link between tradition, sexuality and ritual is closely bound in this early work.[20]

■ *We never step twice into the same Auden.* – HERACLITUS

In the first part of this article I want to analyze the general position Auden makes for himself in his early poems, and to show how the very different attitude of the later poems developed from it . . . I have borrowed several terms from an extremely good book – Kenneth Burke's *Attitudes toward History* – and I should like to make acknowledgments for them.

The date is *c.* 1930, the place England. Auden (and the group of friends with whom he identifies himself) is unable or unwilling to accept the values and authority, the general world picture of the late-capitalist society in which he finds himself. He is conscious of a profound alienation, intellectual, moral, and aesthetic – financial and sexual, even. Since he rejects the established order, it is necessary for him to find or make a new order, a myth by which he and his can possess the world. Auden synthesizes (more or less as the digestive organs synthesize enzymes) his own order from a number of sources: (1) Marx-Communism in general. (2) Freud and Groddeck: in general, the risky and nonscientific, but fertile and imaginative, side of modern psychology. (3) A cluster of related sources: the folk, the blood, intuition, religion and mysticism, fairy tales, parables, and so forth – this group includes a number of semi-Fascist elements. (4) The sciences, biology particularly: these seem to be available to him because they have been only partially assimilated by capitalist culture, and because, like mathematics, they are practically incapable of being corrupted by it. (5) All sorts of boyish sources of value: flying, polar exploration, mountain climbing, fighting, the thrilling side of science, public-school life, sports, big-scale practical jokes, 'the spies' career', etc. (6) Homosexuality: if the ordinary sexual values are taken as negative and rejected, this can be accepted as a source of positive revolutionary values.

Auden is able to set up a We (whom he identifies himself with – rejection loves company) in opposition to the enemy They; neither We nor They are the relatively distinct or simple entities one finds in political or economic analyses, but are tremendous clusters of elements derived from almost every source. Auden is interested in establishing a dichotomy in which one side, naturally, gets all the worst of it, and he wants this *all the worst* to be as complete as possible, to cover everything from imperialism to underlining too many words in letters. . . . I am going to treat this We – They opposition at the greatest length – a treatment of it is practically a treatment of Auden's early position; and I shall mix in some discussion of the sources of value I have listed. Auden begins: The death of the old order is inevitable; it is already economically unsound, morally corrupt, intellectually bankrupt, and so forth. We = the Future, They = the Past. (So any reader tends to string along with Us and that perpetual winner, the Future.) Auden gets this from Marxism, of course; but never at any time was he a thorough Marxist: it would have meant giving up too much to the enemy. He keeps all sorts of things a Marxist rejects, and some of his most cherished doctrines – as the reader will see – are in direct contradiction to his Marxism. At the ultimate compulsive level of belief most of his Marxism drops away (and, in the last few years, *has* dropped away); his psychoanalytical, vaguely medical beliefs are so much more essential to Auden – 'son of a nurse and doctor, loaned a dream' – that the fables he may have wanted to make Marxist always turn out to be psychoanalytical. But Marxism as a source of energy, of active and tragic insight, was invaluable; it was badly needed to counteract the passivity, the trust in Understanding and Love and God, that are endemic in Auden. Marxism has always supplied most of the terror in his poetry; in his latest poems all that remains is the pity – an invalid's diet, like milk toast.

Obviously They represent Business, Industrialism, Exploitation – and, worse than that, a failing business, an industrialism whose machines are already rusting. Auden had seen what happened to England during a long depression, and he made a romantic and beautifully effective extension of this, not merely into decadence, but into an actual breakdown of the whole machinery, a Wellsish state where commerce and transportation have gone to pieces, where the ships lie 'long high and dry', where no one goes 'further than railhead or the end of pier', where the professional traveler 'asked at fireside . . . is dumb'. . . . The thought of those 'beautiful machines that never talked /But let the small boy worship them' (*C.P.*, p. 255), abandoned and rusting in the wet countryside – the early Auden sees even his machines in rural surroundings – was perhaps, unconsciously, quite as influential as some political or humanitarian considerations.

Auden relates science to Marxism in an unexpected but perfectly orthodox way: Lenin says somewhere that in the most general sense Marxism is a theory of evolution. Auden quite consciously makes this connection; evolution, as a source both of insight and image, is always just at the back of his earliest poems. . . . There are many examples of this coalition of Marxism and biology; probably the prettiest is IX, a poem with the refrain, 'Here am I, here are you:/But what does it mean? What are we going to do?' (*The English Auden*, p. 42). The I of the poem is supposed to be anonymous and typical, a lay figure of late capitalism; he has not retained even the dignity of rhetoric, but speaks in a style that is an odd blank parody of popular songs. He has finally arrived at the end of his blind alley: he has a wife, a car, a mother complex, a vacation, and no use or desire for any. All he can make himself ask for is some fresh tea, some rugs – this to remind you of Auden's favorite view of capitalism: a society where everyone is sick. Even his instincts have broken down: he doesn't want to go to bed with Honey, all the wires to the base in his spine are severed. The poem develops in this way up to the next to the last stanza: 'In my veins there is a wish,/And a memory of fish:/When I lie crying on the floor,/It says, "You've often done this before".' The 'wish' in the blood is the evolutionary will, the blind urge of the species to assimilate the universe. He remembers the fish, that at a similar impasse, a similar critical point, changed over to land, a new form of being. Here for the millionth time (the racial memory tells the weeping individual) is the place where the contradiction has to be resolved; where the old answer, useless now, has to be transcended; where all the quantitative changes are over, where the qualitative leap has to occur. The individual remembers all these critical points because he is the product of them. And the individual, in the last stanza, is given a complete doom ('I've come a very long way to prove/No land, no water, and no love'). But his bankruptcy and liquidation are taken as inevitable for the species, a necessary mode of progression: the destructive interregnum between the old form and the new is inescapable, as old as life. The strategic value in Auden's joining of Marxism and evolution, his constant shifting of terms from one sphere to the other, is this: the reader will tend to accept the desired political and economic changes (and the form of these) as themselves inevitable, something it is as ludicrous or pathetic to resist as evolution.

When compared with the folkish Us, They are complicated, subtle in a barren Alexandrian-encyclopedia way. They are scholarly introspective observers, We have the insight and natural certainty of the naive, of Christ's children, of fools, of the third sons in fairy stories. They are aridly commercial, financial, distributive; We represent real production, the soil. They are bourgeois-respectable or perverted; We are folk-simple, or else consciously Bohemian so as to break up Their system and morale – there is also a suggestion of the prodigal son, of being reborn through sin. They represent the sterile city, We the fertile country . . . They are white-collar workers, executives, or idlers – those who neither 'make' nor 'do'; We are scientists, explorers, farmers, manual laborers, aviators, fighters and conspirators – the real makers and doers. Auden gets Science over on Our side by his constant use of it both for insight and images . . .

Since Auden has had to reject Tradition, he sets up a new tradition formed of the available elements (available because, rejected, neglected, or misinterpreted) of the old. . . . One can see this working even in the form of Auden's early poetry: in all the Anglo-Saxon imitation; the Skeltonics; the Hopkins accentual verse, alliteration, assonance, consonance; the Owens rhymes; the use of the fairy story, parable, ballad, popular song – the folk tradition They have rejected or collected in Childs. Thus Auden has selected his own ancestors, made from the disliked or misprized his own tradition. In *The Orators* Auden shows, by means of the regular Mendelian inheritance chart, that one's 'true ancestor' may be neither a father nor a mother, but an uncle. (His true ancestor wasn't the Tradition, but the particular elements of it most like himself.) This concept is extremely useful to Auden in (1) family, (2) religious, and (3) political relations. (1) By this means he acquires a different and active type of family relationship to set up against the inertia of the ordinary bourgeois womanized family. (2) God is addressed and thought of as Uncle instead of Father: God as Uncle will help revolutionary Us just as naturally and appropriately as God as Father would help his legitimate sons, the Enemy. This Uncle has a Christlike sacrificial-hero representative on earth, who is surrounded with a great deal of early-Christian, secret-service paraphernalia. This hero is confused or identified with (3) the political leader, a notably un-political sort of fantasy Hitler, who seems to have strayed into politics with his worshippers only because he lives in an unreligious age. There is hardly more politics in early Auden than in G. A. Henty; what one gets is mostly religion, hero worship, and adventure, combined with the odd Lawrence-Nazi folk mysticism that serves as a false front for the real politics behind it – which Auden doesn't treat.

When Auden occasionally prays to this Uncle he asks in blunt definite language for definite things: it is a personal, concrete affair. In his later poetry Auden is always praying or exhorting, but only to some abstract eclectic Something-or-Other, who is asked in vague exalted language for vague exalted abstractions. . . . Most of this belongs to the bad half of what Burke calls secular prayer: the attempt, inside any system, to pray away, exhort away, legislate away evils that are not incidental but essential to the system. . . . When Auden prays for anything specific at all; when he prays against the organization of the world that makes impossible the moral and spiritual changes he prays for, it will be possible to take the prayer as something more than conscience – and face-saving sublimation, a device ideally suited to make action un-urgent and its nature vague. . . . . . .[21]

But let me return to We and They, the early Auden. We are Love; They are hate and all the terrible perversions of love. There is an odd ambivalent attitude toward homosexuality: in Us it is a quite natural relationship shading off into comradeship (like Greek homosexuality in Naomi Mitchison), in Them it is just another decadent perversion. . . . Where the members of a class and a sex are taught, in a prolonged narcissistic isolation, to hero-worship themselves – class and sex; where – to a different class – unemployment is normal, where one's pay is inadequate or impossible for more than one; where children are expensive liabilities instead of assets; where women are business competitors; where most social relationships have become as abstract, individualistic, and mobile as the relations of the labor market, homosexuality is a welcome asset to the state, one of the cheapest and least dangerous forms of revolution. One gets no such analysis in the early Auden, though a real uneasiness about Our condition is plain in the allegorical *Letter to a Wound,* implicit in the Airman's kleptomania. A contempt for women sometimes breaks out in little half-sublimated forms; 'there is something peculiarly horrible about the idea of women pilots', writes the Airman, whose love for E. has not managed to give him any prejudice in her sex's favor. Sometimes this contempt is openly expressed. 'All of the women and most of the men/Shall work with their hands and not think again' is the early Auden's lyrical premonition of the ideal State of the future. Words fail me here; this is not tactics, not sense, and certainly not Marxism: compare Engels's contempt at Dühring's ingenuous belief that the Ideal State would have professional porters. All this is related to a Lawrence-Hitler-*Golden Bough* folk mysticism – complete with Führer, folk, blood, intuition, 'the carved stone under the oak-tree' – which crops up constantly; it is partly literary, partly real. What is wrong with it is too plain to say; what is right about it – the insistence on a real society, the dislike of the weird isolation and individualism, the helpless rejection, forced on so many of the members of our own society – may be worth mentioning. Auden has forgotten the good with the bad, and now takes the isolation of the individual – something that would have seemed impossible to almost any other society, that is a tragic perversion of ours – as necessary, an absolute that can only be accepted.

We are health, They are disease; everything Auden gets from Freud and Groddeck is used to put Them into the category of patients, of diseased sufferers who unconsciously will their own disease. This makes Our opposition not only good for Them but necessary – Our violence is the surgeon's violence, Their opposition is the opposition of madmen to psychiatrists. We are Life, They are Death. The death wish is the fundamental motive for all Their actions, Auden often says or implies; if They deny it, he retorts, 'Naturally you're not *conscious* of it'.

These earliest poems are soaked in Death: as the real violence of revolutionary action and as a very comprehensive symbol. Death is Their necessary and desired conclusion; often poems are written from Their increasingly desperate point of view. Death belongs to Us as martyrs, spies, explorers, tragic heroes – with a suggestion of scapegoat or criminal – who die for the people. It belongs to Us because We, Their negation, have been corrupted by Them, and must ourselves be transcended. But, most of all, it is a symbol for *rebirth*: it is only through death that We can leave the old for good, be finally reborn. I have been astonished to see how consistently most of the important elements of ritual (purification, rebirth, identification, etc.) are found in the early poems; their use often seems unconscious. The most common purification rituals (except that of purification by fire) are plain. There is purification through decay: physical and spiritual, the rotting away of the machines and the diseased perversions of the men. There are constant glaciers, ice, northern exploration – enough to have made Cleanth Brooks consider the fundamental metaphorical picture of the early poems that of a new ice age.[22] There is purification by water: in the second poem in *On This Island* a sustained flood metaphor shifts into parent-child imagery. There is some suggestion of purification through sin. There is mountain climbing: from these cold heights one can see differently, free of the old perspectives one returns, like Moses, with new insights. This is akin to the constantly used parable of the fairy-tale search, the hero's dangerous labors or journey. And the idea of rebirth is plainest of all, extending even to the common images of ontogenetic or phylogenetic development; of the fetus, newborn infant, or child; of the discontinuities of growth. The *uncle* is so important because he is a new ancestor whom We can identify ourselves with (Auden recommends 'ancestor worship' of the true ancestor, the Uncle); by this identification We destroy our real parents, our Enemy ancestry, thus finally abolishing any remaining traces of Them in us. These ideas and their extensions are worth tracing in detail, if one had the space. Here is a quotation in which rebirth through death is extremely explicit; seasonal rebirth and the womb of the new order are packed in also. Auden writes that love

> Needs death, death of the grain, our death,
> Death of the old gang; should leave them
> In sullen valley where is made no friend,
> The old gang to be forgotten in the spring,
> The hard bitch and the riding-master,
> Stiff underground; deep in clear lake
> The lolling bridegroom, beautiful, there. (*C.P.*, p. 49)

I want my treatment of Auden's early position to be suggestive rather than exhausting, so I shall not carry it any further; though I hate to stop short of all the comic traits Auden gives the Enemy, wretched peculiarities as trivial as saying *I mean* or having a room called the Den. The reader can do his own extending or filling in by means of a little unusually attractive reading: Auden's early poems.[23] □

The influence of Jarrell's criticism has been wide-ranging, and has dictated many of the subsequent readings of the poet.[24] In his book *Reading Auden: The Returns of Caliban* John R. Boly usefully makes visible the ubiquity of the 'Jarrell Scheme', whereby Auden's career between 1930 and 1945 can be divided into three distinct sections. This scheme is based on the second major Jarrell essay 'Freud to Paul: Stages in Auden's Ideology' (1945).[25] Here Jarrell describes Auden's early work (Stage I) as trapped within a causal necessity, marked out by a rugged and heartless landscape which neatly frames the 'unconscious, the primitive, the childish, the animal, the natural'.[26] A transitional Stage II shows Auden in the 'Realm of Logical Necessity' which is dominated by the need to choose; this is the realm of choice. Stage III is given the single name *Paul* in which all has arrived at stasis: 'man's ultimate accomplishment is *sitting still'*.[27]

Boly wants to move away from such a division, as it implies an abnegation of social responsibility on Auden's part, and unfairly sets the scene for many of the important works written about Auden in the last thirty years. Instead, Boly looks toward an emphasis on the *textual* and the *ludic* as well as the *dialogic* interplay of Auden's texts. These elements appear in the later phases of Auden commentary with a greater attention to the *discursive* effects of both poetry and its criticism as well as the important text that runs alongside these arguments: the biography.[28]

■ The question of Auden's social commitment is not completely dead. In a once infamous essay, 'From Freud to Paul: The Stages of Auden's Ideology,' Randall Jarrell attacked Auden for a lack of high intellectual seriousness.[29] Jarrell argued that during the period of his most intense political involvement (or at least his reputation for that involvement), Auden was a spiritual magpie, stealing ideas from first a crackpot psychology, then a puerile Marxism, and finally a Kierkegaardian fideism. Jarrell's argument may be the most influential criticism ever written about Auden. Its idea of a three-step development, from personal, to social, and then back to personal (religious) concerns, has furnished a framework that both Auden's defenders and detractors have been obliged to accept. . . . So one of the most durable truisms about Auden is that he marched under the successive banners of psychology, politics, and at last religion. But Jarrell's study has also shaped the critical tradition in a subtler way, by fostering a tendency to separate the early secular Auden from the later religious convert (temporizer, reactionary, sellout). . . . It would seem that Auden either lost or never had the high seriousness required of a social poet.

. . . As might be expected, the early commentaries on Auden are dominated by his detractors. When the disappointed hopes of thirties radicalism were still painful, and the resentment of Auden's abrupt departure for America still fresh, critics had a greater tendency to assail what Hynes calls the Auden Myth. . . . . . . Still, Auden does have his defenders. Yet these rescue missions are oddly unfortunate in that their arguments, however perceptive as readings, have unwittingly confirmed the framework of Jarrell's assumptions. Until that framework is challenged, the question of Auden's social commitment remains at an impasse. The defenders might be divided into two camps, the polemicists and the humanists. Taking the high road, the polemicists maintain that Auden did indeed have a prophetic message. This is certainly the most direct line of defense. But even with a deft selection of materials, the polemicists run athwart the obvious posturing of the texts. Auden's poetry retains the sense of a mask or pose, as of someone miming a part in an unnervingly overdone way. The performance has the quality of an impersonation, so that it seems less a statement than a dramatization. . . .

The other camp, the humanists, also retain the ideal of a unified message, but they shift its site from the treacherous plains of history to the more congenial sanctum of psychology. For the humanists, Auden is the upholder of individual rights and personal freedom against the insidious encroachments of mass culture and its mechanized bureaucracies: the poet of works such as 'The Unknown Citizen', 'The Managers', 'The Chimeras', and 'Progress?' . . . . . .

Like any thematic approach to Auden, the humanist defense captures certain elements of his practice, but at the cost of ignoring many others. It cherishes the notion of a free and autonomous individual, set apart from social currents and detached from ideological frays. This idea, however, runs counter to Auden's insistence that human beings are historical entities: 'For we are conscripts to our age/Simply by being born' (*C.P.*, p. 183). . . . Certainly, the humanists can point to numerous passages in which Auden requires a 'change of heart' or demands a new beginning. But such texts must be approached carefully. One example is a retrospective passage from 'Authority in America': 'Looking back, it seems to me that the interest in Marx taken by myself and my friends . . . was more psychological than political; we were interested in Marx in the same way we were interested in Freud, as a technique of unmasking middle-class ideologies, not with the intention of repudiating our class, but with the hope of becoming better bourgeois.'[30] Auden says nothing here about an autonomous inwardness or a heroic decision making. Instead he emphasizes analytical procedures. Both Marx and Freud offer strategies for recognizing and reassembling discursive structures: the assumptions and practices through which meaning is fashioned. It is this 'technique of unmasking', not any privileged interior or independent will, that is cited as the important contribution of psychology. To argue, as the humanists do, that a change of heart must precede any significant social reorganization is in effect a reactionary tactic. It conveniently overlooks that what is meant by 'heart' (an ideologically approved

value, *anthropos,* an inwardness subject to state and economic formation), or what is acceptable as 'change' (a move toward carefully
restricted goals), has already been fashioned by the social organization
it proposes to alter.

It does not follow that Auden was either a behaviorist or a relativist.
He did not believe that acculturation imposes an invincible order, nor
did he maintain that any one society is as good as another. But he did
insist that human freedom begins in an understanding of the discursive structures and techniques through which well-entrenched social
interests attempt to supervise meaning and truth.[31] □

Boly describes Auden as 'dedicated to a play of contrasts' and this would
be a fitting description of Auden's lighter verse. In his book *The Poetic
Art of W.H. Auden,* John G. Blair writes about Auden's interest in and
composition of 'light verse' and thinks carefully about exactly what
Auden achieved by writing in this form. Blair suggests that Auden's
'unserious' techniques actually reveal serious questions beneath their
jester's masks. What is important here is that we get a sense of the seriousness of Auden's light verse, and a partial refutation of those critics
like D.S. Savage, who see Auden's interest in light verse as simply
another example of his immaturity of judgement.[32] As with the
'defection' to America, the apparently trivial, 'comfy' style of the later
years has caused, unsurprisingly, a polarity of views on the value of his
work:

■ Moraine, pot, oxbow, glint, sink, crater, piedmont, dimple . . . ?
Just reeling off their names is ever so comfy. (*C.P.,* p. 563) □

In this piece Blair explores the ambiguous and difficult relationship in
Auden's poetry between the serious and the unserious, a problem that
accompanied criticism of the poet from the early years of the dangerous
The Orators to the apparent complacencies of *Thank You Fog.*

■ The appeal of light verse for Auden goes beyond personal pleasure.
In the perspective of cultural history he finds that lightness in poetry
reflects an intimate relation between the poet and his audience. The
modern poet who inherits no sense of community with his readers
finds himself in a paradoxical situation. His estrangement from society
allows him to see its faults; yet that same isolation makes communication of his insights proportionately more difficult. What Auden *can* do,
recognizing the problem, is to manufacture lightness as a possible
means of reopening communication. In the late 1930s light verse
seemed to Auden for a time a promising means for reaching a large
audience. It also served indirectly as a stimulus to developing his

unserious technique. It suggested striking variations on old saws or folk figures presumably having wide cultural dissemination. It sanctioned verse forms in which colloquial diction and witty rimes were appropriate. It provided a vehicle for treating serious subjects in an ironically lowbrow manner.

Auden never succeeded in reaching as wide an audience as he had hoped. Even in 1936, in the midst of his most direct efforts at public appeal, he remarked, 'Personally, the kind of poetry I should like to write but can't is "the thoughts of a wise man in the speech of the common people"'.[33] The subjects he wanted to treat in verse became, especially after 1940, less amenable to presentation in a popular mode, and he resigned himself to the fact that for poetry that is not propaganda, the audience is inescapably limited. He continued to extol the virtues of lowbrow art but less in hopes of a real rapprochement than with the intent of unsettling highbrow prejudices. More recently he labels himself a highbrow while mourning the extinction of popular art in the postwar culture built by mass media.

From his attempts at popular light verse, however, Auden did preserve an inclination toward unserious poetic technique. . . . . . . The single most important facet of technique that Auden explored primarily in such light verse and then carried over into more serious works involves what we might call the principle of poetic unexpectedness. Like all the memorable comic and satiric poets, he seems to have understood instinctively what his reading of Kierkegaard reinforced: the most direct source of aesthetic interest is the unexpected or incongruous. Thus a clergyman who steals is aesthetically interesting; one who simply performs all his duties properly is dull.[34] To exploit this principle, Auden establishes in the reader's mind a series of expectations which he then disappoints by injecting the incongruous. The expectations can either be generated within the poem itself or be assumed to exist in the reader's mind. . . . . . .

The diverse application of poetic unexpectedness or incongruity seems at the heart of Auden's mature technique and his inclination toward making serious points in an unserious way. Among other things this technique reinforces his characteristic kind of ambiguity. Unlike the unresolvable obscurity of some of his early poems, this is the temporary ambiguity of a riddle. Once the reader has exerted the conscious effort required to solve it, he can see the riddle as a rhetorically arresting and elegant combination of words that also contains an unforeseen yet inescapable comment on human nature or a human problem. Because the poem's comment is made by upsetting and reordering his previous associations with the words or situations involved, the reader may be startled into accepting a fresh evaluation of himself and his world. Ideally, he will go on to take the verbal meaning 'seriously' by attempting to rethink his life on the basis of the poem's insights. . . . . . .

Stephen Spender has suggested that a kind of frivolity is dominant in Auden's mode of poetry. He calls it a 'serious insistence on unseriousness – on reducing the cosmos to the personal and gossipy even'.[35] Certainly Auden's handling of intensely serious subjects in apparently trivial terms is one of his most pervasive and delightful uses of poetic incongruity. His aim, however, is not often simply reductive. Auden's position as he has extended it in the last fifteen years [before 1965] comes close to being a serious insistence on the impossibility of being serious in poetry.

This rather paradoxical position grows by stages out of Auden's mature conception of man. We have seen that by 1940 or so he was convinced that direct sincerity is a pretense which can only lead to self-deception and falsehood. As 'New Year Letter' indicates, an unserious technique seemed to Auden at that time an aid to trapping the elusive truth and making it available to the conscious mind.

[Cites from 'New Year Letter': 'Though Language may be useless . . . The candid psychopompos spoke' (*C.P.*, p. 206)]

The psychopompos, Hermes, the guide of the souls of the dead, may be induced to speak through a joke which can look two ways; if on one side it is not intended to be honest self-expression, it has the chance of being truthful on the other. The truth that the poem as joke reveals, of course, may turn out to be that the human being cannot speak truth. Even then the poem, which is itself an instance of human play-acting, can reveal to men something of themselves as actors who may never be able to catch themselves off-stage to see what they are 'really' like.

This line of thinking is developed more fully in 'The Truest Poetry is the Most Feigning' (1955), originally subtitled 'Ars Poetica for Hard Times'. It concludes:

What but tall tales, the luck of verbal playing,
Can trick his lying nature into saying
That love, or truth in any serious sense,
Like orthodoxy, is a reticence. (*C.P.*, p. 621)

Reiterating Auden's conception of man as actor, this poem implies that the poet can say something true only by accident, by the 'luck of verbal playing' with an unserious technique within the limitations of verse form. The final 'truth' that emerges, however, is paradoxical: the poem asserts that truth in any serious sense is a reticence, something that is unspeakable in poetry or in prose. In the words of an earlier couplet from the same poem, 'No metaphor, remember, can express/A real historical unhappiness'. The most feigning poetry is the truest because its artifice gives public recognition to its inability to state directly a truth that has any necessary validity outside the poem; hence, it is truest to the limitations of poetry.[36] □

In this context Justin Replogle's book *Auden's Poetry* (1969) is pertinent. There he makes a case for Auden's poetry as a site of struggle between the poet and his essential companion the *anti-poet*, the fundamental dialectic set up between these two figures providing the animus and energy in the poetry.[37]

John Bayley's essay on Auden from his book *The Romantic Survival* (1957) is an illuminating and weighty piece of criticism. He describes Auden's acute self-consciousness in relation to the way that his poetry is being read and received. A useful comparison with Eliot demonstrates that although both poets are self-conscious of their role as poet, Eliot surprisingly remains the public poet, while Auden is seen as the more private. This reading does indeed fly in the face of much Auden criticism to date, but has the virtue of looking beyond the simple fact of Auden's politics into a world where those politics assume more than the transient importance of fashion.

■ [Auden] shares with T. S. Eliot this enormous self-consciousness – it is one of the few points which they have in common. In Eliot it takes the form of a deprecation, an honest enquiry, an implied refusal to posture before the reader and dazzle him with a display of poetical virtuosity.

> That was a way of putting it – not very satisfactory,
> A periphrastic study in a worn-out poetical fashion
> Leaving one still with the intolerable wrestle
> With words and meanings. The poetry does not matter.
>   ('East Coker')

Following a passage that is, as it were, wearily rhetorical and artificial ('What is the late November doing'), this disclaimer may baffle and irritate the reader, but it certainly leaves him in no doubt about the poet's honesty. It is almost a device for creating an atmosphere of sincerity. In Auden's case the fact that 'the poetry does not matter' is rather differently conveyed: the poet does not attempt to disguise the fact that he is a virtuoso whose job it is to give a good performance, but his gestures as he does so are ironical, and the irony is often directed at the poet himself. In both cases the idea that the poetry is important is not entertained, but whereas for Eliot the poetry is part of a general ethos which is of the very first importance, for Auden it is not. This is perhaps why we can take Eliot seriously even when he is being his most exasperatingly deprecating and self-conscious, whereas the Auden irony and urbanity we follow gladly for their own sake and can only be persuaded of their final seriousness by external means, i.e. by the subject matter – refugees, war, etc. – which the poet puts before us. Auden has always shown a great interest in light verse and the ironic approach, . . . but our point for the moment is the connection between such an approach and the contemporary poetic self-consciousness. Deprecation in Eliot, irony in Auden, are symptoms of the same condition. . . . . . .

'No artist,' writes Auden, 'not even Eliot, can prevent his work being used as magic, for that is what all of us, highbrow and lowbrow alike, secretly want Art to be.' And it is a guilty secret.

> Shame at our shortcomings makes
> Lame magicians of us all.
> Forcing our invention to
> An illegal miracle
> And a theatre of disguise. . . . . (*The English Auden*, p.455)

The shame of Magic is that it solves easily what in life can only be solved partially and with continual effort. And this consciousness of the possibility of poetry being used as an incantation, as a quick way to a satisfaction of the feelings, haunts Auden, perhaps because the 'magical' power of his own poetry is so obvious and so impressive. But it is a quick self-contained 'magical' satisfaction that the Auden quotation, divorced from its context, gives us, and though the poet is careful to dissipate such impressions as much as he can by descent into irony – 'wit that spoils Romantic art', as he calls it – or into flat statement or exhortation, it is the 'magical' passages that remain with the reader. Irony does not necessarily destroy magic, for, as we shall see later, it may itself be one of magic's expedients. What does destroy it is Eliot's deliberate and weary refusal to keep up the incantation: by shrugging his shoulders with a 'that was a way of putting it' he effectively checks any attempt of the reader to repose in an insulated enjoyment of the passage. And at what a cost! If this is a preventive against magic, we should have good grounds for preferring magic instead. Whether true or not, Auden's admission that magic is what we want poetry to be gives the clue to the real source of vitality in his own poetry.

None the less, Auden's attitude implies a certain desperation. How can 'magic' and parable ever be reconciled by a poet who is so obsessed with the difference between them? How can our reaction be anything but ambiguous towards a poetry that is by implication telling us: 'I may read like a charm but you must not take me for one.

My subject is Love, the Just City, right conduct, the nature of moral and religious choice, etc.' . . .

Nor is the rigour of the dichotomy apparently lessened by existentialist theories of art. 'One must get out of the poetical into the existential' is one of Auden's favourite Kierkegaard quotations; another, 'the poet's sin is to poeticise instead of being'. And by implication it is his readers' sin to read the poetry instead of living. In Kierkegaard the Aesthetic and the Ethical are sharply divided – two stages from one to the other of which the individual must move. And Sartre is similarly emphatic. 'The real is never beautiful,' he writes. 'Beauty is a value which can apply only to the imaginary, and whose essential structure involves the nullification of the world. This is why it is foolish to confuse ethics and aesthetics. The values of the Good presuppose being-in-the-world; they are concerned with behaviour in real contexts and are subject from the start to the essential absurdity of existence.' The debt of Auden's critical outlook to pronouncements of this type is obvious, and it is this bleak critical climate which is accepted in the context of his poems. And not only accepted, but exploited sometimes with a positive buoyancy. Auden delights in turning into poetry – in 'nullifying' into the poetic as Sartre might call it – the most ragged and 'viscous' aspects and experiences of life. He seems to find its randomness and existential absurdity a challenge to his skill. *The Age of Anxiety* is particularly full of such passages.

> In a vacant lot
> We built a bonfire and burned alive
> Some stolen tyres. How strong and good one
> Felt at first, how fagged coming home through
> The urban evening. Heavy like us
> Sank the gas-tanks – it was supper time.
> In hot houses helpless babies and
> Telephones gabbled untidy cries,
> And on embankments black with burnt grass
> Shambling freight-trains were shunted away
> Past crimson clouds. (*C.P.*, p.466)

The brilliancy of description ends there. It does not lead anywhere – (indeed it is difficult to see where anything in *The Age of Anxiety* can be said to lead) – but it conveys a sense of the occasion at once and with vivid accuracy, and gives the reader the unpursuing satisfaction of contemplating a formal triumph. It is difficult for the most conscientious reader – if he enjoys the passage at all – not to repose upon the event described, upon its sense of the particular and upon the flavour of nostalgic recollection which it holds.[38] □

Both Blair and Bayley mention Søren Kierkegaard, and the Danish philosopher offers many clues to a positive understanding of Auden's attitude in his later years. From the writing of *The Sea and the Mirror* and the interest in artists which he pursued at the end of the 1930s, there is a sub-theme that runs through Auden's work concerned with the loss of his poetic power. Prospero's renunciation of his magic sets the tone for this theme, and his farewell and freeing of Ariel remains ambiguous as we are uncertain whether his actions result from necessity or from choice. The Kierkegaardian aspect of this uncertainty is that the truth will never be discovered. Many critics, beginning with Leavis, have suggested that the best work came first, but I am more inclined to believe, like Clive James (see chapter six), that Auden was always *reining in* a precocious power, and certainly was always one step ahead of his critics.

CHAPTER THREE

Early Auden – The Making of a Poet

WHAT VOICES inhabited Auden's early poetry? How did he arrive at a voice of his own? The following passage is taken from the Introduction to Katherine Bucknell's important work on Auden's early poetry: *W.H. Auden: Juvenilia*. Bucknell is the joint editor, along with Nicholas Jenkins, of the scholarly *Auden Studies* series and in her editing of the *Juvenilia* she provides an intelligent and sensitive reconstruction of Auden's transformation from an imitator to a poet with his own distinct voice. From Thomas Hardy, Edward Thomas and Robert Frost, to the importance of Eliot and the refining fires of Yeats – these influences were taken on and worked through by the young Auden. Bucknell also looks at Auden's sexual and familial situation as a portrait of Auden's father emerges, at once longed for and yet distant, missing so critically from Auden's important years of development. The ambiguity of the maternal and its relation to landscape, and the increasingly sexually charged references to borders and limits, show the extent of the presence in the early Auden of the interests and concerns of the older poet. Bucknell also usefully locates Auden's relation to modernism through her discussion of his relation to Eliot.

■ In the summer of 1923, according to Auden's recollection in his 1940 essay 'A Literary Transference', Hardy struck for him 'the authentic poetic note'. Although Auden exaggerated when he wrote that 'for more than a year I read no one else', Hardy awakened in him an intense and long-lasting 'passion of imitation',[1] which, for the first time, established the pattern of obsession and assimilation that was to prove characteristic not only in his early development but throughout his career. By early 1924, he was writing poems that sounded like Hardy himself. As Auden explained, Hardy was not such a good craftsman as to make Auden feel he could never equal his achievements; on the contrary, Auden could easily see his faults: 'his rhythmical clumsiness, his outlandish vocabulary were obvious even to a schoolboy.' And, far more than Wordsworth might have done, Hardy showed Auden the use of 'direct colloquial diction'.[2] . . . . . .

To a poet whose earliest compositions show uncertainty before the natural world and ambivalence about his attachment to the earth, Hardy offered a key to the baffling maternal landscape. And Hardy's basic philosophical outlook – of disillusioned modern scepticism – may also have seemed to Auden like his father's. . . . . . . Auden's search for a poetic father, a figure who might balance the natural visionary power of Wordsworthian Romanticism and the emotional intensity apparently generated by his early relationship with his mother, did not end with Hardy. The search itself became part of the pattern of his general intellectual development and a theme of many of his poems. But Hardy served as his poetical father for nearly a year. In some of his poems Auden uses the voices of Hardy and Wordsworth together, like mingled parental voices, arguing with or balancing each other. Hardy was as unconvinced as the young Auden was by the Romantic vision of nature. He had already made the limitation of human insight a successful theme in his poems, and he provided a suitably ironic tone, free of self-pity, in which to write about it. . . . . . .

In 'A Literary Transference' he wrote that what he valued most in Hardy was his 'hawk's vision, his way of looking at life from a very great height'. He went on to explain that 'from such a perspective the difference between the individual and society is so slight' that it appears as if 'reconciliation is possible'.[3] From the 1930s onwards, whenever Auden writes about Wordsworth, for instance in 'Letter to Lord Byron' (1936), the introduction to *The Oxford Book of Light Verse* (1938), or the introduction to *Poets of the English Language* (1950), he uses Wordsworth as the example of Romantic poets in general, who, as a result of the break-up of traditional communities at the time of the industrial revolution, 'turned away from the life of their time to the contemplation of their own emotions and the creation of imaginary worlds'.[4] . . . The hawk's vision reduced the rift between poet and society; it was a substitute for Romantic vision, replacing the advantages of intimacy with the advantages of distance, of intensity with panoramic perspective, of intuition with judgement.

Then, in the autumn of 1924, Auden discovered Edward Thomas, and Hardy 'had to share his kingdom'. Soon Auden's passion extended to Thomas's friend and mentor, Robert Frost. He was attracted to their gentle reticence and their down-to-earth natures perhaps more than anything else. . . . Auden wrote about everyday experience by imitating Thomas and Frost. These models brought him back during 1925 to the natural themes of Wordsworth, and although he now dealt with such themes more confidently, his old ambivalence persisted. His descriptions of the natural world were calm, understated, even reticent, but images such as gates or mountains blocking his access to the landscape reappeared, now more overtly associated with his sexual nature. . . . . . .

When Auden went up to Christ Church in October 1925, his search for poetic models continued, but the search now became more eclectic and less personal and he no longer needed his poetic forebears to resemble his own father. He decided to change schools, and he read Philosophy, Politics, and Economics during the spring of 1926 while he completed, as required, the first year of Natural Science; by the autumn of 1926 he settled on English. His wide academic reading, as well as the discovery of many new poets, is reflected in his work. He read and imitated Housman, Sassoon, Gordon Bottomley, Emily Dickinson, and others, but not until he discovered T. S. Eliot, in about May 1926, did he reach another great watershed. His tutor, Nevill Coghill, recalled that Auden once arrived for his tutorial claiming to have torn up all his poems 'because they were no good. Based on Wordsworth.' He told Coghill, 'I've been reading Eliot. I now see the way I want to write.'[5] Within a few months everything Auden had achieved until then seemed to be lost in the self-conscious sacrifice of his poetic personality to a version of Eliot's tradition. He filled his work with arcane allusions, used the most difficult and awkward-sounding words he could think of, added epigraphs and footnotes, and splintered his verse into syntactically discrete shards. . . . In Eliot, Auden admired both classical learning and apparent modernity, and he added to his version of Eliot some attributes borrowed from his own father, so that Auden himself seemed for a time to be part scientist, part doctor, and part poet. . . .

. . . Auden's obsession with Eliot, like his obsession with Hardy, lasted about a year. During this period, he drew not only on Eliot, but also on the work of other modernists, such as Gertrude Stein, Virginia Woolf, Ezra Pound, and especially Edith Sitwell, whose influence on his work during 1926 is not easy to distinguish from that of Eliot. He also discovered Gerard Manley Hopkins, Wilfred Owen, and Katherine Mansfield, and he read Joyce, D.H. Lawrence, Kafka, and Thomas Mann. Then in the late spring of 1927 he read, apparently at the suggestion of his friend Cecil Day-Lewis, some of the recent work of Yeats. He wrote to Isherwood that of the modern poets he was reading that summer term, 'the later Yeats alone seems to me to be α+'. Soon after this he wrote again asking, 'Have you seen Yeats' poem in the June *Criterion* [?] It is very good.' The poem was 'The Tower', and it brought about a revolution in Auden's work. His 1927 poem beginning 'I chose this lean country' is modelled on the third part of 'The Tower' – Auden especially liked this section of Yeats's poem and later printed it on its own in his 1935 anthology, *The Poet's Tongue*. In 'I chose this lean country' Auden once again took up the old theme of the unhappy lover confronting an unyielding landscape, and in it he made clear for the first time, as he was much later to do in poems such as 'In Praise of Limestone' and especially 'Amor Loci', that this was the land-scape of his choice, satisfying to him precisely because of its austerity. . . . 'I chose this lean country' marks Auden's first move away from the cerebral, multi-layered, artificial Eliot productions of his middle Oxford years towards the simpler, tougher, more reticent, and essen-tially English plain style that he had first begun to learn as a schoolboy under the influence of Hardy, and later Thomas and Frost. Yeats's influence was tempered in the poem by the sinewy strains of Robert Graves, another student of Hardy whom Auden had first read at school in *Georgian Poetry 1918–1919* and had recently rediscovered. And the Old English poetry in which Auden had been immersed partly for academic reasons now added to his new, shorter lines a bold, haunting drive that lingered through *Poems* (1928) and after. . . .

. . . Although he preserved in some collections of his adult work a few of the poems written in Oxford when he was twenty and twenty-one and printed in *Poems* (1928), it was not until after Auden arrived in Berlin that he began steadily to produce mature, publishable work. . . . Alone in Berlin, cut off from family, friends, and familiar institutions, he had started to come to terms with the gift of his own weakness. The student began to transform himself into a master.[6] □

Bucknell usefully shows us what was going on up to the point of Auden's entry into the public critical gaze, and although there is now a critical canon surrounding Auden's work, we must try to imagine how the poetry appeared to his contemporaries reading the poems for the first time. One is struck by how little contextual information Auden provides. For example, the seminal poem 'The Watershed' (*C.P.*, p. 32) is packed with the mystery and power of Auden's early work, and contains all the ingredients that characterise the landscape and aura of the early poems. 'The Watershed' portrays an abandoned mine, whose deserted presence echoes with old narratives of adventure. The scene is watched by a young stranger, alienated from the old world and strangely out of place in the new. Yet there is no answer to questions of 'who' the young stranger may be, or 'why' or 'when' these events take place; the poem *begins* with these problems rather than assuming their clarity. Critics often felt that Auden had clipped too much information out of his work, leaving his poetry floating in a strange, obscure world containing ele-ments of oddly assorted narratives and themes. Much of the early criticism, then, is infused with an uneasiness over Auden's aims. What was he trying to say? And yet they knew that he was speaking to them, and often *about* them in a voice that offered hope, yet which also spoke with menace, and hinted that it was all going to be over soon for a class that had 'had its day'.[7]

It is instructive to listen to those lone voices from the early days, speaking without the benefit of hindsight (but often with the spirit of prophecy) about the young poet and his work. Critics dealt with Auden's poetry in their own way; Robert Graves, for example, accused him of plagiarism, claiming that Auden lifted lines directly from the poems of Laura Riding. F. R. Leavis, on the other hand, contented himself with tracing the signs of adolescence that were visible in the poetry. This belief in Auden's essential immaturity remained axiomatic for criticism produced under Leavis's influence, and the entire 'Scrutiny' school followed his example.[8]

In the Introduction to his *Auden: A Collection of Critical Essays* (1964) Monroe K. Spears summarises the important negativity of Leavis and his followers, noting how they played a major part in forming critical opinion of Auden up to that time:

■ The most influential of all hostile criticism of Auden was that of F. R. Leavis and his followers, whose criteria appeared to be aesthetic but were, it seems clear in retrospect, basically moral and social. Though Leavis allowed Auden promise and published occasional reviews by him in *Scrutiny* from 1932 to 1935, Auden soon became the whipping boy for the group's profound antipathy to Oxford, Bloomsbury, and the academic and literary establishments which had, they thought, made Auden fashionable. The recognition of Auden's promise was accompanied by forebodings for the future: as early as 1933 Leavis pronounced that *The Orators* was an ominous falling off from the *Poems* of 1930. Soon Auden was 'placed' as immature, 'arrested at the stage of undergraduate "brilliance".' Leavis established this view so early in Auden's career that one wonders at the assurance with which he dismissed Auden's future as hopeless and damned him for good; one suspects that the judgment, being an integral part of *Scrutiny* orthodoxy, was an article of faith and not subject to change. As Leavis summed it up in the 'Epilogue' to the second edition of *New Bearings in English Poetry*,[9] speaking of *Paid on Both Sides* (1930): 'It seems to me that Auden has hardly come nearer to essential maturity since, though he made a rapid advance in sophistication.' Auden's arrested development is then considered as a case history, a cautionary tale showing the effects of 'uncritical acclamation,' the 'failure of the function of criticism,' the 'disintegration of the educated reading public,' and the domination of the literary world instead by a coterie and the values of fashion and social class. In the 'Retrospect' appended to the recent reprint of *Scrutiny*, Leavis reveals the extent to which Auden became a mythical figure, a kind of culture villain, or victim, for the group. He asserts that *Scrutiny's* major negative service 'was to deal firmly with the "Poetical Renascence," the coterie movement that opened triumphantly in the early thirties.' *Scrutiny* pointed out 'that Auden, with his modish, glib, and sophisticated immaturity couldn't go on being credited with promise if, gainsaying the ominous characteristics, he didn't soon begin to prove himself capable of developing.' But he didn't develop, and in spite of Keynes, Bloomsbury, the *New Statesman*, and the Public School Communists and fellow travelers, *Scrutiny* repeatedly affirmed and enforced the verdict. Leavis concludes with some complacency:

> Thirty years after we put the case against Auden it passes as a commonplace. True, there is a suggestion that he has 'gone off,' and that it is the late Auden who compels the current adverse criticism. But if the criticism is admitted, then the Auden of no phase can be saved. And in fact that has been implicitly granted. Quietly, by tacit consent, his spell of glory has lapsed. . . .[10]

Scrutiny was, of course, negative toward almost all contemporary poetry, with the partial exceptions of Yeats, Eliot, and Ronald Bottrall, but the case against Auden was pressed with special vigor, and with motives at least in part transparently extraliterary. His defects could be dealt with more in sorrow than in anger, as not so much his own fault as the result of the lack of critical standards and an educated public: an object lesson in the effect of Oxford frivolity and coterie standards. The verdict was spelled out by many of Leavis's followers. In 1945 R. G. Lienhardt, reviewing *For the Time Being* in *Scrutiny*, called his review 'Auden's Inverted Development.' His severity exceeds even Leavis's: Auden's 'only claim to importance rests on effects produced almost casually in his early work,' and he is dismissed finally with the contemptuous observation that he has 'the mental equipment only of a minor poet.' The *Scrutiny* campaign exerted a powerful and continuing influence: Richard Hoggart, writing the first full-scale book on Auden in 1951, acknowledged that his view of Auden's career had been influenced by Lienhardt's review and R. G. Cox, in the chapter on Auden in the *Pelican Guide to English Literature*, plainly still reflects it.[11] □

Partly, these criticisms were coping strategies for a poetry that challenged the very world that the critic inhabited. In an unsigned review from *The Listener* Leavis embodies the bafflement felt by many at the encounter with this difficult poetry.

■ A recent writer has remarked that poetry, as a result of modern mechanization, has become more and more removed from the external

common life of men: that its material is found more in the inner life of
the individual, and its interpretation depends increasingly upon the
individual's private and personal knowledge. . . . Many passages in
[Auden's *Poems* (1930)] are baffling, if not unintelligible, because they
lack that measure of normality which makes communication between
one individual and another possible. For mental idiosyncrasies, if they
are extravagantly indulged, isolate a writer as completely as if he
spoke in an unknown tongue. Thus in the first of his poems Mr.
Auden invites us, so far as we understand him, to discover, amid the
horrors and humiliations of a war-stricken world, the 'neutralizing
peace' of indifference. But the manner of his invitation is often so
peculiar to himself and so eccentric in its terminology that, instead of
communicating an experience of value to us, it merely sets our minds
a problem in allusions to solve. For example:–

[Quotes stanzas 5–9 of 'Will you turn a deaf ear' (*C.P.*, p.42)]

To Mr. Auden himself the meaning of these last three stanzas is
doubtless as clear as day, because they fit the peculiar habit of his
mind and his experience. But although we can sense his general
meaning, it requires a kind of effort to discover the exact relevance of
his allusions which, even when we are sure of having done so,
destroys the possibility of real enrichment. Such poetry, indeed, completely contradicts Keats's axiom that 'poetry should surprise by a fine
excess and not by singularity': that it should 'strike the reader as a
wording of his own highest thoughts, and appear almost a
remembrance'; and it fails to make a living contact with us because
it is the fruit of a too specialized kind of concentration. For intellectual
analysis of emotional states, however sharp its focus, is poetically
as barren as emotional diffuseness. And although Mr. Auden can
write –

Coming out of me living is always thinking,
Thinking changing and changing living,
                                        (*C.P.*, p.46)

the thinking process in most of his poetry is either arbitrarily imposed
upon the living or the living impulse, weakened by uncertainty and
disillusion, begets a symbolism which is full of personal caprice. For a
sense of chaos and defeat not only underlies but determines the very
texture of his verse and particularly of the strange 'Charade', entitled
Paid on Both Sides, with which his book begins and which, in its combination of seriousness and flippancy, presents in the form of a feud
between two hostile parties, the stultifying division in his own consciousness which wrings from him the cry –

Could I have been some simpleton that lived
Before disaster sent his runners here;
Younger than worms, worms have too much to bear.
Yes, mineral were best: could I but see
These woods, these fields of green, this lively world
Sterile as moon. (*C.P.*, p. 11)[12] □

When E.R. Dodds was shown the little 1928 book of poems that Spender
had tried to print on a chemists' press, he remarked:

■ I recognized the tones of a new, completely individual voice and the
presence of some highly compressed message which was trying to
force its way into expression.[13] □

and this was a sentiment shared by many of Auden's early commentators
including the poet and literary critic William Empson who wrote a perceptive analysis of *Paid on Both Sides*. Empson recognised Auden's insight
into the problem of attempting 'to change radically a working system',
the poet being both an agent of change and a part of the system. *Paid on
Both Sides* depicts a psychological landscape, steeped in Auden's reading
of Freud and Adler, which has the uncanny ability, as Empson affirms,
'to define the attitude of a generation'.

■ One reason the scheme is so impressive is that it puts psycho-
analysis and surrealism and all that, all the irrationalist tendencies
which are so essential a part of the machinery of present-day thought,
into their proper place; they are made part of the normal and rational
tragic form, and indeed what constitutes the tragic situation. One feels
as if at the crisis of many, perhaps better, tragedies, it is just this
machinery which has been covertly employed. Within its scale (twenty-
seven pages) there is the gamut of all the ways we have of thinking
about the matter; it has the sort of completeness that makes a work
seem to define the attitude of a generation.[14] □

After Empson's review of *Paid on Both Sides* Leavis dived into the fray
with another review which looked at the Charade in the light of
Empson's remarks. He found Auden wanting on the question of class,
unhappy at what he saw as Auden's lazy rendition of working-class
dialect in *The Dance of Death* (1933). Leavis countered Empson's praise,
reminding his readers that a 'Charade' should not be taken too seriously,
and again noticed a pronounced lack of 'maturity' in Auden's work. This
became a catchphrase for Leavis, as well as the damning element in his
opinion of Auden, a poet who had fundamentally failed to grow up.[15]
Given that Leavis did not have the benefit of hindsight, he could be

forgiven for adhering to his own criteria of maturity in order to judge Auden. But from where we stand now, Auden's use of public school rhetoric, the antics of Officer Training Corps (OTC) cadets, and the *simulated* adventures of the grown-ups, are closer to a postmodern ironical critique of the time in which he lived, and the sexual overtones of many of these games would also have been passed over quietly at the time. Leavis once more tackled Auden in the early thirties, this time over the strange piece *The Orators* (1932) in which Auden blended surreal verse and prose in a depiction and analysis of the simultaneous breakdown and release of the 'Airman', a heroic, rebellious homosexual, who realises that his own resistance to the system has been the cause of his downfall. Leavis looked at this work with a mixture of scepticism and admiration.

■ Mr. Auden's first book of poems has already won him a reputation; yet it is safe to say that no reader put the book down with a comfortable sense of having understood. The present book makes no easier reading, and since Mr. Auden obviously has unusual gifts, it becomes important to examine into the nature of the difficulty; – for snobbism – (such as attends upon every cult) is fickle, and will desert a writer after having encouraged his faults. We expect some measure of difficulty in modern verse; indeed we are suspicious when we find none. But now that fashion has come to favour modernity there is a danger that difficulty may be too easily accepted. The publishers of *The Orators*, on the dust-cover, have almost an air of boasting that their author is obscure.[16] Yet the general nature of what he has to say is plain enough, and the obscurity of the particulars seems to a great extent weakness. *The Orators*, we are told, 'is not a collection, but a single work with one theme and purpose, partly in prose and partly in verse, in which the author continues his exploration of new form and rhythm.' The exploration is still in the early stages, groping and inconclusive, and the roughness of the jottings must not be mistaken for subtlety of charting. The opening piece of prose, 'Address for a Prize Day', is very good, but the standard of precision and coherence introduced here in the part is not maintained generally. Mr. Auden seems apt to set down too readily as final what comes, on the tacit plea that modern poetry has vindicated the right to demand hard work from the reader. But we demand of the poet that he should have done his share, and in Mr. Auden's case we are not convinced. Too often, instead of complexity and subtlety, he gives us a blur; and again and again it is evident that he has not taken enough trouble to make his private counters effective currency. One gathers assurance to put the judgment in this way from the signs, here and there, that he does not know just how serious he is: the diagrams, for instance, . . . (*The English Auden*, pp. 74–5) represent what looks like satisfaction in undergraduate cleverness. Certain characteristics appear to go back further. The frequent images of war seem to betray, in part at least, a romantic habit, deriving from a boyhood lived in the years 1914–1918.

Vadill of Uirafirth, Stubbo, Smirnadale, Hammr and Sullom, all possible bases: particularly at Hubens or Gluss. Survey to be completed by Monday. (*The English Auden*, p.76)

Those names come from a boy's romantic map.[17] □

The importance of the 'romantic boyhood' and its relation to the First War is something that needs to be thought through quite carefully today. Christopher Isherwood's *The Memorial* (1932) covers similar ground to sections of *The Orators* and was written at roughly the same time: questions of memory, heroism, and the need to build a 'New Country' are shimmering in both texts, and at this distance we can see more clearly that it is a generational difference, mainly between those who missed the war (this would be the kind of 'romantic' picture of the war that Leavis detected) and those who took part, but who are now irretrievably tainted by their involvement. It is not surprising that Leavis (who took part in the war as a medical orderly) should have misread Auden's serious interest in the war and its effects as a light, romantic pastiche.

The Orators mixes together the adolescent hero-worship and manoeuvres of the public school OTC, with the language and imagery of St John Perse, combined with a surreal and subversive homosexual subtext. In this extract from his 1935 book *The Destructive Element*, Stephen Spender lays out his reading of the political and sexual meanings of Auden's 'Airman':

■ The symbolic position of the airman is, as it were, to be on the margin of civilization. Being an airman, it is obvious that he is not tied down in any way; he is up in the air, and in the position of artists like Rilke or Lawrence who travel; and yet he is the man of action, flying, planning Fascist (?) coups, circulating leaflets.

It is important to realize that this particular airman is not only an airman with an aeroplane, but he is a psychological airman as well. He has another mythology besides the ancestral relationship with his uncle. This mythology has to do with the association, amongst certain natives, of epilepsy with the idea of flying. Perhaps the airman is an epileptic: certainly he is homosexual, and also a kleptomaniac. The *Journal* leaves one in no doubt that his uncle was homosexual, and on this fact depends the ancestor relationship.

The airman symbolizes the homosexual, because, like him, he is incapable of exploiting the old, fixed relationships: he has involuntarily broken away from the mould of the past and is compelled to experiment in new forms; his life, being comparatively disinterested, may result in an experiment of value to society, so long as he does not become obsessed with his own personal problem. His chief danger is his remarkable irresponsibility which leads him to indulge in Fascist day-dreams of fantastic and murderous practical jokes. The airman, therefore, with his bird's-eye view of society, sees everywhere the enemy. The most brilliant passages in the book are those in which he classifies the enemy. We are never, of course, told directly who the enemy is, but only (i) how he behaves; (ii) symptoms by which we may recognize his influence on individuals; (iii) how, regarding him as a disease, we may recognize his symptoms in ourselves.

The study of his behaviour is very largely an ingenious application of the Marxist analysis of capitalist society. E.g.: 'The effect of the enemy is to introduce inert velocities into the system (called by him laws or habits) interfering with organization. These can only be removed by friction (war). Hence the enemy's interest in peace societies.' (*The English Auden*, p. 73)

This is a brilliant but partial application of the Marxian conception of history. But it is not a formula. It is a generalization which is also a very striking psychological observation of behaviour.

Combined with Marxism is psychology, and a very acute analysis of the behaviour of individuals. The 'enemy' sections are the strength and also the weakness of the *Journal*. They are strong because they contain the same true vision as does the wider, social observation. The weakness is, firstly, that the enemy tends to be too easily recognizable as one of several public school types. Secondly, that, in this context, psychology combined with Marxism tends to produce a peculiarly ingenious form of heresy-hunting. Heresy-hunting is not dangerous because one wishes in any way to spare the Enemy, but because it justifies narrow personal dislikes, universalizes petty criticism, and because in many cases it encourages a kind of masochistic self-abuse. . . . . . .

After indulging in fantastic dreams of violence, the airman suddenly goes back on these Fascist plans. 'My whole life has been mistaken, progressively more and more complicated, instead of finally simple.' (*The English Auden*, p. 93) . . . . . . The airman's end is now not far off. The last entry in his *Journal* is that his 'hands are in perfect order.' So he has triumphed; but it is a secret victory. We have seen him torn between ideals [ed. 'ideas'?] of revolution, ideas of religion, and ideas of cure. The acceptance of his hands, which is followed by the hands being in perfect order, is his psychological victory.

The airman, being who he is, is bound to fail, because he is alone. So long as he is alone he is bound, like pacifists, to answer war by non-resistance of a kind which he believes to be anti-toxin. That is, as long as the airman's observations, whilst they make an enemy of the governing class, do not find an ally in any other class. There is never any really revolutionary issue in *The Airman's Journal*, because the airman has no friends.

The airman is particularly interesting because he is, in fact, in much the same position as the contemporary writer who hates the social system under which he exists, and lives, and writes in a dream of violence on behalf of himself and his friends. He is ignored by the greatest part of society, and neither directly nor indirectly does his work penetrate to it. Yet he may represent the most intelligent and critical forces in society. Supposing that he is living in a society that is self-destructive and actively preparing for war, he seems to be completely powerless. His elimination is *no loss* to society, as Fascist governments have discovered who have been able to dispose of all the groups representing culture in their countries, because this culture had no deep roots in the life of the whole people. . . .

He has, therefore, like the airman, got to defeat the enemy. There are two methods of attack. The first is to become an active political agent, to take part in the immense practical joke of destruction. But then he is using the enemy's own weapons: he will become an enemy to the enemy; and, besides that, his hands steal. The second is to learn how he may escape from his own isolation; not to resist the enemy, but to absorb him. To make an art that is infected by – that is about – society, and which it is impossible for society to discard, because it is essentially a part of it; and to make it a part which will transform the whole.

One sees then in *The Orators*, the victory of the idea of the psychological cure, which is always predominant as an aspect of Auden's work.[18] □

For a more recent reading of the meaning of homosexuality in *The Orators*, see Richard Bozorth's essay in *Auden Studies 2*.[19] Early reviews consider Auden as a solitary poet, writing for and from himself. It was not long until the sense of an Auden 'group' began to form around Auden, in part because of the references he lodged in his work to 'Wystan, Stephen, Christopher, all of you!'[20] – proper names and places that built up an intertextual set of references that had their own power and momentum. As Spender's piece affirms, the Airman is ultimately powerless because he 'has no friends' and this was the problem being addressed by the formation of a group of poets whose work, although widely different in style, were linked in their aims for a 'New Country'. Justin Replogle has written well on this in *Auden's Poetry* and in his article 'The Gang Myth in Auden's Early Poetry'[21] where we can see the myth of the group being constructed in both the poetry and the critical discourses that surround it.

One of the 'gang' was the poet Cecil Day-Lewis, and in this extract from *A Hope for Poetry* (1934) he expresses his admiration for Auden while at the same time pointing to his weaknesses.

■ His first book, *Poems*, is full of psychological examples and inferences. It ought, by rights, to have been nothing more than an illustrated case-book. Yet no one can read it without feeling again and again, however baffled he may be for a meaning, the impact of poetry. It is his astonishing capacity for assimilation and his ability to distil poetry out of the most forbidding retorts of science, which make me think that Auden more than any other young writer has the essential qualifications of a major poet. The subject-matter of his verse would seem to be irretrievably 'prosaic'; yet, if we try to express almost any poem of his in prose, we find it impossible; its rare spirit evaporates in the process. The attitude of the satirist is for him halfway between the attitudes of the psycho-therapist and the faith-healer: sometimes he is carried to ridiculous lengths by the latter, infuriating the reader with an apparently superstitious belief in the functional nature of all disease. But even when he is being most ridiculous, his work keeps its poetic interest intact. . . .

'What do you think about England, this country of ours where nobody is well?' Auden asks at the beginning of *The Orators*: and by consistently maintaining this attitude he has done more perhaps than any other writer to replace in our minds the idea of the wickedness of society by the idea of the sickness of society. The force of his satire is, however, diminished in two ways. First, he does not seem to discriminate sufficiently between the really sick and the merely hypochondriac: the old satirists had to have a very definite criterion for measuring good and evil; the new one, to be thoroughly successful, must have equally definite standards of sickness and health. Auden is an adept at saying Boo to invalids and taking away their rugs; but one feels that he does not really care whether the invalid is a malingerer or just recovering from pneumonia. He is an expert at diagnosis, but has only one treatment for all ailments: we should feel happier if he evinced a love of health and a knowledge of its nature equivalent to his love and ability of diagnosis. In the second place his treatment, his method of satire is apt to defeat its own ends. Spender has correctly called it 'buffoon-poetry'; and in guying his victims Auden too often becomes identified with them, so that, instead of the relationship between satirist and victim which alone can give significance to satire we get a series of figures of fun into each of whom the satirist temporarily disappears. Where light and darkness merge into one, the visibility is poor and our eyes will play us tricks. If Auden could maintain an objective attitude to his victims, if the part of him that writes buffoon-poetry could be brought into closer relationship with his positive poetic force and be modified by it – or, in other words, if he had a coherent philosophy at his back, nothing could stop him from writing major poetry. At present he suffers from an extreme sensitiveness to the impact of ideas combined with an incapacity to relate them with any scheme of values, which is apt to give his work a flavour of intellectual dilettantism.[22] □

Louis MacNeice was the other member of the 'MacSpaunday' group. The extract below from the interesting collection *The Arts To-Day* (1935) is taken from MacNeice's summary of the state of modern poetry. The admiration for Auden's work is tempered here by MacNeice's pragmatic approach to the writing of poetry.

■ Three notable elements in the poetry of Auden, Spender, Day-Lewis, etc., are the topical, the gnomic [proverbial], and the heroic. These elements qualify and reinforce one another. To be merely topical, by mentioning carburettors or complexes, is not truly modern. To be merely gnomic, without a concrete foreground, is boring and ineffective. To be merely heroic is escapism, shallow decoration. The value of a poem consists in a ratio. The ratio is, naturally, difficult to maintain. Day-Lewis e.g. is sometimes too facile in introducing his culverts, gasometers, cylinders and other modern properties; similarly Auden in enumerating (often for purposes of satire) his heterogeneous strings of things or people who are 'news.'[23] In these three poets there is a strong personal element (contrast the professions of Eliot); thus *The Orators* by Auden, an admittedly personal work, is made very obscure by a plethora of private jokes and domestic allusions. The personal element is a bridge between the topical and the heroic; these poets make myths of themselves and of each other (a practice which often leads to absurdity, e.g., Day-Lewis's mythopoeic hero worship of Auden in *The Magnetic Mountain*). This personal obsession can be collated with their joint communist outlook via the concept of comradeship (see again Mr. Roberts' preface to *New Signatures*).[24] Comradeship is the communist substitute for bourgeois romance; in its extreme form (cp. also fascism and youth-cults in general) it leads to an idealisation of homosexuality. . . .

By far the most important work yet produced by any of this group is Auden's *Charade, Paid on Both Sides* which appeared first in *The Criterion* in 1928. It can be very profitably contrasted with *The Waste Land*. It is tragic where *The Waste Land* is defeatist, and realist where *The Waste Land* is literary. *The Waste Land* cancels out and ends in

Nirvana; the *Charade* (cp. once more the Greeks) leaves you with reality, an agon [conflict between two protagonists] (see the final chorus). The obscurity of the *Charade* is not the obscurity of *The Waste Land* but mainly an obscurity of method (condensed syntax, etc.). Auden has been very much influenced by the Icelandic Sagas; the plot of *Paid on Both Sides* is the simple saga plot of the vendetta; a chorus does the moralising. The result is an illusion of history. Poetry to-day is seen (contrast Aristotle with twentieth-century philosophers) to have affinities with history. History is not, for most people, a science; they read it because they take its persons and events as symbols. But symbols of what? The whole point, perhaps, is that we do not know what they symbolise. Philosophies of history over-simplify and cheapen, just as psycho-analysis tends to over-simplify and cheapen our dreams. . . .

Auden's great asset is curiosity. Unlike Eliot, he is not (as a poet) tired. It is significant that in *The Rock* where Eliot attempts to give his poetry a social reference, the passages which ring truest are still those which are non-social, individualist, even suicidal. (There is nothing so individualist as suicide.) Auden is not so sophisticated; he is not old with reading the Fathers. He reads the newspapers and samples ord-nance maps. He has gusto, not literary gusto like Ezra Pound, but the gusto which comes from an unaffected (almost ingenuous) interest in people, politics, careers, science, psychology, landscape and mere sen-sations. He has a sense of humour. . . . His job is to go on observing things from his very unusual angle and recording them (need I say that the combined process of observing and recording = creation?) in his very individual manner. His style is still changing, towards a wider intelligibility; and he has a strong tendency towards satire and burlesque. He may therefore be expected to produce either further 'serious' work as in the *Charade* and the earlier poems, or comic work ranging from mere satire to Aristophanic fantasy. His recently pub-lished little play, *The Dance of Death*, was not interesting as verse, but it is a good sign that his eye was on the stage; the new poetic drama, if it is to exist, must have entertainment value. Auden's versatility and fertility are invaluable at a time when too many writers are hampered by the fear of not being modish.[25] □

Auden's own sense of what poetry should be about was captured in an introduction to an interesting anthology of poetry put together in collabor-ation with John Garrett called *The Poet's Tongue* (1935).[26] Auden's view of poetry is far from elitist, and the way that the anthology was laid out was intended, in part, to prevent readers from the 'automatic response' at the sight of a famous name.[27] Auden included non-canonical material such as nursery jingles and popular ballads and songs in an attempt to demonstrate a continuum between the discourses of the academy and those of the street.

He suggests that poetry is not a rarified or unusual activity, but a condition we cannot avoid, arising whenever we swear or make love. Poetry is not an elitist discourse (even if it often looks that way) but is ever present in the form of a 'good joke' or a limerick or riddle. In fact, says Auden, poetry arises whenever we allow our language to be more than purely referential. When he states that 'The test of a poet is the frequency and diversity of the occasions on which we remember his poetry', we need only think about the way that Auden's poetry found a new and contemporary context in the film *Four Weddings and a Funeral* (1994). The resulting surge of popularity and interest in the poet's work (including the publication of a small collection of poems) showed that Auden could speak clearly to a new generation.

This introduction, and indeed, the content of the anthology itself, give readers a good sense of what absorbed Auden in the mid thirties: the social usefulness of the poet, the democracy of writing, and the ubiquity (rather than the elite rarity) of poetry. Poetry is 'memorable speech', says Auden:

■ Memorable speech then. About what? Birth, death, the Beatific Vision, the abysses of hatred and fear, the awards and miseries of desire, the unjust walking the earth and the just scratching miserably for food like hens, triumphs, earthquakes, deserts of boredom and featureless anxiety, the Golden Age promised or irrevocably past, the gratifications and terrors of childhood, the impact of nature on the adolescent, the despairs and wisdoms of the mature, the sacrificial victim, the descent into Hell, the devouring and the benign mother? Yes all of these, but – not these only. Everything that we remember no matter how trivial: the mark on the wall, the joke at luncheon, word games, these, like the dance of a stoat or the raven's gamble, are equally the subject of poetry. . . . . . .

In spite of the spread of education and the accessibility of printed matter, there is a gap between what is commonly called 'highbrow' and 'lowbrow' taste, wider perhaps than it has ever been.

The industrial revolution broke up the agricultural communities, with their local conservative cultures, and divided the growing population into two classes: those whether employers or employees who worked and had little leisure, and a small class of shareholders who did no work, had leisure but no responsibilities or roots, and were therefore preoccupied with themselves. Literature has tended therefore to divide into two streams, one providing the first with a compensation and escape, the other the second with a religion and a drug. The Art for Art's sake of the London drawing-rooms of the 90s, and towns like Burnley and Rochdale, are complementary.[28] □

Auden mentions the idea of the parable in this Introduction, and although a comparatively simple concept, it has a bearing on how we think of Auden's political and religious statements. He remarked in *The Dyer's Hand* that 'The only kind of literature which has gospel authority is the parable'.[29]

Samuel Hynes, in his important book *The Auden Generation: Literature and Politics in England in the 1930s* (1976) provides an excellent survey of writing and politics in the 1930s, usefully depicting the historical context in which Auden's work can be assessed. The extract selected here introduces the idea of the parable through a discussion of Auden's key essay 'Psychology and Art To-day'. Hynes examines the relation between politics and psychology in Auden's thinking: 'Art, Auden is saying, can effect a revolution, but it will be an inner and moral one.' Auden's pragmatic and realistic assessment of the power and the role of the artist can easily look like weak liberalism from some angles, but this would be to forget Auden's continuous *construction* of an audience receptive to his poetry and the ideas it contains. The parable provided Auden with a structure that enabled him to preach without overtly hectoring.

■ At about the time that Spender was writing his book, [*The Destructive Element* (1935)] and changing his mind about its direction, Auden, with his friend John Garrett, was preparing *The Poet's Tongue*, a poetry anthology for use in schools. It appeared in June 1935, with an introduction that is clearly the work of Auden. The anthology is, in its way, a political document. The editors chose poems from all literary levels – standard anthology pieces, skipping-rhymes, runes, riddles and word games, anonymous poems – with the intention of erasing the social distinction between highbrow and lowbrow, and presenting poetry as the whole variety of 'memorable words'. The poems were arranged (as Auden later arranged his *Collected Poetry*) alphabetically by first word, and without the author's name on the page – a method that stresses the community of poetry and eliminates the authority of individual status.

Left-wing critics took the political point at once. 'It is an anthology,' the *Left Review*'s critic wrote, 'that claims, not explicitly and so more weightily, that real English poetry has been shaped by the people in every generation.' In addition to its general political point, he found another significance in the anthology; it was, he said, a kind of manifesto of the Auden generation:

It is as if the younger poets addressed us: 'Our writing is based on another tradition of literature than the one that has been usual lately with amateurs of the subject. We present our anthology as an indication of the tradition we mean. It will also help you to understand how we are writing, what we are writing about and the direction we are moving in.'[30]

Each of these remarks, taken separately, is more or less true: certainly *The Poet's Tongue* does contain more 'poetry of the people' than most anthologies do, and could be used to support the Marxist theory of the collective origins of poetry; and certainly some avant-garde poets – notably Auden – were drawing upon traditional popular forms like the riddle, the ballad, and the music-hall song that had not been a part of the art-tradition. But taken together the two remarks imply (and that was certainly the critic's intention) that there was a movement in modern poetry toward popular forms for explicitly political reasons, and this simply was not true.

One can see in Auden's introduction, for example, how he argues for a living and popular cultural tradition, but draws back defensively from the notion that this tradition should be used to advance any causes. . . . . . .

In the introduction to *The Poet's Tongue* Auden remarks in passing on the relation between poetry and psychology: poetry is not, he says, a neurotic symptom as psychologists maintain; in fact, 'poetry, the parabolic approach, is the only adequate medium for psychology'.[31] He developed this extravagant claim further in 'Psychology and Art To-day', an essay that he contributed to Geoffrey Grigson's symposium, *The Arts To-day* (also 1935). Auden's essay is ostensibly intended to give a psychological account of the genesis of the artist and his place and function in society, drawing upon Freud but rejecting those Freudian concepts that diminish the value of art and the role of consciousness in creation. But in the end it is not so much an account of the art-psychology relationship as a defence of art against the reductions of any system.

Auden's strategy is to see psychology as an analogue for art, and with the same moral function:

> The task of psychology, or art for that matter, is not to tell people how to behave, but by drawing their attention to what the impersonal unconsciousness is trying to tell them, and by increasing their knowledge of good and evil, to render them better able to choose, to become increasingly morally responsible for their destiny.[32]

The effect of this claim is to elevate art as a moral force; psychology cannot cure, it can only reveal, and art can do that better. Here Auden repeats the key passage from the *Poet's Tongue* introduction.

> You cannot tell people what to do, you can only tell them parables; and that is what art really is, particular stories of particular people and experiences, from which each according to his immediate and peculiar

needs may draw his own conclusions. (*The English Auden*, p. 341)

It is here that *parable*, in the sense that I have been using it in this book, enters Auden's critical language, though in this passage the meaning is not altogether clear – how, for example, does it differ from mimetic realism? And does it include, as it seems to, all stories? It seems, in this context, to be merely a name for indirection, and a way of asserting the moral function of literature.

'Psychology and Art To-day' is not primarily a political essay; nevertheless, politics enters the argument in two important ways. It enters first when Auden, at the end of the essay, compares Marxism and Freudianism as therapies for a sick society. The relation between these two modern systems was a problem that troubled many left intellectuals; Auden saw them as complementary, neither adequate to the whole task of curing the world:

> As long as civilisation remains as it is, the number of patients the psychologist can cure are very few, and as soon as socialism attains power, it must learn to direct its own interior energy and will need the psychologist. (*The English Auden*, p. 341)

By arguing the mutual dependence of psychological and political 'treatment', Auden was in effect declaring his independence from either; both systems were useful analytical instruments, but neither was the Truth.

Auden's other political point comes in the last paragraph of the essay, when he returns to his idea of the moral function of art:

> There must always be two kinds of art, escape-art, for man needs escape as he needs food and deep sleep, and parable-art, that art which shall teach man to unlearn hatred and learn love. (*The English Auden*, pp. 341–2)

Since this is a statement about changing the relations among men, it is political. Art, Auden is saying, can effect a revolution, but it will be an inner and moral one, the kind that he prayed for in the last line of 'Sir, no man's enemy': 'New styles of architecture, a change of heart.' (The whole passage, with its emphasis on love and its denial of the necessity of enemies and hatred, is directly opposed to the Marxist idea of inevitable class warfare; Auden remained what he always essentially was: an individualist, inclined more to Christianity than to any other system.) Like *parable*, this phrase 'a change of heart' turns up again and again in the writings of the thirties, as a name for the individualist's hope of a new world.[33] □

Hynes shows how Auden's political position was ambiguous during the 1930s, and this ambiguity was probably part of the powerful effect of the poetry. Not reducible to 'mere' propaganda (the main problem with the 1932 poem 'A Communist to Others'[34]), Auden's work was always alive to the contradictions that inevitably built up between himself and those he addressed.

In his Introduction to *Thirties Poets: 'The Auden Group'* (Casebook series), Ronald Carter suggests that despite members of the so-called 'Auden Group' being so different in temperament, it was the fact that they were faced with similar political and historical problems that ties them together; Carter makes these shared concerns explicit. He usefully describes the way we can think about the *politics* of Auden and his friends as a struggle to recognise their own social and political situation, which meant, in turn, an examination of the social patterns encoded into the identity of the individual. Here too, Carter emphasises the importance of the *parable*.

■ Auden, MacNeice, Spender and Day-Lewis came to poetic maturity within the context of a decade the character of which is well-defined by Michael Roberts who, as an editor, was responsible for publishing some of their earliest verse:

> Those of us who grew up to manhood in the post-war years remember how, in that period, it seemed to us there was no finality. We learned to question every impulse until we became so self-conscious, so hag-ridden by doubts, indecisions, uncertainties that we lost all spontaneity, and, because we learned to account for the actions of others, we learned neither to praise nor blame them. It was not any one thing which caused this scepticism: it appeared in various guises – the theory of relativity breaking up our neat mechanical world, science learning to doubt whether it could approach any finality, psychoanalysis discovering how many actions, apparently spontaneous, were rigidly determined; and beyond all this a feeling that the middle-class world, the world of the nineteenth century, was definitely breaking up, and that it would be replaced in the near future by a world of communism or big business.[35]

This 'context' gave rise to fundamental literary questions to which the poets responded collectively and uniquely. Many of their essays of the time attempt theoretical discussion of these questions; their poetry constantly reflects the effort to realise some practical resolution of them. The questions are ones which had been put before, but in these years they were forced on all writers with a particular intensity and

urgency. Questions such as: can or should a poet stand above the contemporary struggle going on around him? Should he put his talent at
the service of specific causes? If he does the latter, what *kind* of poetry
does he write? What is the relationship between political poetry,
propaganda and art? How can literature become an effective moral
force? If – as Louis MacNeice pleads in the Preface to his book on
Modern Poetry . . . – poetry should become 'impure', that is 'conditioned
by the poet's life and the world around him', then what place is there
for the private world of the poet? These and related questions were not
put as part of some kind of generational ideology, nor all in one single
year by the same group of poets, nor were they always framed in quite
this way, but they do form a common basis to the thinking about poetry
undertaken by poets in these years and they do constitute, as it were, a
Thirties 'poetic' providing a common structure and theme in many of
the key poems of the age.[36] □

How did Auden specifically respond to the questions that Carter
describes above? By way of answer, I have selected a recent pithy reading of Auden's 1933 poem 'A Summer Night' from Michael O'Neill and
Gareth Reeves' book *Auden, MacNeice, Spender: The Thirties Poetry*. Their
discussion begins to disclose some of Auden's political strategies and formal techniques, showing how they were merged in his poetry. They
remark that 'Auden's use of traditional form reveals its subversive cunning', and this is a key element of the power of Auden's work. It was in
evidence in *Paid on Both Sides* when Auden used the Mummers' Plays and
Anglo-Saxon forms in order to articulate the needs of the contemporary
moment.

■ Certainly the poem is musical and initially invites the reader to be
lulled by the music: 'Out on the lawn I lie in bed,/Vega conspicuous
overhead/In the windless nights of June'. But any security into which
we are lulled is false, and here Auden's use of traditional form reveals
its subversive cunning. Heaney may be right to say that 'A poem floats
adjacent to, parallel to, the historical moment',[37] but he fails to see that
'Out on the lawn I lie in bed' sets its poise, craft and elegance against
a 'historical moment' recognized as being chaotic, dangerous and
brutal. Moreover, Auden is defeating his contemporary readers' expec-
tation: for a poet to alter his style can delight but it can also unsettle.
The use of 'we' in this poem is an index of Auden's changed mode of
address; the pronoun does not hector in a self-incriminating way;
rather, it urbanely extends itself from the group whose intimacy is
celebrated at the poem's outset (where Auden is 'Equal with colleagues in a ring') to absorb quite casually the – middle-class – reader.
At any rate such a reader finds it difficult to escape the indictment

wittily made by this stanza (subsequently omitted along with the two following):

> The creepered wall stands up to hide
> The gathering multitudes outside
> Whose glances hunger worsens;
> Concealing from their wretchedness
> Our metaphysical distress,
> Our kindness to ten persons. (*The English Auden*, p. 137)

By this stage in the poem Auden has faced up to the privileges which allow 'Our freedom in this English house,/Our picnics in the sun'; indeed, his irony (evident in the pinprick of 'Our kindness to ten persons') is in danger of negating the real, if vulnerable, validity of the well-being with which the poem began. Yet, in fact, it is the interplay of irony and uncomplacent self-acceptance that gives life to the poem and keeps Auden from imitating himself. . . . . . . 'Out on the lawn I lie in bed' is written when premonitions are beginning to prove all too justified, and insists on a historical world beyond the enclosures of class and poem. This insistence is, however, conveyed through a series of smoothly uninsistent transitions, of which the most crucial is this stanza (the seventh) following the account of the moon looking down on 'Those I love':

> She climbs the European sky;
> Churches and power stations lie
> Alike among earth's fixtures:
> Into the galleries she peers,
> And blankly as an orphan stares
> Upon the marvellous pictures

The first line's adjective widens the poem's scope: 'European' in 1933 is a politically loaded word. But Auden does not bang a verbal drum; instead, he is content to let implications look after themselves. The blankness and indifference of the moon's stare hint at that existential desperation which is one of Auden's strongest notes (it is heard again at the end of 'Spain', 'We are left alone with our day'). The 'galleries' full of 'marvellous pictures' upon which the moon stares like an 'orphan' (later changed to 'butcher') have a chill, comfortless effect. 'Marvellous' takes on a polite hollowness – not that Auden denies that the pictures are 'marvellous' but that he denies that they (or the culture they stand for) can alleviate the lot of anyone who is or will become an 'orphan'. If that way of putting it seems melodramatic, it needs to be re-emphasized that Auden successfully avoids melodrama, relying on his reader's awareness of the political gravity of a year in which Hitler had come to power in Germany. . . . . . .

The reticence here differs from the reticence of an earlier poem like 'From the very first coming down'; where that poem signals its reticence, referring to the country god's stone smile 'That never was more reticent,/Always afraid to say more than it meant', 'Out on the lawn I lie in bed' does not. A major reason for the later poem's strength is the alliance between this lack of underscoring and the measured control evident in, say, 'unlamenting', with its hint that the impulse to lament the passing of an old order is being disciplined, not disregarded; will the new way of things come about and, if so, will it be desirable? The poem wants to answer 'yes' to both questions, but its inability to do so with complete confidence gives it pathos. So the last stanza is more anxious diminuendo than climax as it prays that what is now called 'it' will 'All unpredicted . . . calm/The pulse of nervous nations'. But if Stan Smith is right to assert that 'The last impression is of an unresolved contradiction',[38] the contradiction and lack of resolution are acknowledged by the poem, part of its 'unpredicted' alertness to its own procedures.[39] □

The small, select group of friends that Auden used as the conceptual centre of 'A Summer Night', was part of a larger group which made up the 'nervous nations' of Great Britain, and it is Auden's depiction of these 'nations' that concerns the next piece, which is taken from the chapter 'Eliot and Auden' from Steve Ellis's book *The English Eliot* (1991). Ellis performs a twofold task in this chapter: firstly he places Eliot back into the 1930s from whence he has been conventionally displaced by the impact of Auden, and secondly he traces the reciprocal influence that the two poets exerted on each other, stressing the role of Eliot as Auden's publisher, as well as the two poets' distinctive use of the definite article.[40]

In the extract cited here, Ellis discusses Auden's awkward and difficult use of the term 'England' in the poetry of the thirties, taking as the archetypal instance the opening poem of *Look, Stranger!*, 'O Love, the interest itself in thoughtless heaven', which, far from celebrating an essential 'Englishness', describes the country as a 'complex and changing entity'. Ellis finally suggests that Auden's most famous poem, 'In Praise of Limestone', successfully fuses together the public 'classic' landscape with its 'hill-top temples' with the more private, secretive world of 'caves and conduits'. As a metaphor for England, the co-existence of these worlds alongside the malleability and possibility of its rocks suggest once more that England is far from the fixed, paternal granite of Victorian ideology in which Auden grew up. Ellis performs a useful task by demonstrating the ambiguous relation between identity and England throughout Auden's work. Back in 1929, Auden was thinking of the vital differences between the sexuality of Berlin and the family home of England:

■ Being alone, the frightened soul
  Returns to this life of sheep and hay
  No longer his: he every hour
  Moves further from this and must so move (*C.P.*, p. 48) □

This social and sexual distancing from England, a parting ten years before he *actually* went, left a scar on the surface of the early poetry that never healed, being aggravated by his trips abroad (see chapter four). His relation to England was a central problem for a child of a 'country where nobody is well'. At the beginning of the extract Ellis remarks how Auden avoided privileging the 'south-country' in his poetry:

■ In the treatment of England in his writings of the 1930s, Auden is similarly concerned to explode any south-country epitomizing of the type we have looked at, and is constantly stressing the opposing force of regional variegation, often via the aerial view. A unitary England is indeed often set up in his work, only to be subsequently challenged, as in 'O Love, the interest itself in thoughtless Heaven' (*The English Auden*, pp. 118–9), which, as Hynes noted, begins with an evocation of John of Gaunt's 'this England'; what Hynes omits to add is that we immediately move on into economically distressed regions of the island – Lancashire, Glamorgan, Dumbarton – that deliberately complicates and unsettles any narrowly 'projectile' nationhood such as that called for by Sir Stephen Tallents, as if his England is being countered by the untidier sprawl of Britain . . . . This poem is indeed one instance (the opening chorus of *The Dog Beneath the Skin* being another) where as Edward Mendelson has noted,[41] Auden is indebted for his geographical details to Anthony Collett's *The Changing Face of England* (1926). Collett's insistence on 'drawing attention to the contrasts of shire and shire', and the extensive travelogue round the island his book incorporates, themselves contrast with the attempt of many writers of the period to 'find' England in some particular corner. Such a work undoubtedly fed Auden's sense of the country as a complex and 'changing' entity, not easily susceptible to being 'fixed'.

The poem 'O Love, the interest itself' acted as the prologue to Auden's 1936 volume *Look, Stranger!*, and the setting-up/discomfiting strategy seems to be encapsulated in the relation between the title-poem of this collection and the book's contents. 'Look, stranger, at this island now' is an exercise in presenting England as abstract chalk idyll, . . . or indeed of a Batsford book-jacket:

[Cites: 'Look, stranger, at this island now' (*C.P.*, p. 130)]

The emphasis of *Look, Stranger!* is precisely to oppose such a picture of 'this island', to go into the details that reveal a much more composite national identity. Such a project is already at the heart of *The Orators* (1932), the first book of which opens with an imagined inspection of the nation by 'a picked body of angels', sent out into 'rain-wet Scotland', the 'furnace-crowded Midlands', Cornwall, the Severn, King's Lynn (a deliberately eccentric choice) and so forth to report back to the capital with the famous question 'What do you think about England, this country of ours where nobody is well?' (*The English Auden*, pp. 61–2). In an ode from the final section of *The Orators* this plurality is recomposed in the form of a boarding-school rugby fifteen, where team-mates from conspicuously far-flung and contrasting regions – Skye, the Wash, Aberdovey and Cornwall are highlighted – are saluted in their cup-winning triumph (*The English Auden*, pp. 96–8). Whatever vein of irony runs through this poem, there is no doubt that the 1930s Auden feels a deep attraction towards an England thus reconstituted, *e pluribus unum* [Latin: 'One out of many'], and that his attacks on national reductivism of the Pressan Ambo type, as in *The Dog*, are part of a nationalist affiliation not subject, I believe, to the deep qualifications about nationalism we find in Eliot.

Thus a sense of detail and difference is combined in Auden with an ideal of the composite whole, something of a federalist notion of England which embodies Eliot's insistence throughout *Notes Towards the Definition of Culture* on a nation's requisite 'variety in unity', though the *Quartets* themselves as we have seen emphasize the reverse of such a viewpoint. Certainly much of Auden's work is too close to the land it surveys to permit that comfortable view of a unitary England where distancing hides division and composes the island into wholeness – 'this precious stone set in the silver sea', and so forth. Many of Auden's poems are rather like an ordnance survey of individual localities, where every feature (and blemish) is seen, as in 'industrial slump' poems like 'Who stands, the crux left of the watershed' (*C.P.*, p. 32). At the same time the urge to find some panoramic viewpoint in which such details, while not being lost, will take their place in a national whole is marked, a 'hawk's-eye' viewpoint in which keen-sightedness is combined with aerial breadth. Auden wants both the whole and the part, and we can often find a bias in individual poems to either of these viewpoints. Thus in 'O Love, the interest itself' he seems as we saw to resist any Gaunt-like glossing of England by unearthing the intractable details of regions like Glamorgan that 'hid a life/Grim as a tidal rock-pool's in its glove-shaped valleys' (*The English Auden*, p. 119). Another state-of-the-nation poem from *Look, Stranger!*, 'Here on the cropped grass of the narrow ridge I stand', has, however, a rather more cursory reference to regionality, with the meditation on

'England' afforded by the station of the Malvern Hills taking in its purview only a brief glimpse at Wales. . . . . . . That somewhat reductive emblematization of England we find in the title-poem of *Look, Stranger!* then might be seen to embody the pull towards central-ization in Auden which is elsewhere resisted, the volume itself like *The Orators* showing a highly ambiguous relationship towards nation-hood. . . . . . .

The foregoing observations may throw some light on what is Auden's most famous landscape poem, 'In Praise of Limestone', writ-ten in 1948 (*C.P.*, p.540). Such a poem presents a classic landscape indeed, one that is temperate, non-extremist, 'homocentric', 'a stone that responds' to any will to form humans exercise upon it. The poem carries on from the sonnet 'Wandering lost upon the mountains' in converting such a lost prelapsarian landscape into an image of the para-disal garden after time, of 'a faultless love/Or the life to come'. Yet limestone synthesizes the idea of the classic norm with an element of abnormality, taking the form of hill-top temples and secret systems of 'caves and conduits', a stone both tractable and irregular, smooth and intricate, well-behaved yet mysterious, open yet 'underground', and supporting inhabitants confederate yet not totalitarianized:

> Watch, then, the band of rivals as they climb up and down
> Their steep stone gennels in twos and threes, at times
> Arm in arm, but never, thank God, in step. (*C.P.*, p.541)

Limestone is, of course, related to chalk, but has none of that national-ism or authoritarianism with which chalk has been repeatedly inscribed, . . . far from being a landscape of what we have called stripped classicism it metamorphoses itself in Auden's poem into features like 'Innocent athletes and gesticulating fountains'. It becomes indeed a (romantically infiltrated) landscape of the traditional antique ideal, precisely that place of empathy which the harsher neo-classicism considered in this book rejects. Its actual location is also crucially important: limestone is the landscape of the dales and moors of northern, not southern England, not the fully 'romantic' mountain-landscape of the northern Lakes but a kind of *via media* between that and the chalk. Here qualities of north and south converge and are yet retained, the one not precluding the many.

Even if, in Auden's England of the 1930s, the representation of the many is foregrounded, one hesitates . . . to salute Auden as the voice of freedom and plurality in opposition to the monologic emphases of Eliot. In spite of the individualistic components of Auden's picture, there remains an ambitious urge towards totality that seeks out some detached, omnipotent prospect whence all of England, History, or the

World is magisterially surveyed. Ultimately the all-inclusive England is but the reverse of the all-exclusive one; that which gives the work of these poets its immense power is in part precisely that which to this reader at least is intellectually and politically specious.[42] □

The next chapter will explore this political side of Auden's work through to the crucial 'defection' to America in 1939.

CHAPTER FOUR

Turning Points

THIS SECTION focuses on the important transitions that took place in Auden's work from the middle of the 1930s to the beginning of the 1940s. 'Never talk about religion or politics' is useful advice if one wants to avoid controversy, but in Auden's case – a popular political poet who renounced his role and resumed the Christian belief of his adolescence – the controversy is unavoidable. The complexity of this transition will be traced through the ambiguity of Auden's politics, and in the next chapter, in the non-representability of Auden's religion. Contained within the overall scheme is a further move, that between England and America. The importance and timing of Auden's 'defection' ramifies to the furthest reaches of Auden's *oeuvre*: from the exploration and modification of 'Englishness' taking place in the very early work ('Consider this', 'Doom is dark', 'Since you are going') to the construction of a new American identity ('September 1, 1939', 'In Memory of W.B. Yeats'). The fundamental quality of Auden's work is often linked to the move to America, for many critics were left with a gnawing sense that when he moved to the States, Auden gave up more than his citizenship – he had turned away from the urgent immediacy of politics, to the cosy self-satisfied solipsism of his faith. The extracts here will help to expose this as a myth, and to let us read the poetry with a new sense of power and politics in place, preparing the way for the difficult and dark religious narrative that was being played out beneath the apparently calm surface of his life.

Auden was active in the theatre throughout the 1930s and I would like to take his first publicly performed drama *The Dance of Death* as an example of how Auden's political position was transformed into a concrete set of attitudes and actions on the stage. The fact that these 'concrete' actions were highly ambiguous is the main point, and I would like to reproduce here Michael Sidnell's discussion of *The Dance of Death* from his book *The Dances of Death: The Group Theatre of London in the Thirties* (1984). The Group Theatre was led by the dancer and choreographer Rupert Doone, who with his partner, the painter Robert Medley (the school friend who asked Auden if he wrote poetry) put on a series of Auden's plays as well as work by Eliot. The company was ramshackle, but keen to experiment with untried work.

Sidnell provides an excellent account of Auden's theatrical work of the thirties. Through his careful and painstaking research he re-creates the early performances of plays such as *The Dance of Death* and *The Ascent of F6* enabling an insight into these productions that a simple reading of the text itself could never provide. This section is interesting as it portrays Auden's politics as double-edged and far from clear. Although the play was 'thematically unified and stylistically coherent' Auden anticipated the problems of audience reception and how they would identify with the action on the stage, and the critical responses that Sidnell presents demonstrate the subtle modes of address taking place within an unsubtle play.

The ambiguity of tone is a vital element here. Looking through criticism of Auden's work in the 1930s, one is struck by the uneven reception of his tone: where some see seriousness, others see levity, where some see commitment, others see a poet playing with ideas. This is not a problem, but a fundamental part of the power of Auden's work. To make us see our peculiarities, but not to accuse us of a crime, to entertain while leading us to new possibilities, these qualities are encapsulated in *The Dance of Death*:

■ The production called for the kind of mobilization that went into the making of pageants and such communal celebrations, its ludic spirit embracing a whole (though hypothetical) community. It was up to the Group Theatre to realize Auden's Marxist hypothesis of an advance party of the doomed middle class celebrating and perhaps accelerating its own imminent destruction.

Whether Auden was acquainted with the German agitprop groups or the British ones that took them as a model, he was obviously familiar with the style, elements of which he commandeered. Even in aspiration, though, *The Dance of Death* was not an attempt at workers' theatre proper but a newer phenomenon: an adaptation for a middle-class audience and partly professional company of agitprop techniques. With its political message couched in blatantly didactic terms, its use of a chorus in a collective role, strict choreography on a bare stage, doggerel verse and simple words, caricature and revue structure, *The Dance of Death* was the first attempt to forge a link between 'bourgeois' and workers' theatre in England.

Auden's depiction of the historically inevitable death of the middle class was unabashedly by, of and for the middle class, and there was deep consistency in his assumption that a middle-class audience would be entertained by the spectacle, since he assumed that its fatal disorder was its death wish. The reviewer who thought that Auden was 'consciously trying to write poetry for the ideal proletarian' and supposed that 'a technique . . . so simplified that it required the help of the stage, with song and dance' must have been adopted in order to reach the simple workers was decidedly off the mark.[1] He would have been nearer to it if he had accused Auden of artfully picking the proletarian pocket in order to bring the English theatre into new country aesthetically, as well as politically.[2]

At a time when literary Marxism was an unfamiliar feature on the landscape, its middle-class variety was hard to comprehend. *The Times Literary Supplement*, having an inkling of what was going on, was irritated by the cheek of it.

> We find Mr Auden in the attitude of one desiring revolution . . . he is a gamin [mischievous street urchin] jeering at the tumbril [wagon that transported aristocrats to the guillotine during the French Revolution]. . . . Those on stage are the outmoded who, like the damned in a foundering ship, are occupied with trying to escape and being frustrated: a situation which is supposed to delight us, which we are expected to enjoy without pity – this is the fundamental and rather adolescent flaw.[3]

'Tumbril' and 'damnation' suggest some unwilling assent to Auden's (or Marx's) prophecy, but the reviewer did not quite see that Auden was himself in the cart and, with merry irony, inviting his fellow passengers to join the dance.

From its different viewpoint, the *Socialist Review* was also rather dissatisfied with Auden's attitude. Seeing that it was 'good that Auden should be on our side', and 'waving the red flag', it had to admit his Marxism 'seemed to misfire'.[4] And a severer comrade, diagnosing the ideological weakness more precisely, objected that 'the death of capitalism is not accompanied and promoted by any conscious and accelerating pressure. Its theoretic deficiency is that of the intellectualistic, deterministic approach.'[5] Far from simply promoting the revolution, Auden presented the emergence of a new proletarian order ambivalently and since the Marxist prognosis was offered in anything but a serious manner, a Communist might well have suspected that Communism was being made a game of; as, rather in the manner of the games played with Christianity in the medieval cycle plays, it was. With its air of detachment, Auden's political ballet-charade adumbrated some happy, far-off, post-revolutionary period in which the passions of yesterday's struggle would long since have been distilled into myth and play.

There were other ways in which *The Dance of Death* was quite unlike the workers' theatre that influenced it. The allusions that the overt simplicity of language and form slyly concealed were decidedly highbrow. . . . . . . *The Dance of Death* was also distinct from workers' theatre in making use of the techniques of symbolist theatre and ballet. . . . . . .

Auden was using Marxist dogma as an intellectual scaffolding but the result was less Communist propaganda (though that is what it looked like to its first audiences) than an ethically timeless – even religious – memento mori. . . . . . . In such a manner Auden made the actors hold up the glass to themselves and to the audience. T. S. Eliot, as one of those present, responded enthusiastically – at first – and some of the enthusiasm he felt for *The Dance of Death* may be attributed to his recognition of a spiritual lamb in Marxist clothing, an example of the celebratory reality that he thought vital for the regeneration of the theatre.

Celebrating the longings and fears of his time and class, Auden focused particularly on the Group's own yearnings for renewal and its particular dance of death. He did so by designing a mask for the Group Theatre so like its face as to be more a revelation than a disguise. . . . In *The Orators*, Auden had exhibited a few of his friends as part of the fantasy but in *The Dance of Death* the Group Theatre as a whole was imaginatively deployed. If there was a risk that this theatrical verism would lead to a self-indulgent display, the risk was offset by the conviviality and the possible therapeutic value of a performance that was, in itself, what it represented.[6] □

The *Dance of Death* may have been ambiguous in a party political sense, but Janet Montefiore's book *Men and Women Writers of the Thirties* (1996) explores the parallel issues of gender politics that were played out (literally and dramatically) during the 1930s. In the following extract Montefiore brings into view the question of gender which is often overlooked when critics look at the work of the homosexual Auden. In her analysis of the role of stereotypical figures such as the spinster and the vamp, as well as the easy archetypes of the mother, she begins to question the assumed and tricky underside to the masculinist thrust of thirties poetry. Encapsulated in the question: 'What sort of meanings did their sexual signifiers carry?', her section on the mother unpicks the importance of this figure, and argues that the venom directed to women goes beyond the expected indifference of the predominantly homosexual theatrical milieu in which Auden and Isherwood wrote their plays.

■ It is important here to take account of context. Many of the most stereotypical representations of women by the 'Auden Generation' poets occur in the experimental verse-plays which they wrote for the

Group Theatre, an association of actors and dancers who were inspired, trained and organized by the dancer and director Rupert Doone, between 1932 and 1938. As Michael Sidnell has shown in *Dances of Death*, his excellent history of the Group Theatre, Doone and his colleagues attempted, with genuine if finally limited success, to change the naturalistic face of English drama by producing deliberately stylized, often avant-garde plays. . . . It is hardly surprising that, when left-wing ex-public schoolboys wrote and produced deliberately extravagant, non-naturalistic plays that satirized their own class, they represented the females of this species as caricature villains, just as they did with the figures of male authority like the Fascist leader, the mad Vicar or the corrupt Press Baron. Nevertheless, the representation of women in the Group Theatre plays is done with a venom which cannot be wholly accounted for by their satirical intent and deliberately simplified characterization.

The female characters in the plays of Auden, Isherwood and Spender are almost uniformly threatening and treacherous. Older women represent the deadly power of reactionary authority, either as mothers who give their sons up to death, or worse still as childless women who vent their frustration at their own barrenness in a death wish against young men. Young women, less threateningly, are expensive temptresses or, very occasionally, brides. These images of women represent both the ideological demands and the often illusory rewards with which a reactionary State bullies and tempts the revolutionary hero. . . . . . .

All the experimental dramas written by Auden and his colleagues in the 1930s are autobiographical parables about the relation between private and public worlds, in which the hero's life represents the characteristic dilemma of the whole 'Auden Generation'. Though not central to the hero's story, Woman is, typically, important in it. As temptation or threat, she represents part of the hero's problem, while, as reconciling bride, she may also represent a possible symbolic solution.

Clearly I am drawing the terms of this description from Samuel Hynes' influential account of the work of the 'Auden Generation' male writers as creators of non-naturalistic 'parable art', representing public, political issues through a private mythology.[7] The public-private dichotomy tends to efface women as subjects, because the feminine is conventionally associated with the world of private life. This is certainly true of the Group Theatre plays: the mother or maiden aunt is part of a domestic scenario, while the siren belongs in the bedroom, or at best the shopping arcade. . . . Yet these 'privatized' female characters also carry a much wider, public significance. The devouring Mother who dooms her son to destruction represents the bitterness famously felt by the younger wartime generation against its patriotic elders in the Great War, and thus personifies a whole blameworthy generation. More than this, she also represents the means whereby the claims of the State get their claws into the young man's psyche. Her near relation, the enraged barren woman who vents her frustration on the young, conversely represents the psychopathology of Fascism. The lovely Vamp is a class signifier as much as a sexual one, for she is the ultimate luxury, affordable only by the rich. Her charm, which resides in her expensive accoutrements as much as in her looks, makes her the prime signifier of the privilege enjoyed by the ruling class, and thus also of their guilt. . . .

Mothers are the chief culprits of Auden's first play, the 'charade' *Paid on Both Sides*, a tragedy of two embattled families, the Nowers and the Shaws, fighting over a 'Northern' landscape. . . . Auden called the play 'a parable of English middle class (professional) family life 1907–1929'[8] – a period which runs from the year of his birth to the year he completed it. . . . . . . The autobiographical application of Auden's parable of English family life is obvious. The image of the son brought up in a world of murderous conflict, without a father and with a dominating mother, is transparently drawn from the poet's own childhood and adolescence during the First World War. On the other hand, the play ignores Auden's own homosexuality, representing heterosexual love as the solution of the hero's conflicts: 'Now this shall end with marriage as it ought' (*C.P.*, p.20). It may appear odd, on the face of it, that a satire on the bourgeois family should represent the proper solution of its conflicts as the successful attempt 'to bring home a wife' (*C.P.*, p.26) and to found a male dynasty. But as Lucy McDiarmid has pointed out, the image of a symbolic heterosexual reconciliation appears as a consistent ideal in Auden's plays, though one invariably prevented by adverse circumstances from actually happening. . . .

The Ascent of F6 (1937), which Auden wrote in collaboration with Christopher Isherwood, deals more overtly with the relation between homosexuality, the family, and the needs of an imperialist State, handling the joint themes of Oedipal trauma and the demands of 'England, home and duty' not much less savagely than *Paid*. Its tragic hero, Michael Ransom, leads a doomed British expedition to scale 'F6', a mountain in African 'Sudoland'. The project is financed by a Press Baron, partly as a publicity stunt but mainly to secure the prestige of Britain as a colonial power. The British Empire in Africa is being threatened by the European state 'Ostnia', which has sent out a rival mountaineering party. This threatens English interests in the region . . . Michael Ransom knows he ought to have nothing to do with this imperialist con-trick; but, being a Truly Weak Man who has to prove himself by attempting heroic ventures, he is tempted by F6 as the ultimate challenge to his skill, and finally persuaded to climb it by maternal blackmail. . . . . . . Yeats, who as an Irishman was acutely aware of the imperialist implications of Ransom's venture, suggested to Rupert Doone that the Group Theatre's production should make Mrs Ransom appear in the final tableau as 'Britannia from the penny': an excellent stage image which would have connected the play's 'private' fantasy of the powerful, devouring mother with the 'public' imperialist iconography of Britannia, the Mother Country who rules the waves by sacrificing her sons.

Mothers may be 'Freudian carnivores' in the Auden Generation's plays, but barren women are a great deal worse. The widow/spinster Mildred Luce in *The Dog Beneath the Skin* is a truly bloodthirsty specimen of this pathology. When the hero Alan is sent off on his quest to restore the missing heir of 'Pressan Ambo', the ideal English village, she appears loudly mourning her two sons who were shot by 'a German sniper' in the war. She hates Alan for being young, but neverthless has instructions for him:

> Set off for Germany and shoot them all!
> Poison the wells, till her people drink the sea
> And perish howling. Strew all her fields
> With arsenic, leave a land whose crops
> Would starve the unparticular hyena![9]

Mildred reappears, even more crazy and hate-filled, at the end of the play where Alan returns, having discovered Francis the missing heir to Pressan Ambo, which is no longer an idyllic Eden but a centre of British Fascism. Revealing himself to the villagers, Francis tells Mildred and the assembly that her public hatred of Germany is a lie; Mildred never had any sons, and her real tragedy is her virginity . . . . . .

Another fire-eating female reactionary, Martha Thorwald of *On the Frontier*, similarly takes out her own frustrations in fanatical devotion to Westland's Fascist Leader. . . . . . . As with Mildred's lunacy, Martha's plight has a wider representative meaning: she stands for all those who take out personal frustrations in blind, romantic patriotism. Both these women become destructive through frustration and denial, displacing their private desires on to false 'public' images. Martha really wants a husband and family and Mildred really wants her German lover; deprived of these satisfactions, one woman worships the leader and the other indulges in fantasies of slaughter which turn into real murder. Their predicament thus represents a political variant of the 'Miss Gee' syndrome, whereby repressed desires turn lethal.

But whereas Edith Gee's cancerous repressions are represented as comic, harming only herself, these much more sinister spinsters represent a symptom of social disorder and at the same time a threat to their disordered society.[10] □

Despite providing a location for the negative representation of reactionary women in the dramas of the thirties, Auden and Isherwood would set up the English village as a foil for the alternative views of their questing and cosmopolitan heroes. The international locations of the plays allowed a view of England from the outside, a view which demanded a fresh consideration of entrenched political and moral prejudices. Auden began writing longer pieces as early as 1932 when he produced an idiosyncratic version of the Divine Comedy, 'In the year of my youth when yo-yo's came in';[11] but the first long major piece of poetry, 'Letter to Lord Byron', forms the backbone of the package *Letters from Iceland* (1937), written in collaboration with Louis MacNeice. 'Letter to Lord Byron' is a fascinating work. Not only does it serve to portray Auden's state of mind and obsessions when in Iceland, but it also paints a bold and pithy picture of Britain in the mid thirties – a task that *Letters from Iceland* always had on its agenda. It was a question of distance – and the trip to Iceland was the next important journey for the poet, after Berlin, from which the state of England becomes clearer, and his own position more difficult, as MacNeice wrote: 'Here we can take a breath, sit back, admire/Stills from the film of life, the frozen fire'.[12] When considering *Letters from Iceland* Stan Smith believes that 'All Auden's discoveries of the artifice of cultural identity, the source of the anthropological interest that runs through his work, occur at moments of dislocation'.[13] This statement is particularly apt when thinking about Auden's politics, where Auden's ability to dissect middle-class identity with such clinical precision derives in part from his upbringing and natural precociousness, but also from the important distance that the trips to Berlin, Iceland, Spain, China and America, gave to his sexual and political understanding of himself and his time.

Anthony Hecht devotes a chapter of *The Hidden Law* (1993) to 'Letter to Lord Byron', arguing that

■ So different is this major long poem from the poetry that immediately preceded and followed it as to astonish almost any reader. And what may be most impressive in the final analysis is Auden's extraordinary capacity to pick up the strain of anxiety, the themes of private and public concern, where he had laid them down before embarking on this holiday interlude.

The Iceland trip was a sort of practical holiday: the chance to visit a wholly different and alien landscape with which Auden identified his

Nordic ancestors, and the chance to write a 'travel book', which had a chance at a wide popular sale (as distinguished from the audience for serious poetry).[14] □

Indeed, the arguments for the commonplace nature of poetry expressed in the introduction to *The Poet's Tongue* (see chapter three) are exemplified in the entire presentation of *Letters from Iceland* which couches its poetry amongst 'Press cuttings, gossip, maps, statistics, graphs' (*The English Auden*, p.172). Tom Paulin's essay 'Letters from Iceland: Going North' brings out the historical and political realities underlying the light-hearted front that *Letters from Iceland* presents to its readers. In this extract Paulin shows that Auden's playfulness often has a serious underside.

■ For anyone born after the Second World War the 1930s can seem to take shape as just another literary period, the object of scholarly interest, packaged and safe. If this happens, then the poetry, with its deliberate relevance to politics and society, must cease to affect us in some of the ways which it, often provocatively, aims to.

What I want to argue is that *Letters from Iceland* offers a response to history, politics and society which is not only still valid, but which has still to be followed. For me, the response, in the 1970s, is less to the European situation Auden and MacNeice were writing about, and more to society in Britain, to landscape, and to Ireland. . . . .

It is Auden's and MacNeice's deliberate intention to present their voyage to Iceland as being apparently escapist, like pastoral poetry . . . But, just as with Marvell, this offered rejection conceals a serious political intention. As MacNeice says, 'We are not changing ground to escape from facts/But rather to find them.' And what they found was, for example, Goering's brother taking breakfast at Holar, parties of Nazis visiting Iceland because they had a theory that 'Iceland is the cradle of the Germanic culture.' . . . . . .

[Their] extraordinary sensitivity to politics means that while Auden and MacNeice may at times present their voyage to Iceland as being possibly escapist and solipsistic they are actually raising that criticism in order to insist on their political subject. They are not writing a travel book – they are writing about European culture by focusing on a democratic community which works under the physical shadow of its landscape and the spiritual shadow of its heroic past. Deliberately, then, both poets refuse to describe landscape in isolation from its inhabitants or some of its sinister tourists. Their book is packed with statistics, jokes and photographs which ignore the landscape – photographs of herring factories, a new concrete school, corrugated-iron farms, sports galas – anything but a barren mountain.

Because, Auden says, 'it is the strictly relevant I sing', he has constantly and wittily to defeat our conventional expectations of picturesque descriptions, praise of solitude, etc. He recalls us to the English landscape, to the condition of England:

There on the old historic Battlefield,
The cold ferocity of human wills,
The scars of struggle as yet unhealed;
Slattern the tenements on sombre hills,
And gaunt in valleys the square-windowed mills
That, since the Georgian house, in my conjecture
Remain our finest native architecture.

This is the real North of [Orwell's] *The Road to Wigan Pier* and [Engels's] *The Condition of the Working Class in England*.

What Auden and MacNeice are so importantly saying is that the artist has social responsibilities. He must do everything in his power to avoid 'kissing wives of mist' because, if he doesn't, he will become a Grettir [from the 13th century Icelandic Saga of Grettir the Strong], an enemy of society, a terrorist. . . . . What Auden objected to, as he says in 'The Greeks and Us', was how

In the nineteenth century and in our own the individual artistic genius has sometimes claimed a supreme importance and even persuaded a minority of aesthetes to agree with him; but only in Athens was this a universal social fact, so that the genius was not a lonely figure claiming exceptional rights for himself but the acclaimed spiritual leader of society.

The artist, therefore, has a duty to be responsible both in the content of his work and in his relation to society where he is a private citizen. . . .
. . . This commitment is felt throughout *Letters* because in choosing to organise it as a series of letters to friends and relatives in England Auden and MacNeice selected a pre-eminently *social* form. . . . . . .
The question for us now is where Auden's and MacNeice's initiative leads. For me the total effect of their work, and especially of *Letters from Iceland*, is to make it impossible to read a volume of nature or rural poetry (especially by any poet writing after the Second World War) without being affected by a peculiar feeling of emptiness. Without human or political content nature means very little, and to describe it in isolation from that content is to abdicate the responsibility to be relevant which Auden and MacNeice impose on themselves and us – indeed it is to recommend, however unconsciously, such an abdication. . . . . . .

So, finally, we discover in *Letters from Iceland* something which looks very like a poetic. If there's nothing particularly new about it that is because it's an initiative that is obvious but which hasn't been sufficiently explored. Both Auden and MacNeice suggest that poetry should be responsible, relevant and, at times, narrative – it should not be about the unimaginative fields.[15] □

The social responsibility of the artist is the subject of the next extract, taken from David Trotter's book *The Making of the Reader: Language and Subjectivity in Modern American, English and Irish Poetry* (1984). Trotter, as the name of his book suggests, is concerned with the way that Auden's poetry constructed an audience for itself, based upon recognition and substitution: the reader searching through his or her own experience to find appropriate middle-class characters to insert into Auden's bestiary of bourgeois types. This was an aspect of *The Orators* discussed by Spender in chapter three of this Guide. Like many other commentators, Trotter noticed that *The Orators* had a slippery and imprecise political agenda, and pointed out how the romantic and potentially politically embarrassing imagery of the 'Airman' and the mountain climber could cut two ways, made to speak for either the fascist or communist sides of the political divide.

Trotter emphasises aspects of liminality (threshold), marginality and hesitancy in the poetry of the thirties – and points to Auden's own depiction of 'going over', that terrifying moment so well documented by the poets of the First World War, and taken up as a metaphor of choice and commitment by the generation that followed. He affirms the importance of Auden's poem *Spain*, describing it as articulating 'more powerfully than any other contemporary work the interplay between rebirth and going-over which pre-occupied so many people during the thirties'.

■ 'It is goodbye to *The Tatler* and the *Bystander*,' Orwell said in 1940, 'and farewell to the lady in the Rolls-Royce car.'[16] A Rolls-Royce clearly signifies the privilege about to be destroyed by gas and bomb, but 'the' lady has been put there only for the reader who can consult the pages of a mental *Tatler*: she is the harder to lose.

Auden had pursued such strategies for more than a decade, for example in the first stanza of '1929', where he detailed the terrible lethargy of 'the loud madman' and announced 'the destruction of error'. It is time, the poem says, for regeneration:

The old gang to be forgotten in the spring,
The hard bitch and the riding-master,
Stiff underground; deep in clear lake
The lolling bridegroom, beautiful, there. (*C.P.*, p.49)

The old gang, which we must identify through our knowledge of hard bitches and riding-masters, will transform itself by shedding its definite articles, 'deep in clear lake'. Auden's friend Rex Warner advised any of his readers who might still belong to the old gang to throw away, before it was too late, 'the eau de Cologne which disguised you', not to mention 'the tennis racquet' and 'the blazer of the First XV'.[17] Day-Lewis was more militant, suggesting that the proud possessors should be junked along with their trophies. His long poem *The Magnetic Mountain* (1933) attacked all those who had nothing to fight for except 'the silver spoon', 'the touched hat', 'the expensive seat'. Silverware seemed to cause particular offence, and even the mild-mannered Louis MacNeice was ready to pour scorn where tea might have been expected. How would the gentry feel, he asked in 'An Eclogue for Christmas',

> Without the bandy chairs and the sugar in the silver tongs
> And the inter-ripple and resonance of years of dinner-gongs?

The eau de Cologne, the blazer, the touched hat, the expensive seat, the silver tongs: it is goodbye to all that.

Finding things to say goodbye to had been a more or less full-time occupation for many writers since the end of the First World War. But Auden and his contemporaries were also looking for things to say hello to. They required their readers to spot both decadence and signs of the birth of a new social order. 'If the poet reproduces within his audience his own sense of disintegration,' wrote Day Lewis, 'he also recreates within them his instinctive movement towards a life which is forming and gathering strength.'[18] Guilt felt at association with the old order might be cancelled by an altruistic embrace of the new one. . . . . . .

Some poems also encouraged the reader to identify the means by which present was to be transformed into future. Spender touches on this problem when discussing his attitude to a proletarian friend: 'I imagined, I suppose, that something which I was now beginning to call in my mind 'the revolution' would alter his lot, and I felt that as a member of a more fortunate social class I owed him a debt'.[19] But how much of the debt was owed to the friend and how much to that provocative definite article? *The* revolution was a kind of club, a meeting-place for the like-minded, a readership. . . . . . .

But the poem which most coherently imagined the interplay between organic metaphors of rebirth and a going-over provoked by definite articles was Auden's 'Spain, 1937'. (In discussing this poem, I shall base my remarks on the longer 1937 text, which represents his immediate and unqualified response to the Spanish Civil War.)[20] Its first six stanzas concern a past whose identity clearly lies in our keeping: 'yesterday the invention/Of cart-wheels and clocks', and so on. It is a rapid summary, a classroom version of the past whose importance lies less in its truth than in the security it offers us – the sense of a knowledge encapsulated and possessed. Soon, however, a more enigmatic and unresolved present intrudes: 'But to-day the struggle.' Samuel Hynes suggests that this is not simply the class-struggle, but also 'the struggle or moral choice that goes on occurring *every* today, because in the present in which men live they must choose and act'.[21] It is the process of going-over, the shifting of a centre within oneself which would produce a new political alignment and a readership.

In the next eight stanzas, poet and scientist and pauper request the intervention of History. They long for some superior force, some rite of passage, which will elide their struggle and usher them smoothly into a new life:

> O descend as a dove or
> A furious papa or a mild engineer, but descend
> (*The English Auden*, p.211)

It is a supremely witty summary of the age's demand for an accelerated and thoroughly modern rebirth. However, History's reply throws the responsibility for decision back on to the human subject: 'I am whatever you do.' There can be no rebirth which is not supported at every point by particular willed acts of going-over.

Or can there be? In 1937, of course, a particular struggle beckoned: 'I am your choice, your decision: yes, I am Spain.' The next five stanzas (two of which were dropped in 1940) describe a journey to the margin, a Romantic quest which promises the new life at a stroke. For those who went to Spain, Bernard Bergonzi points out, 'crossing the frontier from France meant a transition to a new world of faith and hope and meaning'.[22] Suddenly it seems that a particular willed going-over might after all amount to regeneration, as Auden imagines a release from social structure ('the institute-face, the chain store') into liminal comradeship:

> Madrid is the heart. Our moments of tenderness blossom
> As the ambulance and the sandbag;
> Our hours of friendship into a people's army.
> (*The English Auden*, p.425)

. . . Tenderness *blossoms* into a sense of community, and the organic metaphor concludes (as Mendelson has pointed out) a sequence of naturalising terms: the volunteers 'migrated like gulls or the seeds of a flower,' they 'clung like burrs' to the sides of trains and 'floated over the oceans' like clouds. In no previous poem had Auden so exuberantly thrust such metaphors into the centre of political occasion.

The dream of organic change inspires the vision of the future which unfolds over the next four stanzas. . . . The details of the future rest in our keeping, as though Auden had realised that he could not carry his account of the blossoming in Spain through, and that it was already dissolving into what each of us can make it. . . .

Finally the poet resigns himself to the present, to 'the expending of powers/On the flat ephemeral pamphlet and the boring meeting' (which were what Auden expended his powers on during his brief visit to Spain). The concluding stanza registers the exhaustion of organic and natural metaphors, and a new pragmatism:

> The stars are dead, the animals will not look;
> We are left alone with our day, and the time is short and
> History to the defeated
> May say Alas but cannot help or pardon.
>
> (*The English Auden*, p.212)

. . . As organic process on one hand and History on the other draw back into their oblivious shells, we are left alone with our day and with the imperfect continuing of utterance.

'Spain, 1937' attempts to locate a Romantic rite of passage amid contemporary political circumstances, to describe a journey to the margin. But the organic metaphors sponsored by such a project do not 'take'. They are ornamental, a frivolous sub-plot to the main (and true) story of a guilty and incomplete going-over. That story is told by the definite articles, as they tempt us to dismiss a past which only we can identify, or join in a struggle which will be intensified rather than resolved by our participation, or put our names to a blueprint of the future. When Auden left for Spain, he may have thought that he was embarking on a regenerative rite of passage; when he came back, he knew that he had simply gone over and come back. His poem testifies to the reality of that experience, and to its failure to become a metaphor for rebirth.

When he came to revise 'Spain, 1937' for publication in *Another Time* (1940), Auden excluded its major commemoration of liminality (the hours of tenderness blossoming into a people's army); by that time the fantasy perhaps seemed too dangerous even to acknowledge. Later, of course, he disowned the poem altogether. But I believe that in its original form it articulated more powerfully than any other contemporary work the interplay between rebirth and going-over which preoccupied so many people during the thirties (and which is not exactly unheard-of today). Orwell's response to it is well-known, and has formed the basis for much subsequent comment. Less well-known is Eliot's oblique rejoinder to its final stanza in the third section of 'Little Gidding'; he had, after all, seen *Another Time* through the press. Eliot suggested that if History cannot help or pardon the defeated, we can:

> Whatever we inherit from the fortunate
> We have taken from the defeated
> What they had to leave us – a symbol:
> A symbol perfected in death.

He at least tried to meet the force of Auden's argument.[23] □

Trotter's sense that *Spain* holds the tensions and uncertainties of an historical moment suspended in its images and metaphors is echoed in Arnold Kettle's 1979 essay 'W.H. Auden: Poetry and Politics in the Thirties'. Kettle provides a political reading of Auden which has the virtue of understanding how *narrow* conceptions of the political will miss out on much that Auden has to offer in the way of a political explanation of the 1930s. Comparing Auden's view with that of Eliot, we are presented with a situation in which Auden, an 'impure' poet, is able to refract and absorb the political feeling of his time into a poetry that never forgets its human scale, yet does not seek to let the reader off lightly either.

Kettle witheringly suggests that Auden's short lyric 'Our Hunting Fathers' (1934) was a shrewder assessment of the political moment of the thirties than the entire content of Spender's *Forward from Liberalism*. Auden's revisions are also considered here, mainly the eventual rejection of both 'Spain, 1937' and 'September 1, 1939'. Kettle's is a warming and human critical view of a poet who was tolerant of the weaknesses of the common man or woman. His remembrance of 'Spain, 1937' as a poem that refused to 'hector' its audience is an invaluable insight into the way the poem worked its parabolic magic: slowly bringing the relevance of the events into view through the careful converging proximity of the individual choice, and that 'tableland scored by rivers' where 'Our thoughts have bodies' and the 'menacing shapes of our fever/Are precise and alive'.[24]

■ 'September 1, 1939' can be read, quite properly, as a vital step in Auden's movement away from political poetry. But, again, it is not a simple story. Auden and Isherwood went to America not just because they were disillusioned with European politics (though, of course, like everyone else they were depressed and fearful about the advances of fascism and the growing likelihood of a new world war). They also went to America for personal reasons connected with their search for satisfactory homosexual relationships. . . . . . .

The left-wing poets of the thirties were primarily interested neither in the Soviet Union nor in Communism in the abstract but in the problem of making sense of their own dilemmas and of the society and the world into which they had been born. It was the First World War, its consequences and, above all, its *meaning*, that lay behind their lives and consciousness. The differences between the Britain of 1907, when W. H. Auden was born, and that of 1931, when he was twenty-four, were so great that no one could be unaware that he or she was living through some sort of deep social and political crisis: yet at the same time, because there had been no invasion, no occupation, and 'victory' rather than 'defeat', it was surprisingly easy to pretend that nothing much (except the slaughter, softened into the word 'sacrifice') had really happened. The Empire remained, the City of London remained, the General Strike failed, only the Liberal Party seemed to have taken an irrevocable knock. The death of liberal England was something that writers, especially the middle-class writers with their traditional education and most of their traditional privileges intact, had to discover. . . . . . .

Auden's involvement in political struggle during the thirties, though it never brought him to a theoretical position which Marxists would be likely to consider very satisfactory, seems to me to have been an altogether positive factor in his development as a poet for several reasons. In the first place, it led him to explore continuously the connections between his private or purely personal experience and the public, historical developments of the time. In the second, it encouraged him to find out what he had in common with other people and to see himself as a part of a social situation, not merely as one lonely man, uncertain and afraid. In the third place it helped him, at least for a time, towards a view of language and indeed of poetry itself which was fruitful precisely because it was outward-turning and socially orientated. . . . . . .

What he is saying – that the private is entwined with the public life, that our conceptions of love and its possibilities are themselves determined by the sort of society we live in and our attitudes to it – is not of course in itself profoundly original; but I do not think any previous English poet had made so vigorous an attempt to write poetry that absorbed and coped with the relation of the mass media to the nature and quality of our perceptions and assumptions.

'Spain, 1937' was one of the poems Auden himself was to mutilate most drastically. It is also – partly for this very reason – a poem one has to return to in any attempt to define or assess the nature of Auden's political poetry. Why did he come to dislike it quite so much? It is not in any crude sense a propaganda poem exhorting the already converted to support a clearly-defined cause. It centres around the importance of choice, and Spain becomes the moment of choice for reasons which, embodied as they are in a series of disparate images, are – purposely one feels – not easy to disentangle or fix priorities to. . . . . . .

In an interesting and sympathetic discussion of this poem Samuel Hynes has said

> The striking thing about these lines is that they treat the Spanish war in psychological, not political terms, as an eruption of the sickness of modern society: in Spain, the enemy is *us* – our fears and greeds (as usual Auden involves himself in the class he condemns), and the people's army is psychological, too, a sort of metaphor for loving feelings. It is more than a metaphor, though; in Spain 'our thoughts have bodies', what was mental has become physical, and therefore mortal.[25]

I am not sure that this is the right way to put it (and I quote Hynes because the way he reads the poems seems to be a usual one). It is true, of course, that . . . the whole poem, keeps associating or linking psychological attitudes with a political situation, private neuroses with public events, and that the public events – the war – are never analysed in an overtly political way. But when the speaker of the poem says that in Spain 'the menacing shapes of our fever are precise and alive' is he really interpreting the Spanish war in psychological terms, that is to say treating the mental as more basic than the real? I would have said that the precise relationship between the private and the public in 'Spain' is left open and that the general view of that relationship emerging from the poem is similar to that implied by MacNeice when in *Autumn Journal* (written in 1939) he looks back at his pre-war visit to Spain and writes that he could not then know that

> . . . Spain would soon denote
> Our grief, our aspirations;
> Not knowing that our blunt
> Ideals would find their whetstones, that our spirit
> Would find its frontier on the Spanish front,
> Its body in a rag-tag army.[26]

Auden in 'Spain, 1937' seems to be saying that the political decisions or choices which have to be made about Spain today are essential because history (a keyword in the poem) is not a force outside men and their dilemmas and neither are men and their dilemmas outside history. I would suppose that the reason he took so violently against the poem, particularly the final statement, later on was indeed because he recognized that in it the balance between materialism and idealism was so fine. . . . . . .

Its strength, as it seems to me, lies in the way, for example, Auden succeeds in giving the words 'Madrid is the heart' a remarkable sense of the way political action can become central, involving choices whose implications and consequences reverberate through every area of life and consciousness. He isn't saying, 'We must forget our personal obsessions for a bit and take part in the struggle, which is the "real" thing', or 'The Spanish War is "really" a kind of reflection of our personal problems'. Rather, he is asserting a close and complex connection between personal fears and political possibilities and leaving the precise nature of the connection open.

This is what, from the first, gave 'Spain' its particular power and no doubt explains Auden's strong subsequent revulsion against it. . . .

. . . Political Poetry, I would suggest, is Poetry in which the question of power gets recognition and expression. . . . Too strong an emphasis on the autonomy of any human experience or activity always tends to remove it from the pressures, the power-forces, which go towards making it what it is. Poetry that makes us conscious of power opens up the world rather than attempting to enclose a part of it in some sort of mystic purity. One of the virtues of the best poetry of the thirties was that it arose out of and helped define the power struggles of the time.[27] □

Kettle's distrust of criticism that overemphasises the 'autonomy of any human experience or activity' would be at once awakened and quelled by Joseph Brodsky's essay on Auden's important poem 'September 1, 1939'. It was soon after Auden's experiences in Spain that he decided to move to America, and Brodsky sets himself the task of discovering how Auden's 'defection' in 1939 manifested itself in his writing. In his loving and almost fanatical attention to the detail of Auden's poem 'September 1, 1939' he describes the poet testing out the new language in which he had landed, in a poem that obliquely answers the questions bristling around his decision to leave England. In the passage cited Brodsky looks only at the first few lines, but this is enough to show the potential contained within this poem. It is instructive to see Auden's poem read with Brodsky's microscopic attention: a fellow poet following path after path into Auden's poem (the entire essay lasts for fifty-two pages) combining biographical, historical and metrical analysis into a coherent and entertaining performance.

Brodsky is aware that Auden was paying careful attention in this poem to the nature of his audience. Recently 'fled' from a Britain that considered his 'defection' of sufficient interest to raise a question in the

House of Commons, Auden is here establishing his American identity by literally writing himself into the American scene. Brodsky's assertion that 'in the beginning, there is still the word' anticipates writers such as Stan Smith (see chapter six) who discuss Auden's awareness of the power of *discourse* in his poetry. This is important to remember from a poet who claimed that fictional situations could excite him more than the real thing, for whom the power of the word was literally true.[28] Here, Brodsky recognises Auden's immediate assimilation of and love for the new terms offered by American English, and as always with Auden, the words chosen both construct and transform the sense of history and identity woven by the poem.

Brodsky notes the prophetic nature of Auden's poem, reminding us of the significance of the date – events had not yet been officially recognised as a state of Total War, and the uneasy recognition that his predictions for the fate of Europe were beginning to come true permeates the tone of this poem.

■ This poem, whose title, I hope, is self-explanatory, was written shortly after our poet settled on these shores. His departure caused considerable uproar at home; he was charged with desertion, with abandoning his country in a time of peril. Well, the peril indeed came, but some time after the poet left England. Besides, he was precisely the one who, for about a decade, kept issuing warnings about its – the peril's – progress. The thing with perils, though, is that no matter how clairvoyant one is, there is no way to time their arrival. And the bulk of his accusers were precisely those who saw no peril coming: the left, the right, the pacifists, etc. What's more, his decision to move to the United States had very little to do with world politics: the reasons for the move were of a more private nature. . . . Presently what matters is that our poet finds himself at the outbreak of war on new shores, and therefore has a minimum of two audiences to address: those at home and those right in front of him. Let's see what effect this fact has upon his diction. . . . . . .

Let's start with the first two lines. 'I sit in one of the dives/On Fifty-second Street . . .' (*The English Auden*, p.245). Why, in your view, does the poem start in this way? Why, for instance, this precision of 'Fifty-second Street'? And how precise is it? Well, it's precise in that Fifty-second Street indicates a place that can't be somewhere in Europe. Good enough. And I think what Auden wants to play here a bit is the role of a journalist, of a war correspondent, if you wish. This opening has a distinct air of reporting. The poet says something like 'your correspondent reports to you from . . .', he is a newsman reporting to his people back in England. And here we are getting into something very interesting.

Watch that word 'dive'. It's not exactly a British word, right? Nor is

'Fifty-second Street'. For his posture of reporter they are obviously of immediate benefit: both things are equally exotic to his home audience. And this introduces you to one aspect of Auden with which we are going to deal for some time: the encroachment of American diction, a fascination with which was, I think, among the reasons for his move here. This poem was written in 1939, and for the five subsequent years his lines became literally strewn with Americanisms. He almost revels in incorporating them into his predominantly British diction, whose texture – the texture of English verse in general – gets considerably animated by the likes of 'dives' and 'raw towns'. And we'll be going over them one by one because words and the way they sound are more important for a poet than ideas and convictions. When it comes to a poem, in the beginning there is still the word.

And in the beginning of this particular poem there is this 'dive', and it's quite likely that this dive is responsible for the rest of it. He surely likes this word if only because he never used it before. But then again he thinks, 'Humph, back there in England they might think that I am just kind of slumming, in the sense of language; that I am simply rolling these new American morsels over my tongue'. So then, first of all, he rhymes 'dives' with 'lives', which is in itself telling enough, apart from animating an old rhyme. Secondly, he qualifies the word by saying 'one of the dives', thereby reducing the exoticism of 'dives'.

At the same time, 'one of the' increases the humbling effect of being in a dive in the first place, and this humbling effect suits well his reporter's posture. For he positions himself fairly low here: physically low, which means in the midst of things. That alone boosts the sense of verisimilitude: the guy who speaks from the thick of things is more readily listened to. What makes the whole thing even more convincing is 'Fifty-second Street', because numbers after all are seldom used in poetry. Most likely, his first impulse was to say, 'I sit in one of the dives'; but then he decided that 'dives' may be too linguistically emphatic for the crowd back home, and so he puts in 'on Fifty-second Street'. This somewhat lightens the matter, since Fifty-second Street between Fifth and Sixth Avenues was at the time the jazz strip of the universe. Hence, by the way, all that syncopation that reverberates in the half-rhymes of those trimeters. . . . .

To Auden's British audience, the poem starts in earnest right here, with this amusing yet very matter-of-fact air that 'Fifty-second Street' creates, in a fairly unexpected fashion. But the point is that by now our author isn't dealing only with Britons; not anymore. And the beauty is that this opening cuts both ways, since 'dives' and 'Fifty-second Street' inform his American public that he speaks its language as well. If one bears in mind the immediate aim of the poem, this choice of diction is not surprising at all.

Some twenty years later, in a poem written in memory of Louis MacNeice, Auden expresses a desire to 'become, if possible, a minor Atlantic Goethe' (*C.P.*, p.693). This is an extremely significant admission, and the crucial word here is, believe it or not, not Goethe but Atlantic. Because what Auden had in mind from the very outset of his poetic career was the sense that the language in which he wrote was transatlantic or, better still, imperial: not in the sense of the British Raj but in the sense that it is the language that made an empire. For empires are held together by neither political nor military forces but by languages. . . .

Well, this is, perhaps, demagoguery; but it won't hurt. To get back to Auden, I think, one way or another, the above considerations played their role in his decision to leave England. Also, his reputation at home was already very high and presumably the prospect facing him was to join the literary establishment: for in a carefully stratified society there is nowhere else to go, and nothing beyond. So he hit the road, and the language extended it. In any case, for him that empire was stretched not only in space but in time as well and he was ladling from every source, level, and period of English. Naturally, a man who was so frequently charged with fishing out of the OED very old, obscure, dated words hardly could ignore the safari America was offering.

At any rate, 'Fifty-second Street' rings enough of a bell on both sides of the Atlantic to make people listen. In the beginning of every poem, a poet has to dispel that air of art and artifice that clouds the public's attitude to poetry. He has to be convincing, plain – the way, presumably, the public itself is. He has to speak with a public voice, and all the more so if it is a public subject that he deals with.

'I sit in one of the dives/On Fifty-second Street' answers those requirements. What we get here is the level, confident voice of one of us, of a reporter who speaks to us in our own tones. And just as we are prepared for him to continue in this reassuring fashion, just as we've recognized this public voice and have been lulled into regularity by his trimeters, the poet plummets us into the very private diction of 'Uncertain and afraid'. Now, this is not the way reporters talk; this is the voice of a scared child rather than of a seasoned, trench-coated newsman. 'Uncertain and afraid' denotes what? – doubt. And this is precisely where this poem – indeed poetry in general, art in general – starts for real: in, or with, doubt. All of a sudden the certitude of that Fifty-second Street dive is gone and you get the feeling that perhaps it was displayed there in the first place because he was 'uncertain and afraid' in the very beginning: that's why he clung to their concreteness. But now the preliminaries are over, and we are in business indeed.[29] □

Brodsky's image of an Auden simultaneously addressing two audiences aptly evokes the difficult, transitional period at the end of the thirties and the beginning of the forties. The theme of transition is dominant in Walter Perrie's piece from the collection *W.H. Auden: The Far Interior*. Stamped with the unmistakable mark of Mendelson's arguments in *Early Auden*, Perrie offers a useful synthesis of Auden's position at this time, describing him as a moralist and a lukewarm political figure. Striving for a *public* voice, Perrie shows us how 'Riven by loneliness and self-doubt the last thing he wanted was a poetry of "self-expression", that is, organized around his own self-divisions'. The complex interplay between public and private modes of expression that Kettle discussed above is well presented here: the sense that the poetry contained autobiographical elements, but that these were transformed into something less banal than the egotistical facts of life that they are often asked to represent. Auden followed a fundamental left-wing path, but with personal intellectual demands that made a pure observance of the party line impossible. Not, I think, as Perrie suggests, that the Marxism was too crude, but that Auden's demands were obviously too idiosyncratic – such as when in the essay 'The Good Life' from 1935, he attempted the monumental task of holding together Christianity, psychology and Marxism in a unified whole.[30] Perrie argues that 'After the transformations which Auden experienced in 1939–40 he did not stop changing. His development through the 1940s, '50s and '60s is as complex as that through the '20s and '30s'. Perrie's evaluation of these transformations leads us into the concerns of the later chapters:

■ In his early poetry [Auden] sees people simply as instruments of the Life Force or evolution – sometimes called Love – who, when they no longer serve its purposes are discarded by it. Auden absorbed this view from Groddeck, D.H. Lawrence and others, and it was not a large step in the mid-'30s to deck it out in a new costume and call it the *Force of History*. Auden retracted this fatalist element from his writings but did keep the materialism he had absorbed from his readings in Marxism and never went back on the general view he stated in 1938 that:

> Man has always been a social animal living in communities. This falsifies any theories of Social Contract. The individual *in vacuo* is an intellectual abstraction. The individual is the product of social life; without it, he would be no more than a bundle of unconditioned reflexes. Men are born neither free nor good. Societies and cultures vary enormously. On the whole, Marx seems to me correct in his view that physical conditions and the forms of economic production have dictated the forms of communities. (*The English Auden*, p. 373)

Auden's reconciliation of that materialism with a religious outlook was to occupy him for much of the '40s.

Marxism, however, was not, for Auden, an adequate account of the world and he had certainly never accepted the Leninist view of the historical rôle of the Communist Party. He had never lost his interest in religion and of his time in Spain recorded almost nothing beyond the detail of his sudden awareness that he was shocked by the closed churches. By late 1938 Auden was weary of his quest and near to despair. He had come to suspect again that his loneliness was inescapable. His experiences in Spain, China and elsewhere had convinced him, if he ever needed convincing, that there was no natural goodness in man. Not only had he rejected any messianic illusions he may once have nourished about himself, he had rejected most of the thinkers in whom he had been interested over the past decade. . . . . . .

Auden's denial of any immediate political function for poetry was stated explicitly in 'The Public v. the late Mr. W.B. Yeats' ['The Public v. the Late Mr. William Butler Yeats'] (1939) (*The English Auden*, pp. 389–93) and reinforced in *New Year Letter*. His view was, and remained, unequivocal and a note he wrote for a commonplace book in 1970 restates it in almost identical terms:

> By all means let a poet, if he wants to, write *engagé* poems, protesting against this or that political evil or social injustice. But let him remember this. The only person who will benefit from them is himself; they will enhance his literary reputation among those who feel as he does. The evil or injustice, however, will remain exactly what it would have been if he had kept his mouth shut.[31]

Whether or not one agrees with Auden's fairly extreme statement of his view, it was fundamental to his later work. It should be kept in mind, though, that Auden's target is directly political poetry and that he is not denying *any* social function to poetry. Indeed, he continued to think of it as having an educative function, albeit in the negative sense of something which can disintoxicate and disenchant.

Clearly, between 1938 and 1940 some radical transformation had taken place for Auden but it was one for which the whole of the later '30s was a preparation. In late 1938 he had begun to read Kierkegaard. By 1940 he had rejoined the church and, perhaps most importantly, had fallen in love and had that love returned.

From Marx and Freud to Kierkegaard is a shorter step than some of Auden's detractors have thought, but why take the step at all? Auden had realized that his divisions could not be healed by an act of will or by their submergence in any external force, whether a group, an ideology or a career, but simply had to be accepted. Accepting his own imperfect nature he learned, however painfully, to accept others, warts and all:

Throughout the 1930s he had hoped for some political or visionary or predestined end to division. It could not happen. In America, when he had given up his last hopes for Utopia, he learned instead to 'honour the fate you are', with all its incorrigible divisions, 'Travelling and tormented,/Dialectic and bizarre'.[32]

He began to believe that life, once accepted and despite its absurdity, could be celebrated and this transformation is the key to the later poetry: 'He had thought he could love for a faithless moment, before beauty and vision died, now he knew that he might love faithfully if he accepted imperfection and change'.[33] Kierkegaard, the intellectual peg on which Auden hung his new coat, was, at the least, convenient: 'In Kierkegaard he not only found philosophical reasons for accepting life, but a theology insisting that it must be accepted'.[34] And, for all the apoplexy of his critics, 'in reality the leap had been only a small hop, and, in retrospect at least, anything but surprising'.[35] Kierkegaard insists that God is wholly beyond the reach of human knowledge. Therefore, the worldly realms – the ethical and aesthetic – have to be confronted on their own terms and within those realms man has free will to choose either good or evil. This view enabled Auden to retain his whole materialist analysis of economic and literary history with which to approach the world, but rooted now in his assurance that his values of truth and love were ultimately validated in his religious experience. Auden was very much a rationalist on worldly topics, but that his religious foundations should be beyond the reach of rationality suited him very well.

Auden's attitude to the Good Place underwent a similar transformation. It was no longer somewhere to be looked for but somewhere to be made. Auden's work deals consistently with moral choice, the capacity which Auden understood to distinguish man from animal. . . . . . . Because men can choose good or evil, they must not allow themselves to be misled by fantasies of past and future if that entails any sacrifice in the real present of the virtues of love and truth. This shift in attitude places the accent very firmly back on the individual and on subjectivity. Auden came now to a new determination to live in the present, a determination revealingly evident in a letter he wrote to E.R. Dodds in 1940 about his decision to live in the United States: 'At least I know what I am trying to do, which most American writers don't, which is to live deliberately without roots'.[36]

. . . . . . From 1940 until nearly the end of the decade Auden sought to learn to celebrate life and to find an appropriate language in which to do so. The kind of overt political references which had appeared in his poems throughout the '30s stopped and it was widely assumed that Auden had become a non-political or even an anti-political and private poet. . . . . Now, for Auden, the Just City and the Good Place can be created only by a measure of realism, charity and pardon in our personal lives coupled to a defence of rationality. Auden thought of the world as fundamentally hostile to the individual: not only nature, but the social-historical world as well since, for both, the individual is disposable. The Good Place is wherever we can be left in peace enough to get on with creating it. The metaphor of the journey was not discarded but its significance changed: 'All the long works of the 1940s after *New Year Letter* are dialectical landscapes dramatizing the journeys men make to get across frontiers separating Aesthetic, Ethical and Religious existence – Kierkegaard's dialectical triad'.[37] For Auden it was a difficult journey frequently punctuated by despair, but now the despair was kept private. Gradually, however, Auden did find an increased capacity for acceptance and by the end of the decade he had learned not just to accept life but to praise it:

> The works of the 1940s all show that the human world is blessed in a religious sense. God made it. But its earthly satisfactions, while considerable, never quite deserve 'blessed' as a secular epithet. After 1950 they do, and Auden will then not only affirm the need to accept secular life but will celebrate the joy of doing so.[38]

After the transformations which Auden experienced in 1939–40 he did not stop changing. His development through the 1940s, '50s and '60s is as complex as that through the '20s and '30s, and it would need a further essay to follow it through all its twists and turns. Its broad outline, however, is relatively clear in that Auden continued to develop his capacity to celebrate life. It is this Auden who is so often accused of complacency and triviality. Nothing could be further from the truth and the evidence is in the poems. If political poetry means party-political poetry, then Auden after 1940 was not a political poet but, then, he never had been. If, however, that narrow view of politics is put aside and politics can be understood to mean a vision of the *polis*, of human society and its workings, then the late Auden seems to me the most deeply political of English poets of the twentieth century. His politics may be somewhat bleak, but it would be a peculiarly uninformed attitude to find them reactionary.

. . . What seems to have misled some critics is Auden's comic technique, mistaking comedy for triviality. The vision of the later Auden of the comic absurdity of life might be trivial if it did not know about suffering, but suffering is the continual context and background in which it operates. Justin Replogle makes the point well:

In effect, he had to learn how to make poems that mocked poetry, and how to believe in something that laughed at the pretensions of belief. When he learned how to do both, he made some extraordinarily beautiful poems. They were profound, moving, skilful – and comic.[39]

. . . . . . Auden's gift to literature in his later work is a poetically effective language in which to talk about a great range of social experience in a very direct way. That is not so different from the aims set for themselves by such obviously political poets as MacDiarmid, Brecht and Neruda.[40] ☐

As Perrie makes clear, to be a political poet does not necessarily mean to be involved in *party* politics – a point that Trotter and Kettle also affirmed, and this should be kept in mind when considering the surface changes in Auden's attitudes and beliefs at this time. However, the consequences of leaving England were to remain in the critical 'air' for many years. Philip Larkin's acerbic assessment of Auden's career is an interesting example, seeing the move to America as the single most important factor in the poet's 'decline'. As in his poetry, Larkin is sometimes brutally philistine ('As for *The Age of Anxiety* . . . I never finished it, and have never met anyone who has') but these remarks are important, for they display the persistence of a deep-seated resentment at Auden's abandonment of his country, even twenty years later.

■ I have been trying to imagine a discussion of Auden between one man who had read nothing of his after 1940 and another who had read nothing before. After an initial agreement by adjective – 'Versatile,' 'Fluent,' 'Too smart sometimes' – a mystifying gap would open between them, as one spoke of a tremendously exciting English social poet full of energetic unliterary knock-about and unique lucidity of phrase, and the other of an engaging, bookish, American talent, too verbose to be memorable and too intellectual to be moving. And not only would they differ about his poetic character: there would be a sharp division of opinion about his poetic stature.

Only an experiment of this kind could bring home how little the last twenty years have added to Auden's reputation. Why should this be so? He has remained energetic and productive; his later work shows the same readiness to experiment coupled with new and (in theory) maturer themes; he has not lost his sense of humour. And yet no one is going to justify his place in literary history by *The Shield of Achilles* any more than Swinburne's is justified by *Poems and Ballads: Third Series*.

The appearance of his latest collection, *Homage to Clio*, marks the end of the third decade of Auden's poetic life and does not alter the fact that almost all we value is still confined to its first ten years. We need not remind ourselves of his virtues – the wide-angled rhetoric, the seamless lyricism, the sudden gripping dramatizations – but to understand what succeeded it we must understand to what extent his poetry was of its time. He was, of course, the first 'modern' poet, in that he could employ modern properties unselfconsciously ('A solitary truck, the last/Of shunting in the Autumn' (*C.P.*, p.29)), but he was modern also by embracing a kind of neo-Wordsworthianism which, in an effort to put poetry at the service of the working-class movement, called it 'memorable speech' and made no theoretical distinction between *Paradise Lost* and '*The Young Fellow Called Dave*'. This view held that if the poet were not concerned with the historic necessities of the age and akin to the healer and the explorer (typical figures!) his work would be deservedly disregarded.

Few poets since Pope have been so committed to their period. It is not only that to be at home in Auden's poetry we must recognize Bishop Barnes, Coghlan's coffin, Van der Lubbe and all the personalia of 'Last Will and Testament' (*Letters from Iceland*, with Louis MacNeice); we shall also find the Depression, strikes, the hunger marchers; we shall find Spain and China; and above all we shall encounter not only the age's properties but its obsessions: feeling inferior to the working class, a sense that things needed a new impetus from somewhere, seeing out of the corner of an eye the rise of Fascism, the persecution of the Jews, the gathering dread of the next war that was half projected guilt about the last:

> The chairs are being brought in from the garden,
> The summer talk stopped on that savage coast
> Before the storms, after the guests and birds:
> In sanatoriums they laugh less and less,
> Less certain of cure; and the loud madman
> Sinks now into a more terrible calm. (*C.P.*, p.49)

It is precisely this dominant and ubiquitous unease that lay at the centre of Auden's verse and which he was so apt to express. How quickly, for example, he seized on the symbol of 'the Struggle', 'the game . . . that tends to become like a war' (*The English Auden*, p.117); in other writers as well as Auden this concept of the 'Two Sides' was used time and again to represent the young against the old, the poor against the rich, the healthy against the diseased, the class struggle, Spain, the coming war. And whereas the conflict was originally seen as victorious (*The Orators*), as the Thirties wore on disaster became more and more likely. It was in this atmosphere that Auden's sensitivity was quickened and his perceptions heightened, perceptions not only of

> Ten thousand of the desperate marching by
> Five feet, six feet, seven feet high.
> > (*The English Auden*, p. 153)

but also how

> In the houses
> The little pianos are closed, and a clock strikes.
> > (*The English Auden*, p. 157)

I have stressed this identification not for its own sake but to make clear why Auden's outlook was completely dislocated when it ceased. As everyone knows, this came about in two ways – by the outbreak of war in 1939, and by Auden's departure for America a few months earlier. At one stroke he lost his key subject and emotion – Europe and the fear of war – and abandoned his audience together with their common dialect and concerns. For a different sort of poet this might have been less important. For Auden it seems to have been irreparable. . . . .

[O]ne cannot escape the conclusion that in some way Auden, never a pompous poet, has now become an unserious one. For some time he has insisted that poetry is a game, with the elements of a crossword puzzle: it is 'the luck of verbal playing'. One need not be a romantic to suspect that this attitude will produce poetry exactly answering to that description. Here again it seems that Auden was happier when his work had an extraneous social function, and if he feels that poetry is fundamentally unserious otherwise, it is a pity he parted from it, for lack of serious intention too often means lack of serious effect.

In the end that is what our discontent comes down to: Auden no longer touches our imaginations. My guess is that the peculiar insecurity of pre-war England sharpened his talent in a way that nothing else has, or that once 'the next War' really arrived everything since has seemed to him an anticlimax. But these are only guesses. Something, after all, led him to write 'A poet's prayer' in *New Year Letter*: 'Lord, teach me to write so well that I shall no longer want to.' In any case it is our loss.[41] □

Larkin's suggestion that Auden lost 'his key subject and emotion' by moving to America, begs the question of whether the 'common dialect and concerns' that bounded the English Auden would have offered him the necessary distance from his stifling 'family' that he needed in order to move forward with his life and beliefs.

The questions that Auden raises around himself at the end of the 1930s form the basis of his work throughout the 1940s and beyond.

Political events had come to a head in 1939 when a war broke out before his eyes. There was a terrifying access to the reality that had been lurking behind all the political discourses of the 1930s; here the question of fellow-travelling, or of Marxist orthodoxy or heresy fell away. While playing an undeniably useful social and political role as the figurehead of a largely mythical generation of committed writers, Auden had been doing what he did best – working with the material at hand to make the situation his own. Leaving behind the political and historical narratives of the 1930s into which he had been written, Auden started, quite defiantly, with a clean slate in America and the story of his leaving is repeated, cunningly, by the poem 'Musée des Beaux Arts'. The stricken political star of the thirties plunges into the water without trace, while the ploughman – epitome of that Audenesque ordinariness that he was to cultivate for the rest of his life – looks away from the 'disaster', while the ship 'had somewhere to get to' (*C.P.*, p. 179). A career was about to be rebuilt. (See chapter one.)

In the next chapter, we see how Auden's attitude to art and history, and the resumption of his faith, provide important clues to the later poetry.

CHAPTER FIVE

The Longer Poems

IT WAS to be the American distance that shaped Auden criticism from 1940 onward, for many critics considered him to be reborn socially, spiritually and sexually in the early forties. One of Auden's fears was of becoming part of the English literary establishment – part of the 'family' as he put it (see chapter one, note 29). America allowed him to set up with 'no history' and with a completely new set of social relations and problems with which to deal. If the thirties can be crudely categorised as the time when Auden explored the psycho-social elements of middle-class identity in a political frame, then the forties is a time when the psycho-spiritual aspects of his life could be thought through a religious frame. In both cases, paradoxically, the social remains in place. In chapter two Bayley suggested that of Auden and Eliot, Auden was the more personal and introverted poet (even in the 'social' thirties) and that Eliot was the more public. By placing a religious framework around his work, Auden released his earlier, secular self to pursue questions of moral and ethical choice: 'How should we live now?' he asked, and the answer demanded a series of works that would explore and worry this question. Although Auden returned to the faith of his early days, this fact remains strangely incidental to the poetry in ways that will become clear as we listen to the following critical accounts.

In his essay 'The Voice of Exile: Auden in 1940' Samuel Hynes lays out the ground of Auden's later work. Looking at the 'defection' historically, he usefully describes the constituents of what he terms Auden's 'aesthetics of imperfection'.

■ I think Auden's emigration is better explained . . . as a negative response to the historical situation as he saw it. By 1939 it seemed clear to him, as it did to many other Europeans, that the crisis they were facing was not simply another war but the failure of an ideology. If fascism existed, and dominated Europe, if another world war was coming, then the liberal western conception of man must be wrong in fundamental ways – more than wrong, *dead.* By leaving England when he did, Auden was freeing himself from that dead liberal ideology. Man's condition would have to be understood differently from now on: as existentially alone, cut off from the old roots, the old comforts and securities. And if that was true, then England was the wrong place for an English poet. When an old friend opposed Auden's move, on the grounds that it was dangerous for a writer to sever his native roots, Auden replied that the concept of roots was obsolete: 'What I am trying to do,' he explained to E.R. Dodds, 'is to live deliberately *without* roots'.[1] . . . . . . For a European writer who aspired to rootlessness, America was the obvious place to go. . . . . . .

Thinking historically may be the most difficult task that a modern writer can assume, especially in a time of war. In the twentieth century it has been impossible to think about any war in historical terms while it was going on: war-writing, and war-thinking, is always apocalyptic. Auden tried in 'September 1, 1939' to see the war, as it began, as an historical consequence: he mentions Protestantism and imperialism, and invokes Thucydides; but there is really no argument offered, only sketchy materials for one. One way to look at the work that followed is to regard it as a series of expansions and revisions of this first wartime view of Modern Man, in the mess of history that he had made. . . . . . .

If you read through the whole body of Auden's prose for these years, you will find that quotations from these writers keep turning up [Hynes has just mentioned an array of writers that Auden cited in the notes of *New Year Letter* including Hans Spemann, Margaret Meade, Søren Kierkegaard, Friedrich Nietzsche, and Charles Williams], often in quite unlikely places, sometimes more than once. And you will find other repetitions – certain definitions and analyses and formulations. You *could* argue from this evidence that he had simply overextended himself, and was meeting his journalistic deadlines by cannibalizing his own writings. But that doesn't seem an adequate explanation, given the extraordinary fertility of his mind; I think it would be more accurate to say that at this time Auden had certain preoccupations, and that his repetitions express the power of those pre-occupations to force their way into everything he wrote. . . .

You can group those concerns under three general headings: History, Art, and Necessity; *everything* that he wrote during these years had to do with one or more of these subjects. And you might go on to say that in fact these are all aspects of one master question. Auden put that question in a review he wrote of Harold Laski's *Where Do We Go from Here?* Laski's title, he said, posed an unreal question: 'The only real question, and this itself becomes unreal unless it is asked all the time, is *where are we now?*' Everything that Auden wrote – every review, every lecture, every poem – was a draft of an answer to that question. . . .

I have said that Auden's preoccupations during these critical years could be grouped under the headings of History, Necessity, and Art. Let me now try to give you, under these headings, a sense of where Auden thought the world was in 1939–1940.

History: Auden's recurrent theme is that man has come to the end of an epoch. The period that has ended he calls by various names: it is the end of the Renaissance, the end of the Protestant epoch, the end of liberal capitalist democracy. What these have in common is that they all acted to separate men from each other: the Renaissance 'broke the subordination of all other intellectual fields to that of theology, and assumed the autonomy of each'; Protestantism made men's relations to God individual and autonomous; capitalism made men autonomous in their economic relations. The results were the atomization of society, the disintegration of tradition, the loss of community. The war, coming at the end of this process, is not therefore a struggle for the survival of western democracy, or of any other traditional system, but the final term in the disintegrating process, like the last scene of Götterdammerung [*The Twilight of the Gods,* the final part of Richard Wagner's tetralogy of musical dramas *The Ring of the Nibelung*]. The very fact that it was taking place seemed to confirm Auden's analysis: a war involving the whole world was the final disintegration of order. All through the thirties concerned men had said: 'If a war comes, it will be the end of civilization.' And here it was.

A subheading of History is Romanticism. Auden had called his address at Smith 'Romantic or Free?', and early in the speech he explained what he meant:

> The term romantic I have chosen rather arbitrarily to describe all those who in one way or another reject the paradoxical, dialectic nature of freedom. Perhaps heretic would have been a more accurate term, but I chose romantic partly to avoid purely clerical associations, and partly because the particular forms in which these eternal heresies appear today took shape in the period that is historically called the Romantic Revival.[2]

To be romantic, in Auden's view, was to simplify one's sense of man's dialectical existence, to believe that human beings are essentially good, or that they have absolutely free will, or that they are absolutely determined; or that they can live only by instinct; or that they will be happy and good if the structure of society is changed. Auden saw these 'eternal heresies' manifested throughout history, but becoming political with the rise of industrialism, in Rousseau's theory of the General

Will. As long as capitalism was expanding, Auden wrote in 'Jacob and the Angel', 'the inadequacy of rationalist Liberalism to guarantee material happiness was unperceived by the majority, and it was not until after the Great War that political Romanticism became a great force and a great enemy.'[3] To Auden's mind the connection between romanticism and politics was crucial: when he taught a course on romanticism at Swarthmore he called it 'Romanticism from Rousseau to Hitler'. But romanticism was, to him, more than a political term: it was the generic term for all the errors in men's thought – political, philosophical, and religious – that converged at last in Nazism, and in the war. The war was therefore a climactic, terminal event: the ultimate expression of the eternal romantic heresies.

Necessity: Though by 1939 Auden had ceased to be a Marxist (if he can be said ever to have been one), he continued to quote Engels's definition of freedom: that freedom is the consciousness of necessity. The difference lay in what he meant by necessity. In essay after essay of these years he makes one central distinction: between causal necessity ('the external necessity of matter') and logical necessity, which he sometimes calls moral necessity (the internal necessity of moral decision).

[. . .] Today a man has only two choices: he can be consciously passive or consciously active. He can accept deliberately or reject deliberately, but he must decide because his position in life is no longer a real necessity; he could be different if he chose. The necessity that can make him free is no longer his position as such, but the necessity of choosing to accept it or reject it. To be unconscious is to be neither an individual nor a person, but a mathematical integer in something called the Public which has no real existence.[4]

You can see that this account of logical necessity is related to Auden's ideas of history: human society has evolved to a state of total separateness, in which every man has an absolute responsibility to make his own moral choices: that's the necessity. If he does not, if he creates or joins a society that *denies* that necessity, he ceases to be an individual, as in fascist states. (Again and again in the essays Auden defines fascism as a society in which everything that is not required is forbidden: that is, a society which denies the necessity of moral choice.)

Another name for human separateness is *loneliness*, a term which is recurrent and crucial in Auden's writings of this time. Loneliness was, for Auden, a kind of modern categorical imperative: an ethical term, primarily – to be lonely was to be conscious of the real human condition – but with political implications. 'There can be no democracy,' he told the women at Smith, 'unless each of us accepts the fact that in the last analysis we live our lives alone.' Auden's own political position was based on loneliness: 'I welcome the atomization of society,' he wrote in 'Tradition and Value,'[5] 'and I look forward to a socialism based on it, to the day when the disintegration of tradition will be as final and universal for the masses as it is already for the artist, because it will be only when they fully realize their "aloneness" and accept it, that men will "be able to achieve a real unity through a common recognition of their diversity".'. . .

Art: Auden made his most famous statement about aesthetics in the spring of 1939, in his elegy on Yeats: 'Poetry makes nothing happen.' He said the same thing, more elaborately, in his essay 'The Public v. the Late Mr. William Butler Yeats,' written at about the same time:

> Art is a product of history, not a cause. Unlike some other products, technical inventions for example it does not re-enter history as an effective agent, so that the question whether art should or should not be propaganda is unreal. The case for the prosecution rests on the fallacious belief that art ever makes anything happen, whereas the honest truth, gentlemen, is that, if not a poem had been written, not a picture painted, not a bar of music composed, the history of man would be materially unchanged. (*The English Auden*, p. 393)

This is, of course, a repudiation of conventional engagé thinking of the thirties. Its importance to Auden is suggested by the number of times that he repeated it: first in the poem, then in the essay, then twice in 'The Prolific and the Devourer'. . . .

Notice how far Auden goes here: he doesn't simply say that art doesn't affect politics: it makes *nothing* happen, it is not an agent in reality in any sense. Not only that. In 'Mimesis and Allegory' he draws back from another conventional defense of art: 'One of the romantic symptoms has been an enormous exaggeration of the importance of art as a guide to life.'[6]

Most of what Auden had to say about Art at this time is couched in negative terms: he was more certain of what it didn't do than of what it *did*. One can see why this should be so: a theory of Art would have to wait upon the answers to the larger philosophic questions. Still we can see the direction in which his thought about art was moving in two lectures that Auden gave in the autumn of 1940. First these sentences from the final page of 'Mimesis and Allegory':

> [. . .] Art is not metaphysics any more than it is conduct, and the artist is usually unwise to insist too directly in his art upon his beliefs; but without an adequate and conscious metaphysics in the background, art's imitation of life inevitably becomes, either a

photostatic copy of the accidental details of life without pattern or significance, or a personal allegory of the artist's individual dementia, of interest primarily to the psychologist and the historian.

So art has its value: it *orders*. But that order is not self-generated: art needs belief, needs absolutes, needs metaphysics. As Society does; in the same lecture, and in other writings of the time, Auden makes this point very strongly: societies come to grief when they have an inadequate metaphysics, or none.

Auden developed this idea further in 'Criticism in a Mass Society': 'We cannot live without believing certain values to be absolute. These values exist, though our knowledge of them is always imperfect, distorted by the limitations of our historical position and our personal character. However, if but only we realize this, our knowledge can improve.' . . . . . . The key word here is imperfect: it introduces a concept that becomes crucially important in Auden's aesthetic from this point on – what we might call the Aesthetics of Imperfection. Absolute values exist, but man can only know them imperfectly; and his art will mirror his imperfect knowledge. Indeed the very imperfection of a work of art may be a value, since it will enact and so remind us of our own imperfection. The idea of perfection is a romantic heresy.

One can see, in what Auden says about History, Necessity, and Art, a common factor: in every case he is repudiating the convictions and clichés of the thirties. History is not economically determined, man is not perfectible, freedom is not the knowledge of causal necessity, and art is not an agent. But he was also working toward his own alternative ideology, based on the need for absolutes. We sense the form that it will take in the vocabulary that he began to use at this time: words like *sin* and *damnation*, *heresy* and *orthodoxy*. But it is important to recognize that what we are observing in Auden's writings through 1939 and 1940 is not the record of a conversion experience and its consequences, but the evidences of a strenuous and open-minded effort to reconsider his ideas of man and history. . . .

What he found in Christianity was a system of beliefs that could contain his new conclusions: the ethic of loneliness; the aesthetic of imperfection; the paradox of necessary freedom. He found, you might say, that Modern Man and Christian Man were the same.[7] □

Hynes provides a rough sketch of Auden's view of 'Christian Man', but to get a sense of the existential theology that occupied Auden in the early forties we need to turn to Monroe K. Spears's invaluable study, *The Poetry of W.H. Auden: The Disenchanted Island*. The section 'The Shift in Perspective' considers the importance and shape of Auden's religion. In the paragraphs preceding the following extract, Spears has quoted extensively from an Auden essay in a collection called *Modern Canterbury Pilgrims* which allows us to hear, in his own words, one of the stories of his faith. The poetry makes that much more sense when the reader can glimpse what is at stake, spiritually, in its arguments and images. In this extract Spears takes care to lay out some of the key existentialist problems around which Auden's poetry revolves: the questions of dualism, of necessity, and of choice.

■ Auden's religious position is not a denial but a fulfillment of his earlier beliefs; the religious values do not contradict the others, but clarify them and take them to another level. It is no accident nor effect of temporary intellectual fashions that his religious approach should be existential, for this type of religious philosophy starts from the same kind of psychological analysis that had formed the perduring basis of Auden's various attitudes and convictions. . . . . . . Auden has always stressed the unifying factors among all Christians rather than the divisive ones; he is ecumenical, like Charles Williams and Reinhold Niebuhr. An Anglo-Catholic whose attitude is basically existentialist, he interprets the existential tradition with maximum catholicity:

As a Christian, Kierkegaard belongs to the tradition of religious thinking . . . represented by Augustine, Pascal, Newman, and Karl Barth, as distinct both from the Thomist tradition of official Catholicism and from the liberal Protestantism of men like Schleiermacher. As a secular dialectician, he is one of the great exponents of an approach, equally hostile to Cartesian mechanism and Hegelian idealism, to which the Germans have given the name Existential – though it is confined neither to Germans like Nietzsche, Jaspers, Scheler, Heidegger, but may be found, for instance, in Bergson and William James, nor to professional philosophers, for the same approach is typical of what is most valuable in Marx and Freud.[8]

The fundamental approach common to these apparently disparate modes of thought Auden thus describes:

In contrast to those philosophers who begin by considering the *objects* of human knowledge, essences and relations, the existential philosopher begins with man's immediate experience as a *subject*, i.e., as a being in *need*, an *interested* being whose existence is at stake.

Cognition, for these thinkers, is always a historical act, accompanied by hope and fear; not something performed by a timeless, disinterested 'I'. Existentialism, says Auden, is not a surrender to relativism, but an attempt to begin the search for a common truth by being honest about this subjectivity. The relation of the theological, psychological, and political realms for the Christian existentialist he states thus:

> From this viewpoint, the basic human problem is man's anxiety in time; e.g., his present anxiety over himself in relation to his past and his parents (Freud), his present anxiety over himself in relation to his future and his neighbors (Marx), his present anxiety over himself in relation to eternity and God (Kierkegaard).

The last quotation is of special interest both as illuminating Auden's concept of the age of anxiety and as showing how this position transcends, without denying, the earlier Freudian and Marxist analyses. The anxiety viewed by Freud (or Homer Lane) as a disease, a maladjustment, is now seen as purposive, a concomitant of the choice confronting man in his dreadful freedom. . . . . . .

In the early 1940s the effect of Kafka, 'the artist who comes nearest to bearing the same kind of relation to our age that Dante, Shakespeare and Goethe bore to theirs',[9] is also frequently apparent. In these years Auden deals constantly in Kierkegaardian paradoxes, and justifies the 'absurdity' (according to human standards) of the divine; with the shocking patience of Kafka, he juxtaposes the incomprehensible divine and the reasonable human; he points out the theological heresies which have produced our political and social anarchy with the evangelical zeal and large historical generalizations of Niebuhr. . . . . . .

The influence of Kierkegaard has, however, been fundamental and pervasive in Auden's thought since 1940. His fullest discussion occurs in the long introduction to the volume of selections from Kierkegaard[10] that he edited in 1957; this whole volume is of great interest, not only intrinsically as a penetrating and well-balanced presentation of Kierkegaard, but as a useful background for studying Auden's later poetry. Auden draws a parallel between Kierkegaard and Cardinal Newman as the great preachers to a secularized society which was still officially Christian. Kierkegaard's polemic, he says, moves simultaneously in two directions: outwardly against the bourgeois Protestantism of the Denmark of his time, and inwardly against his own suffering.

> To the former he says, 'You imagine that you are all Christians and contented because you have forgotten that each of you is an existing individual. When you remember that, you will be forced to realize that you are pagans and in despair.' To himself he says, 'As

long as your suffering makes you defiant or despairing, as long as you identify your suffering with yourself as an existing individual, and are defiantly or despairingly the exception, you are not a Christian.'[11]

Auden then describes Kierkegaard's three categories of the aesthetic, the ethical, and the religious, putting them in historical terms for the sake of clarity. The Greek gods exemplify the aesthetic religion, which glorifies passion and power; the gods are interested only in a few exceptional individuals, who are heroes, glorious but not responsible for their successes or failures. 'The aesthetic either/or is not good or bad but strong or weak, fortunate or unfortunate.'

The facts on which the aesthetic religion is shattered and despairs, producing in its death agony Tragic Drama, are two: man's knowledge of good and evil, and his certainty that death comes to all men, i.e., that ultimately there is no either/or of strength or weakness, but even for the exceptional individual the doom of absolute weakness.[12]

The ethical religion is exemplified by the god of Greek philosophy. This is the worship of the universal, the First Cause which is self-sufficient. Its 'either/or' is knowledge or ignorance of the eternal and universal truths of reason which cannot be known without being obeyed. Neither in this nor in the aesthetic category is time meaningful or temptation or choice real. Its premise, 'Sin is ignorance; to know the good is to will it', cannot deal with the fact that the will to know must precede knowledge, nor that men do not in practice automatically will the good as soon as they know it. Finally, revealed religion (as in Judaism and Christianity) has a God who is creator, but who is not present as an object of consciousness or knowable as an object. Since He is creator, there is no longer a question of establishing a relationship; the existence of the creature presupposes a relation, and the only question is whether it is the right one:

. . . if I try to banish it permanently from consciousness, I shall not get rid of it, but experience it negatively as guilt and despair. The wrath of God is not a description of God in a certain state of feeling, but of the way in which I experience God if I distort or deny my relation to him. The commands of God are neither the aesthetic fiat, 'Do what you must' nor the ethical instruction, 'These are the things which you may or must not do', but the call of duty, 'Choose to do what at this moment in this context I am telling you to do'.[13]

These three categories have been the basis of a great deal of Auden's thinking in the past two decades. (This is obvious in his various classifications of quests and heroes, and somewhat less so in his interpretations of tragedy and comedy.) Finally, Auden quotes Newman on the absurdity of trying to argue non-believers into belief, for the 'act of faith remains an act of choice which no one can do for another'.

Pascal's 'wager' and Kierkegaard's 'leap' are neither of them quite adequate descriptions, for the one suggests prudent calculation and the other perverse arbitrariness. Both, however, have some value: the first calls men's attention to the fact that in all other spheres of life they are constantly acting on faith and quite willingly, so that they have no right to expect religion to be an exception; the second reminds them that they cannot live without faith in something, and that when the faith which they have breaks down, when the ground crumbles under their feet, they *have to* leap even into uncertainty if they are to avoid certain destruction.[14]

. . . The Christian knows no distinction between the personal and the political; all his relationships are both. Neither an anarchist nor a non-political idiot, he acts in the present, regarding neither past nor future; in theological language, he redeems the time. Man cannot live without a sense of the Unconditional; if he does not fear God, his unconscious sees to it that he has something else, airplanes or secret police, to fear.[15] When anxiety is not kept in its proper theological place, it returns in realms – the moral and aesthetic – where it should not be. . . . The Christian God of love is not self-sufficient; hence matter is not evil, and there is no division into divine reason and mortal body. Man is thus explained as image of God and as a fallen creature. Everything man does is an act of religious worship: 'Man always acts either self-loving, just for the hell of it, or God-loving, just for the heaven of it; his reasons, his appetites, are secondary motivations.'[16] A society is a group associated on the basis of the things the individuals in it love. For the Christian there is no one perfect form of society; the best is that in which at any historical moment love for one's neighbor can best express itself.[17] □

Some of Spears's points are reiterated in Lucy McDiarmid's exploration *Auden's Apologies for Poetry* (1990), but she is also aware of the complex games between reader and poet that Auden's poetry sets in place. This passage, extracted from the beginning of her book, gives a swift and intelligent portrait of Auden's position at the beginning of the 1940s. When McDiarmid considers the problem of truth in poetry she casts light on Hynes's comment that Modern Man and Christian Man had fused in Auden's thought: 'If all human activities were, as Auden came to believe, religiously grounded, no such activity (for instance, poetry) was itself expected to provide absolute truths.' McDiarmid shows us that to be at once a Christian and an artist demanded more from Auden's poetry than a passive repetition of his faith:

■ The wish for the poetic to reach the extrapoetic, for silly, flimsy poetry to invoke a spiritual dimension where something significant might exist, dominates all of Auden's work. His central subject is the elusiveness of what is spiritually valuable, a value uneasily relegated to 'outside' the work of art. This is a subject that only gradually becomes explicit in the poems themselves, as the notion of 'outside' the poem emerges, and as its location changes. In his earliest work Auden voices the tentative hope that poetry can be like loving spoken words, transforming and redeeming, themselves carriers of value. Auden's later essays and poems deny art's spirituality, claiming that 'Love, or truth in any serious sense' is a 'reticence', the unarticulated worth that exists, if at all, outside the words on the page ('The Truest Poetry Is the Most Feigning' (*C.P.*, p. 619)).

Between these two positions, between what critics call 'early' and 'later' Auden, during the late 1930s and early 1940s, Auden's religious views changed. He began attending church regularly and he read widely in theology – so a merely external description of Auden's spiritual development might read. Because this change began soon after his immigration to the United States, the church whose services Auden attended was the Episcopal Church, but the 'faith' was the Anglican faith in which he had been raised. Auden's return, his deliberate choice of religious belief, was gradual. There was no dramatic, clandestine second baptism, such as Eliot had, nor was there a single public announcement of his belief. Even a casual reader of Auden's book reviews in 1940 and 1941, however, could not have failed to notice the author's religious preoccupations and his theological vocabulary: eros, agape, logos, heresy, sin, grace.[18]

Auden's renewed belief may have begun emerging as early as 1937, during his trip to Spain: 'On arriving in Barcelona, I found as I walked through the city that all the churches were closed and there was not a priest to be seen. To my astonishment, this discovery left me profoundly shocked and disturbed.'[19] But some kind of religious attitude was present in his poetry all along; the 'vision of agape' in 'Out on the lawn I lie in bed' occurred in June, 1933, and the redemptive and spiritual possibilities of erotic love underlie the plot of *Paid on Both Sides*.[20] Political events provided a stimulus to this latent faith: the success of the Nazis made Auden feel that it was impossible any longer to believe that the values of liberal humanism were self-evident. Unless one was prepared to take a relativist view that all values are a matter of personal taste, one could hardly avoid asking the question: 'If, as I am convinced, the Nazis are wrong and we are right, what is it that validates our values and invalidates theirs?'[21]

The death of Auden's mother in 1941 gave an emotional charge to his new faith, and a crisis – now well-documented – in his relationship with Chester Kallman made faith a matter of desperate urgency.[22]

The significance for Auden's poetics was enormous. If all human activities were, as Auden came to believe, religiously grounded, no such activity (for instance, poetry) was itself expected to provide absolute truths. The notion that poetry could and ought to provide absolutes constituted the central position that Auden's poetics argued against for the rest of his life. Eliot had fought literature's appropriation of religion in the nineteenth century by having religion reappropriate culture. Auden strove to disentangle the two. Delivering the first of the T. S. Eliot Memorial Lectures in 1967, Auden said, 'Mr. Eliot was a poet writing in English in the twentieth century; he was also a Christian.' This double identity, according to Auden, requires an answer to the question, 'What difference, if any, do my beliefs make, either to what I write, or to my conception of my vocation?'[23] Auden's answer is a diplomatic correction of Eliot.

The imagination is to be regarded as a natural faculty, the subject matter of which is the phenomenal world, not its Creator. For a poet brought up in a Christian society it is perfectly possible to write a poem on a Christian theme, but when he does so he is concerned with it as an aspect of a religion – that is to say, a human cultural fact, like other facts – not as a matter of faith.[24]

In passages such as this one, Auden implicitly undoes the work of [Eliot's] *Notes Towards the Definition of Culture* (1948).

More often irreverent and iconoclastic, Auden writes against the high seriousness of the Arnolds and the Eliots.

To a Christian . . . both art and science are secular activities, that is to say, small beer. . . . There can no more be a 'Christian' art than there can be a Christian science or a Christian diet. There can only be a Christian spirit in which an artist, a scientist, works or does not work. . . . Culture is one of Caesar's things.[25]

That 'small beer' is crucial to understanding the poetics of later Auden, a poetics of apology and self-deprecation, a radical undermining of poetry itself.

Such an undermining of his own art could only come from a poet whose earliest writings had, however tentatively, attributed great powers to art. When Isherwood wrote that he had to 'keep a sharp eye' on Auden in their theatrical collaborations, 'or down flop the characters on their knees', and observed that 'another constant danger is that of choral interruptions by angel-voices', he knew that Auden was seeking some kind of spiritual exaltation through aesthetic means.[26] In the dramatic writings of the 1930s, characters flopped on their knees and angels interrupted (Isherwood was only slightly exaggerating) because Auden did want to invoke some spiritual value. He wanted something like the appearance of Hymen at the end of *As You Like It*, or Hermione's return to life at the end of *The Winter's Tale*, signalling a time of divine blessing and universal forgiveness.

Forgiveness is sought after in these works, but it proves elusive; it is the grand finale of a dramatic work that is rehearsed but never performed, the comic ending that is noticeably manqué. The characters anticipate a reconciliation they never experience. Indistinguishable from its theatrical aspects, forgiveness is associated with weddings, music, dance, ceremony, the words of the marriage service in *The Book of Common Prayer*. Its absence is an aesthetic and literary absence. It lies 'outside' as if the play's fifth act had not been completed.

In the long poems Auden wrote after his move to New York, forgiveness, and indeed all spiritual significance, is explicitly dissociated from its theatrical embodiment. These poems show the scene of reconciliation, the Shakespearean comic finale always missing in the plays of the thirties, but then emphasize its artifice. They offer only what *The Sea and the Mirror* calls 'feebly figurative signs' of a realm where a less artificial forgiveness exists. In the poems' final lines, guilty speakers look beyond the poetic for forgiveness and concede their need for validation from whatever of spiritual value lies outside the poem. In this act of concession, a kind of theatrical *plaudite* [call for applause], the artificial struggles to address a 'real' it is chary of calling anything but nonartificial. 'Outside' means 'not-in-this-poem', as the audience exists outside the actors, as the Virgin exists outside Barnaby. [McDiarmid has previously discussed Auden's poem 'The Ballad of Barnaby' (*C.P.*, p.824).]

Caliban of *The Sea and the Mirror* forms the pattern for most of the speakers in Auden's subsequent lyric poems. The naughty boy, incorrigibly stagy, guilty but charming, trivial but longing for significance, playfully performs his poem and then undermines it. In the late forties, fifties, and sixties, Auden becomes the theatrical 'presenter' of his own lyric poems, his stage the printed text of the poem. The spiritual value the speaker hopes may exist somewhere (it certainly is not in this poem) can only be indicated by *praeteritio* [something mentioned while professing not to be able to mention it], as, for instance, Cicero specifies the crimes of Verres he says he cannot mention. 'Outside' now is a rhetorically hypothetical realm, what-I-can't-write-about.

Ultimately, all Auden can do to indicate spiritual value is to talk about his own and poetry's inabilities. Every poem becomes an apology, undermining its own significance and alluding to the value it cannot contain. Barnaby could at least tumble before a holy icon responsive to his efforts, redeeming his frivolous art. Auden's later poetry anticipates no such redemption for itself: 'I dare not ask you if you bless the poets', he coyly says to Clio, 'Nor do I see a reason why you should' (*C.P.*, p.613). Clio can be invoked and praised, but she will never say, 'Well have you tumbled. . . .'

The poet who, at age twenty-eight, hoped art could 'teach man to unlearn hatred and learn love', recognizes at age fifty-seven the source of his inspiration in naughtiness and 'vices', and imagines a judgmental God 'reciting by heart/The poems you would/have written, had/your life been good'. Only in the imagination of an imagined deity live the poems that do not need apology.[27] □

McDiarmid opens up some important areas of study here, especially through her suggestion that Auden became the 'theatrical "presenter" of his own lyric poems, his stage the printed text of the poem'. This theatrical self-consciousness also attends Auden's *New Year Letter* (which appeared first in America as *The Double Man* (1941)) and which was addressed to Elizabeth Mayer, a patroness of the arts who was in some ways a 'mother-figure' to Auden, and 'a fit recipient of a poem which was to argue itself into a position of detachment and worship of "the powers that we create with"'.[28] Taking the form of a letter, as with the letter to Byron, the tone can be deceptively easy, whereas, as John Fuller suggests, the piece is

■ something between Blake's *Marriage of Heaven and Hell* and a metaphysical treatise, with nutshell political theory and the pragmatic philosophical discoveries of a great talker thrown in for good measure.[29] □

In the next extract, Edward Callan usefully introduces the three Kierkegaardian categories that structure *New Year Letter*: that is, the *aesthetic*, the *ethical*, and the *religious*. The tension and play between these categories can be seen as one of the fundamental concerns through which Auden works his material in the later poetry. Although Fuller is sceptical about the importance of these categories to *New Year Letter*,[30] they nevertheless pervade the writing of the 1940s. Callan has just been discussing the formal elements of Auden's poetry, citing the line from *Poems* (1930): 'look shining at/New styles of architecture, a change of heart' (*The English Auden*, p. 36):

■ Critics generally concede that Auden's work following his emigration to America in 1939 is grounded in a Christian outlook transcending his earlier preference for near-Marxist social theory and his earlier concept of personality derived from Freud, Groddeck, and Homer Lane. In their varying estimates of Auden's later work, commentators have tended to stress the 'change of heart' and to ignore the architecture.

In seeking an appropriate architecture for modern themes Auden found useful models in Jung's theories on the psyche, and Kierkegaard's all-embracing notional scheme of categories. These conceptual schemes provided original structural devices for Auden's four later major works: *New Year Letter; The Sea and the Mirror; For the Time Being;* and *The Age of Anxiety;* as well as new sources of metaphor for many of his later lyrics.

Auden's first long poem of the 1940s, *New Year Letter*, is an initial experiment in an architectural method which he later refined and developed in the other long works. *New Year Letter* is a simple construction: it is a three-part poem in which the parts correspond to Kierkegaard's triad of Aesthetic, Ethical, and Religious spheres. The subject-matter of the poem is the problem of order in each of these spheres and therefore might be said to resemble Dante's *Divine Comedy* in its structure as well as in its theme which ultimately transcends local and temporal order and includes the restoration of Divine order.

Kierkegaard's triad may categorize either individual persons or particular periods of history. The Aesthetic person may, like the artist, see things as beautiful or ugly, or, like the gambler, see them as governed by chance, or even by magic. The Ethical person – the philosopher or logician – envisions a world governed by rational laws, and describes man's actions as right or wrong, not as beautiful or ugly. The Religious person is one whose faith transcends the limitations of fate or reason and accepts what, to the Ethical mind, is absurd, and, to the Aesthetic mind, incomprehensible. Furthermore, the categories permit such classification of historical periods as this: the period influenced by the Aesthetic religion of the Greek pantheon, the period that discovered the Ethical 'good' of philosophy, and the period of 'revealed religion in which neither is destroyed or ignored, but the Aesthetic is dethroned and the Ethical fulfilled.'

The three parts of *New Year Letter* correspond in both structure and subject-matter with Kierkegaard's three categories. Part I corresponds to the sphere of the Aesthetic; its subject is the relation of art and the artistic vocation to ultimate order; its subdivisions resemble a series of figurative devices or devices of art; and it culminates in a key metaphor drawn from the Greek religion. Part II corresponds to the sphere of the Ethical; its subject is the variety of intellectual systems – dualisms or monisms – that logicians have proposed as ultimate order; the verse is rhetorical rather than figurative; and it culminates in a key metaphor concerning the 'double-focus' of dialectical logic. Part III corresponds to the spheres of the Aesthetic and Ethical reconciled; its subject is Love 'set in order,' or restored through penitence; its literary method is a purgatorial Quest analogous to Dante's *Divine Comedy*, developed through an orchestral arrangement of such themes as Being and Becoming, Time and Space, and the One and the Many; and it culminates in a hymn to the Holy Trinity. . . . . . .

The choice of Kierkegaard's scheme of categories as unifying principle for a major poetic composition served Auden in two ways; for this choice provided the necessary bounds for an imaginative construction and at the same time, paradoxically, allowed the imagination free play over 'all that is,' since Kierkegaard's triad is not a restrictive, but an all-embracing, notional scheme. The poet is not chained by a set philosophic formulae, because the essence of Kierkegaard's thought opposes both formula and system. His own thought is not set forth in systematic treatises but in such literary forms as the journal, the diary, the symposium or the character sketch, which keep the existent individual always in view. Auden's choice of a personal letter as the genre of *New Year Letter* is therefore consistent with the whole scheme of the poem. Those who have viewed the poem as a 'loosely constructed dissertation' are at least half right, but they miss Auden's insistence throughout the poem on reconciling dialectical opposites. The poem attempts to represent the dialectical relationship of Freedom and Necessity in its structure as well as in its matter, so that the question of the formality or informality of its structure is not resolved by an 'either/or' but is encompassed by a 'both/and.' It is, in the words already quoted, both 'supple and coherent stuff,' or, like James Joyce's puns, both trivial and quadrivial. [In *Finnegans Wake* (1939) Joyce constructed puns from several languages that contained multiple meanings and allusions.]

Ideally, Kierkegaard's philosophy cannot be formulated; it can only be acted out, and the literary form best suited to representing it is the drama. Auden's later major works, while continuing to depend on the scheme of categories for a unifying principle, are cast in dramatic forms which permit, for example, in *For the Time Being*, the representation of Herod as the type of the rational or Ethical man, and of St. Joseph as the type of 'the Religious hero' who, like Abraham, must transcend the Ethical sphere and accept the 'absurd' on the basis of faith alone.

I have suggested that Auden refined and developed, in other major works, this new style of architecture in which the structure of the work is a formal analogue for its subject-matter. *The Sea and the Mirror: A Commentary on Shakespeare's* 'The Tempest' provides an interesting example of this. The theme of *The Sea and the Mirror* is the relationship between art and reality. The structure of this poem is comparable to a triptych: the first panel represents the artist; the second, the work of art; and the third, the audience. In Part I, Prospero, the 'personified type of the creative,' becomes aware of death as a reality he cannot conjure with. His farewell to Ariel is developed in three stages analogous to Kierkegaard's triad. Part II is an elaborate pageant corresponding to Prospero's masque in *The Tempest*. The group of characters from Ferdinand to Miranda who are 'linked as children in a circle dancing' (*C.P.*, p.422) represent the ideal order possible in art; and the arrangement also suggests a 'Utopian' social order as Alonso holds the center and the courtly and rustic characters are proportioned on either side of him between the lovers. The attitude of Antonio who stands withdrawn from the group represents the tension between his Ethical world of 'will' and their Aesthetic world of 'wish' – a tension present in all Christian art. Part III, 'Caliban to the Audience,' is an artful symposium in which Caliban echoes the Ethical and Aesthetic attitudes of the audience to the relationship of art and reality.

In *For the Time Being* the unifying principle of structure rests on a fusion of the traditional elements of the Nativity play with Kierkegaard's triad, and in a somewhat similar manner the architectural framework of *The Age of Anxiety* rests on a fusion of Kierkegaard's scheme with Jung's 'maps' of the psyche. Auden's continued use of this method would argue his satisfaction with the initial experiment in *New Year Letter*.

Auden had changed the style and the subject-matter of his poetry to accord with the shift in emphasis in his own questions about man's situation. Had he also changed his conception of the poet's function? The tone of *New Year Letter* shows that Kierkegaard's dialectical method helped Auden to solve this problem too. Some have felt that the conflict between Montaigne's 'doubt' and Kierkegaard's 'faith' throughout *New Year Letter* indicates Auden's unsure stance; but could this not be merely a presentation of the dialectical tension between the Ethical and Religious spheres? However this may be, *New Year Letter* certainly resolves the conflict between 'preacher' and 'poet' that some have found in Auden; for this poem is, like *Macbeth*, a product of the art of Christendom which must reconcile the Ethical and the Aesthetic and present 'serious' subject-matter through the 'frivolous' medium of art. Hence the deliberate seriocomic tone of a poem embracing spheres inimical to the purely Aesthetic: 'For through the Janus of a joke/The candid psychopompos spoke.' (*C.P.*, p.206)[31] □

The collection *For the Time Being* which Callan discusses at the end of his piece furthers Auden's exploration of the possibilities of faith. The difficulties and narrative identifications that the two works – *For the Time Being* and *The Sea and the Mirror* – raise are manifold, but what we see is Auden taking over two established stories, and playing with the possibility of inhabiting them. In *For the Time Being* the Christmas story is set in the modern world and in a modern American idiom ('My shoes were shined, my pants were cleaned/and pressed' (*C.P.*, p.362)) to emphasise that the story did not simply take place *then* but is being relived in the now – and its yearly occurrence has a blend of repetition and return that needs to be made relevant beneath the commercial layering of American capitalism. Written in the midst of a triple crisis – the loss of his mother (to whom the piece is dedicated), the infidelity of Chester Kallman, and the resumption of his faith – *For the Time Being* resonates with a passion and identification that makes it regrettable that the piece was too long to be set to music by Benjamin Britten, which would have completed this 'Christmas Oratorio' as Auden wished it. Privately Auden identified with the figure of Joseph, confronted by the fact of Mary's pregnancy, and yet committed still to the relationship – Auden had to believe in Kallman, who he considered as his marriage partner, despite the fact that he knew he had been unfaithful and broken their vows. Here the element of the leap of faith arises, which permeated both *For the Time Being* and its companion work *The Sea and the Mirror*. In the latter it is the question of power – both political and artistic – that comes to the fore, as Auden uses Shakespeare's *The Tempest* to explore the relation between life and art. It is the 'savage' Caliban that Auden comically imbues with the voice of Henry James to analyse the problem at length in finely wrought and well observed prose. Prospero, although not obviously the voice of Auden himself, nevertheless asks some pertinent questions about the loss of poetic power, and more pointedly (in the context of Kierkegaard) rehearses what the renunciation of a previous life may mean for a man of faith.

Caliban's discussion of art and the relation between poem, poet, reader and critic is itself 'mirrored' (although rather perversely) by G.S. Fraser's reading of Miranda's line: 'My dear one is mine as mirrors are lonely.' In this fascinating fragment from Fraser's *Vision and Rhetoric*, the critic begins by complaining about a 'triteness and woolliness' in some of Auden's verse, and then falls under the spell of the line he discusses. The density of the image from Miranda's song in *The Sea and the Mirror* belies its apparently casual appearance and demonstrates the care one needs to take over Auden's poetry before dismissing it.

■ With this advance in metrical accomplishment there goes, however, that tendency towards an impressive vagueness, even towards a triteness or woolliness, of metaphor and simile first noticed by Julian Symons. The contrast with the tightness of Auden's earliest poems is striking and from some points of view depressing. 'My dear one is mine as mirrors are lonely.' That, as reviewer after reviewer has pointed out, is a very lovely line. But just how does my dear one being mine resemble mirrors being lonely? (To anybody with some knowledge of how poems are composed, it must seem possible that Auden may have written first, 'My dear one is mine though mirrors are lonely,' and then, by the alteration of a syllable, created at once a more euphonious and a more mysterious line.) It might be a mere comparison of degree: mirrors are so lonely that they reflect everything which is in front of them, and my dear one just as completely reflects me (or I may be, indeed, comparing myself to the mirror; I am so lonely for my dear one as a mirror is for everything, and for me there is nothing else, my dear one is everything). That is enough to satisfy the syntax, but the sadness and the beauty of the line come partly, I think, from the fact that mirrors are so obvious a symbol both of understanding and separation; I am reflected completely in the mirror, but I also, my real self, remain completely outside the mirror; or, in love with you, I reflect you completely, but you are free, as a person, to move away, while I still possess – for a little time – your image. And if both you and I are like mirrors, we only know each other as reflected in each other, and being in love is important as a way of possessing oneself. But this possession is illusory, for the surface never melts away, never quite dissolves even in love, and we can never, like Alice, enter the looking-glass kingdom, and wander together there, hand in hand. All these ideas are more or less relevant, and there are probably others I have missed. The point is that one can't, of course, stop to work them all out while actually reading the poem. One has the impression, merely, of something moving, intricate, and perhaps true, and passes on. This intricate vagueness has its own fascination and I cannot agree with Mr. Symons in regarding it as mere laziness on Auden's part. He knows very well, I should think, its peculiar effectiveness.[32] □

Fraser experiences the subtlety of Auden's line and defends the poet against charges of 'mere laziness', implicitly acknowledging the poet's right to control his or her work. This right is not so generously allowed by critics when it comes to Auden's revisions of his earlier poetry, and Edward Mendelson's essay 'Revision and Power: The Example of W.H. Auden' explores the issues that underpin Auden's revisions – the power that circulates between author and reader, and also between the author and those who may want to use the poetry either for their own particular aggrandisement or comfort, or by politicians, who in this piece, exemplify the social and discursive possibilities open to the poems of a famous poet. Mendelson helps us see what remains subdued in *The Sea and the Mirror* and *For the Time Being* – that the personal faith of the poet should never be assumed as known, visible or appropriable by others – and as a consequence 'Aloneness is man's condition' as Auden's existentialist belief tirelessly demonstrates.

■ Auden understood that revision was an act of power over his own text, and he therefore revised his texts in ways that renounced the kind of power that he employed in revising. He recognized that when he – like any other writer – altered the words on a page, he was using his authority to manipulate, transfer, alter, or eliminate. And he believed that a writer's pride in his power over words was all too easily transferable into pride in his power over readers.

In 1948 Auden wrote one of the four essays in *Poets at Work*,[33] the first book that studied literary revision in theoretical terms. The other three essays were written by the gestalt psychologist Rudolf Arnheim, the poet Karl Shapiro, and the literary scholar Donald A. Stauffer. Each of the four essays considered the theory of revision, and chose examples from the pioneering collection of modern literary manuscripts at the University of Buffalo. Arnheim, Stauffer, and Shapiro all wrote about revision in terms of literary effect and the psychology of the poet. In contrast, Auden's essay, 'Squares and Oblongs', was the only one that focused on the effect of revision on the poet, and on the psychological power-politics of revision as a variant of the power-politics that connect a work of art and its audience.

Auden's approach remains unique in the theoretical study of literary revision, and his observations were not designed to offer much comfort either to poets or critics. During the quarter-century before he wrote his essay, writers on both sides of the Atlantic had begun to claim special status as political analysts and visionaries. The implicit claim made in most writings on politics by modernist artists is this: because artists, by nature and training, understand matters of composition, order, balance, hierarchy, and relation, they are therefore especially well-equipped to understand those questions as they arise in the political realm.

Auden had little patience for this claim. He wrote in 1939: 'One of the best reasons I have for knowing that Fascism is bogus is that it is too much like the kinds of Utopias artists plan over café tables very late at night.'[34] In 1948, in 'Squares and Oblongs', he emphasized that the craft and vision required to create works of art were precisely those that were most dangerous when creating political systems:

A society which really was like a poem and embodied all the aesthetic values of beauty, order, economy, subordination of detail to the whole, would be a nightmare of horror, based on selective breeding, extermination of the physically or mentally unfit, absolute obedience to its Director, and a large slave class kept out of sight in cellars.[35]

The means by which that kind of society could be created were precisely the same means by which a poet organized the society of a poem. . . . . . .

The acts of revision performed in secret by a poet were acts of compulsion. Auden, recognizing this, worked in his own acts of revision to balance the compulsion that he necessarily practised on his words by renouncing any form of compulsion over his readers. The success of his power over words offered the temptation to use power over persons. So, when he revised his early drafts into publishable form, and, later, when he revised his published works for new editions, he repeatedly rejected his most *compelling* metaphors, and called attention to his own artifice. When he compiled his *Collected Shorter Poems 1927–1957* in 1965, he omitted the best-known public poems that he wrote in the 1930s, 'Spain' and 'September 1, 1939'.[36]

He did not drop these poems because he disagreed with their politics – vaguely Marxist in the first poem, even more vaguely idealistic in the second – but because he distrusted their power to convince his readers that he and they were on the right side in the great struggles of the age, that they were 'the just' who exchanged messages through 'ironic points of light'. Auden also wanted to drop his most popular love poem, 'Lay your sleeping head, my love', apparently because it gave a romanticizing gloss to brief, unfaithful sexual love; but he was persuaded by friends to let the poem remain.

Auden's revisions of his poems, both before and after their first publication, were the chief means by which he put into practice his theory of the effect of poetry upon its audience. In 'Squares and Oblongs' he renounced any theories of poetry that assume that a poem works by *compelling* a response in its reader – as drama, for example, works in Aristotle's account of catharsis. 'Orpheus who moved stones,' Auden wrote, 'is the archetype, not of the poet, but of Goebbels.' . . . . . .[37]

The difficulty of Auden's position, as he acknowledged, is that a poem that disenchants and disintoxicates – a poem that reminds its readers of the flaws not merely in their world but, above all, in themselves – may not be a poem that an audience will want to read. His solution to this difficulty was a dialectical one, in which the formal and verbal beauty of a poem is an *analogy* of the order and coherence of some ultimate goodness, while the poem simultaneously insists that its own order is a fiction, that it is 'an analogy, not an imitation'. A poem can never show how to reconcile contradictions in the world of time and experience, but it can present an analogy of reconciliation through its own formal and verbal order; in that limited realm, contradictory feelings, languages, tones, and voices are contained and reconciled. . . . . . .

[In *The Sea and the Mirror*] Auden's Prospero knows about his own use of others; what he does not know is his own errors about others. Intent on transforming experience into art, he fails to recognize that, precisely because he sees others from the perspective of an artist with purposes of his own, he scarcely sees them at all. During the course of his speech, he presents plausible and authoritative-sounding character sketches of all the other persons in the play. And then the speeches of the other persons themselves prove him to have been utterly and extravagantly wrong about all of them. The other characters speak from their own inwardness and in their own personal voice, while Prospero can only understand them cynically as behaviorist automata, manipulable by their passions and by his art.

The effect of the other characters' speeches is, of course, to affirm that Auden is the kind of artist who can understand them, while Prospero is the kind of artist who cannot. But Auden was aware that one of the ways in which writers and their audiences enter into a relation of mutual congratulation and comfort is the implied contract in which an author assures readers that, as long as they read the author's work, they are in knowledgeable hands, while readers flatter themselves with the feeling that they have found a guiding intelligence that corresponds to their own.

The process of reading *The Sea and the Mirror* is one of progressive disillusionment in which a reader is convinced of one perspective, which is then revised and corrected by a drastically different perspective, which is in turn revised and corrected until no perspective can claim authority over any other. Prospero's authoritative verse speech is corrected by the verse speeches of 'The Supporting Cast, Sotto Voce', and these are in turn exposed as artifice by Caliban's prose speech, his deliberately artificial voice. The poem treats Caliban as an allegory of unintelligible, voiceless erotic energy; for Caliban to speak at all, he must speak in the most artificial of all voices available in literary English, the narrative voice of the later novels of Henry James. And the direct argument of his speech is the inability of any literary or personal vision to be an adequate, accurate, or comprehensive perspective on the real world in which choices must be made.

Auden's sense of the deceptive effect of his own writings led to his most notorious revision. These revisions have been denounced almost unanimously by the critics and reviewers who mention them. But the nature of Auden's revisions makes clear that, from Auden's perspective, his critics and reviewers were insisting on remaining deceived, while he insisted on undeceiving them. Caliban, in *The Sea and the Mirror*, offers a mocking version of the demand by readers to be deceived by art. Those with the leisure to read literature at all demand from Ariel (the poem's allegorical figure of art itself) a release from the intransigent particularity of the real world:

> Deliver us, dear Spirit [so Caliban quotes them as imploring Ariel] from the tantrums of our telephones and the whispers of our secretaries . . .; deliver us from these helpless agglomerations of dishevelled creatures with their bed-wetting, vomiting, weeping bodies, their giggling, fugitive, disappointing hearts, and scrawling, blotted, misspelt minds . . . ; deliver us from all the litter of *billets-doux*, empty beer bottles, laundry lists, directives, promissory notes and broken toys, the terrible mess that this particularised life, which we have so futilely attempted to tidy, sullenly insists on leaving behind it; translate us, bright Angel, from this hell of inert and ailing matter . . . to that blessed realm . . . that Heaven of the Really General Case where, tortured no longer by three dimensions and immune from temporal vertigo, Life turns into Light.
> (*C.P.*, pp. 439–40)

The poems that Auden excluded from his collected editions – notably 'September 1, 1939' – had precisely this quality of flattering generalization. At the end of the poem, in the midst of wartime negation and despair, the poet implicitly invited his readers to imagine themselves as the origins of one of the 'Ironic points of light' that 'Flash out wherever the just/Exchange their messages'. In the 1980s, one of President George Bush's speechwriters remembered this phrase and introduced a sentimental version of it, referring to 'a thousand points of light', into the president's most deceptive speeches. Auden had tried to reduce the self-flattering effect of this phrase in the process of revision before publication. The typescript of the poem that he submitted to *The New Republic* (and now in the Berg Collection of the New York Public Library) has 'The little points of light'; Auden deleted this by hand and wrote in 'Ironic' in place of the first two words.

An earlier stanza in the poem ended with the famous line, 'We must love one another or die'. This sounds unexceptionable enough – and it has biblical authority in a verse from the First Epistle to John: 'He that loveth not his brother abideth in death.' But Auden knew that he intended it to indicate that love is an instinctual drive like hunger, not a personal and moral choice. (He had written about 'the drives of love and hunger' in 'Letter to Lord Byron'.) If we must love one another or die, then the mere fact that we are very much alive indicates that we have adequately fulfilled our instinctual need to love; but the argument that Auden wished to make in his poems was that we have done nothing of the sort. He abandoned the stanza that contained this line before 1945, when he reprinted the poem, without this one stanza, in his *Collected Poetry*. (He abandoned the whole poem when he compiled his next collection, *Collected Shorter Poems 1927–1957*.)

The stanza and poem remained famous and easily available in anthologies, and in 1964, a political speechwriter remembered it during the bitter American presidential election campaign between Lyndon Johnson and Barry Goldwater. One of Johnson's campaign themes was the likelihood that Goldwater would start a nuclear war. (During the campaign, Johnson never mentioned his plans to increase American involvement in the war in Vietnam.) In a famous television commercial – it was broadcast only once by Johnson's campaign organization, but became so notorious that it was rebroadcast in news programs and discussed in all media – a little girl was seen counting the petals of a flower while an ominous male voice counted down from ten to zero. When the male voice reached zero, the image of the little girl was abruptly replaced by the image of an atomic explosion, and Johnson's voice was heard saying:

> These are the stakes: to make a world in which all of God's children can live, or go into the dark. We must love each other or we must die.

In addition to Johnson's closing sentence, the children and the dark also derive from lines in the poem: 'Children afraid of the night/Who have never been happy or good' and 'From the conservative dark/into the ethical life'. Auden's revisions were belated attempts to keep the poem from being put to exactly the kind of use to which it was put by two American presidents. . . . . . .

The choice that Auden faced when he revised his work was whether to flatter his audience or to disenchant it. He invariably chose disenchantment.

In his later years, Auden saw the same process of revision that worked to disenchant his readers as a means of freeing himself from isolation. Around 1970, three years before his death, he wrote this hexameter couplet:

> Blessed be all metrical rules that forbid automatic responses,
>   force us to have second thoughts, free from the fetters of Self.
>
> (*C.P.*, p.856)

Without the self-imposed requirement of metrical rules, the first thought would be sufficient, and the first thought would remain trapped within the fetters of the Self. About fifteen years earlier, in his poem 'Homage to Clio', Auden addressed the muse of the unique historical fact in similar terms. He praised Clio as the keeper of historical time, the medium in which choices are made, and in which it is possible to change one's future. Without history, in a world of determined necessity, 'Only the first step would count and that/Would always be murder'. Revision, for Auden, was the means by which that first step was followed, voluntarily, by a very different one.[38] □

Mendelson's argument bears out Auden's claim in the poem 'In Memory of W. B. Yeats' that 'The words of a dead man/Are modified in the guts of the living' (*C. P.*, p. 247). That Auden self-consciously interfered with the way that his works can be interpreted and understood should always be thought of as a *counter-critical strategy* built into his poetry and his criticism, as well as into the very biographical narratives that the poet conspired to produce in his later years.

Critical uncertainty over the long and difficult poem *The Age of Anxiety* meant that it took several years to emerge as one of Auden's most skilful and important works. Edward Callan lays out the bare structure:

■ One Night of All Souls, during World War II, four strangers meet in a Third Avenue bar in New York. They are Malin, a medical intelligence officer in the Canadian air force; Rosetta, a Jewish businesswoman – British by birth; Emble, a college sophomore enlisted in the U.S. Navy; and Quant, an elderly clerk of Irish origin. Led by Malin, the four discuss 'the seven ages' of man; then, led by Rosetta, they embark on a surrealist dream-journey 'to Grandmother's House' through seven stages of the unconscious. On awakening, they leave the bar and join Quant in a yearning lament for an archetypal father-figure as they drive through the streets to Rosetta's apartment; later, with Emble as bridegroom in a parodied wedding masque, they seek happiness in sensual love; and finally, at daybreak they go their separate ways wiser and less self-centered than before.

The Four Faculties were separately personified in *For the Time Being* to symbolize the fallen state of the psyche. Here the four strangers in the Third Avenue bar also correspond to Jung's psychic faculties. Thought personified by Malin; Feeling by Rosetta; Intuition by Quant; and Sensation by Emble. Jung's notion of the relations among the faculties is commonly represented by a diagram placing them at the cardinal points. If the two evaluative functions, thought and feeling, are placed north and south respectively (thought high in the conscious sphere and feeling submerged in the unconscious and, therefore,

135

described as feminine because the unconscious is the realm of the primordial Mother); and the two perceptive functions, intuition and sensation, are placed east and west, the resulting figure will serve as a diagram of the psyche of the 'Thinking type' which, collectively, the characters in *The Age of Anxiety* constitute.[39] □

When Richard Hoggart looked at the poem in his 1951 *Auden: An Introductory Essay* he admitted that it was 'excessively difficult to read' and that when confronted by the 'Seven Stages' section 'the significance of each stage is unjustifiably difficult to discover'.[40] Indeed, when one looks through Haffenden's collection of contemporary criticism of this work, the near unanimity and depth of animosity directed towards it is startling. Ian Samson, however, refers to Randall Jarrell writing a stinging review of *The Age of Anxiety* particularly to offset the 'mindless adulation' of the poem.[41]

An exception to the hostile critics is Jacques Barzun who defended both the difficulty and the apparent casualness of Auden's language, and made a prophetic claim for the future perception of Auden's work and *The Age of Anxiety* in particular. 'All poetry is difficult', he says, 'because it tries to thicken again, and restore, the experiences we dilute and distort through habit and conventional speech'. His next remarks seem to me particularly apt in the context of this Guide:

■ Whence it is the fate of certain poems to become shorthand notes on history. I have not the slightest doubt that when books analyzing our plight are read only by candidates for degrees, Auden's eclogue will be quoted, in bits, as a sufficient token for our times. His very forms and turns will mean all that we try to say in long chapters. And this implies that besides knowledge he gives pleasure.[42] □

There was not much pleasure for Delmore Schwartz, who thought *The Age of Anxiety* to be 'the most self-indulgent book that Auden has written',[43] while Giles Romilly suggested that to read the text was like 'eating an omelette made with egg-shells'; it is 'the least attractive poem which Mr. Auden has ever written, a desert with scarcely an oasis, with great stretches which seem pointlessly repellent, over which Mr. Auden scurries like a distracted red ant'.[44] This gives a sense of the poem's precarious stance, with critics seeing as faults the very qualities Auden was attempting to construct; for example, Patric Dickinson writes in *Horizon*: 'Purely as a work of art it seems utterly remote from living experience; quite emotionless; full of carefully written words and carefully contrived ideas.'[45]

Such a mixed reception should alert us to the importance of a work, and it is Barzun's prophetic criticism that emerges as the best clue to the importance of *The Age of Anxiety*. The concluding remarks of John Fuller's analysis of this poem, focusing particularly on Malin's last speech, emphasise the subtle play between childishness and historical responsibility which can easily be misconstrued as flippancy:

■ Malin's last words stress the irresponsible childishness of human beings, but Auden's poem is such a subtle and generous effort of understanding that this speech, with its appeal to the traditional Judaeo-Christian God, paternal and inscrutable, seems like a historical position suited to the years of Auschwitz and Hiroshima; it is itself a poetical performance less artistically moving than that 'noble despair of the poets' which Malin condescendingly mentions. Actually *The Age of Anxiety* is rich not only in noble despair, but in a kind of inner glee and inventive response to the conditions of life which is the mark of great literature.[46] □

This childishness is continually mistaken in Auden for immaturity, or adolescent play, but it is nearer to that childishness which John Bayley mentions:

■ But in Auden's poetry . . . the adolescent note – however strong and shaping its influence – is never admitted to be such. The closest that Auden has come to such an admission is his fondness for a Nietzsche quotation – 'Maturity – to recover the seriousness one had as a child at play' – and his references to poetry as a particular sort of game.[47] □

Both Fuller and Callan give extended critical time to this poem, and while Fuller takes delight in revealing sources for the poem that have been hidden in archives, notebooks and letters, he also provides a useful introduction to its themes.

The long poems written in the forties reveal a poet struggling with a series of existential, theological and historical questions, and at the same time contain some majestic poetry. Auden's ability to render argument as art, and art as argument, give to the poems a unique sense of 'double focus', a skill that was maintained in the later poetry which is discussed in the next chapter.

CHAPTER SIX

The Later Collections

F OR A detailed picture of the 'American' Auden, Edward Mendelson's *Later Auden* (1999) is a good place to begin, while John Fuller's *W.H. Auden: A Commentary* (1998) provides the student with intelligent and sympathetic readings of the entire *oeuvre*. In these texts, poems such as 'In Praise of Limestone', 'The Shield of Achilles', and the sequences 'Horae Canonicae' and 'Bucolics' are discussed, and many of their difficulties are addressed and explained. In this chapter I have selected a few close, intelligent readings of some key poems in order to reproduce the depth of allusion and deceptive complexity of Auden's later collections. Again, the themes of art, history and politics emerge as important paths into the heart of these poems.

The later Auden refined his interest in the role of the poet in a modern secular society – his search for the 'Good Place' and the 'Just City' continued as the times became more intractably incomprehensible and difficult. In the post-war period, Auden continued to question the *importance* of art in a world which was trying to come to terms with some of the most terrifying events in recorded history.

In his review of *The Shield of Achilles* Karl Shapiro affirmed that Auden's main theme was 'the quest for the authentic city', adding that 'Nowadays when Auden talks about the Good City or the Just City it is as if he were telling a story about a wonderful place where something terrible happened'.[1] This is a useful remark as it helps us to gauge the depth of Auden's nostalgia for the unattainable city and what it might mean. What emerges is a poet who recognises that Eden is unrecoverable, but who delights in imagining an Arcadia that can make the imperfection of the world that much more bearable. What is important is telling the story of these places to the best of your skill. Tight-lipped maybe, like Hephaestos in 'The Shield of Achilles', but as a skilled craftsman who can do his job *despite* the unreasonable and deluded demands of his audience and critics.

At the end of the 1930s Auden began a series of poems about poets and artists: Rimbaud, James, Housman, for example, as well as a couple of timely elegies – those on Yeats and Freud being the best known. These 'people poems' as he called them, allowed Auden to think about the role of the poet in ways that were drawn from the experience of his new life in America.[2] In the 1941 poem 'At the Grave of Henry James', for example, he directs our attention to the fundamental discrepancies between life and art:

■ All will be judged. Master of nuance and scruple,
Pray for me and for all writers, living or dead:
Because there are many whose works
Are in better taste than their lives . . . (*C.P.*, p. 312) □

It is in the light of the biographical and aesthetic mixture that makes up an artist that the significance of *The Sea and the Mirror* can be felt at its most intense, where Caliban played out the relations between artist, audience, poet and work. Appearing as it did in the same volume as *For the Time Being*, a religious oratorio, a set of religious and aesthetic questions loom into view. What is the value of art? How can the religious attitude or religious meaning be contained in poetry? Auden's claim in the elegy to Yeats that 'poetry makes nothing happen' asks us to consider all the varied ways that poetry fails to make an impact on the world, but we may ask in return, then what *does* it make happen? What *can* it make happen?[3]

In the later poetry, by way of answer to these questions, Auden often exploited the ambiguous relation between the artist as a fictional subject (who inhabits the 'I' of the poem) and the artist as the person who makes the poetry. For example, much of Auden's discussion of the role of religious faith in poetry is made problematic by this ambiguity, for while the artist explicitly rejects a 'Christian Poetry', the 'I' in the poem invites readers to be involved and concerned with spiritual questions that may transform them. So the poetry could make *something* happen even though the poet denies it.

Auden's interest in Kierkegaard is to the point here. By playing upon our automatic reaction to his religion, by undermining our over-quick tendency to assume that we know what he is trying to say, and by anticipating our secular need for rational explanations of even a frivolous poet's behaviour, Auden encourages his reader to experience the terrors and overlooked dangers of the critical situation – the regressive abyss over which the poet and critic dance in blissful ignorance while remaining engaged in a sober discussion of form and meaning.[4]

In Lucy McDiarmid's *Auden's Apologies for Poetry* she reads a group of the later poems as complex dissections of the art of poetry. Discussing 'The Shield of Achilles' she sees Auden musing on the impotence of poetry and its relation to a disappointed audience. The audience play a key role here, and McDiarmid is right to focus on their deflated expectations of what the artist can do.

McDiarmid, then, reads a particular vein running through Auden's work that is concerned quite comprehensively with the role of art and the status and possibilities of poetry in the modern world. She discusses two key poems: 'The Shield of Achilles' (1952) and 'In Praise of Limestone' (1948). The later poem, 'The Shield of Achilles', tells of Thetis, mother of Achilles, looking for the 'classical virtues on her son's shield'.[5] The images seen there, 'An artificial wilderness/A sky like lead' are at odds with the 'Marble well-governed cities' that she expects. The familiar twentieth-century scenes of warfare, execution and inner-city violence confirm that this poem 'puts the post-war scene into just the kind of oblique and dramatically archetypal context that brings out both its full horror and its religious meaning'.[6] McDiarmid argues that the disparity of the two depictions lays out the diverging desires of artist and audience, and that the artist Hephaestos coldly demonstrates the *inabilities* of art, while Thetis expects a truth that will perversely imitate her desires and expectations.

■ 'The Shield of Achilles' (1952) offers the major statement of the aesthetics of postwar Auden. Its subject is what art cannot do; the poem dramatizes its own incapacities. An intertextual reading, by way of introduction to the poem, bears out this definition of its subject: 'The Shield of Achilles' rereads its sources by severely qualifying their assertions of art's significance. [Locates sources in Homer's *Iliad* and Keats's *Ode on a Grecian Urn*.] . . . .

The poem is a parable of the relation between art and its audience. It is structured by a series of escalating demands (on the part of the audience) and escalating denials (on the part of the shield). With each of the three sets of exchanges, more of life is viewed as undepictable.

Thetis is the last of Auden's demanding mothers: like John Nower's and Michael Ransom's mothers,[7] she is implicated in her son's death. It is she who goes to Hephaestos for a shield, implicitly sanctioning the death in battle of 'Iron-hearted man-slaying Achilles/Who would not live long.' As the audience for a work of art, Thetis can also be numbered among Auden's naive aesthetes, like the first speaker of 'O what is that sound that so thrills the ear' (*C.P.*, p.120) and the lover in 'As I walked out one evening' (*C.P.*, p.133). She is someone who desires 'beauty' and assumes it is 'truth.' Her mind does not go beyond the dichotomy of the pretty and the ugly; she must be shocked into moral awareness. Her demands are simple and absolute.

The clearest example of the way the subject of 'The Shield of Achilles' is art's own inabilities occurs in the third contrast between what Thetis looks for and what the shield shows her.

She looked over his shoulder
For athletes at their games,
Men and women in a dance
Moving their sweet limbs
Quick, quick, to music,
But there on the shining shield
His hands had set no dancing floor
But a weed choked field.

A ragged urchin, aimless and alone,
Loitered about that vacancy; a bird
Flew up to safety from his well aimed stone:
That girls are raped, that two boys knife a third,
Were axioms to him, who never heard
Of any world where promises were kept,
Or one could weep because another wept. (*C.P.*, p. 597–8)

Thetis is looking for something like the scene of warmth and pardon
Auden describes in 'City without Walls,' an aesthetically pleasing and
emotionally harmonious vision of reconciliation between men and
women, and between human beings and the universe. The scene
Thetis describes is one in which by long literary and iconographic
tradition aesthetic qualities signify spiritual ones. Thetis wants tran-
scendent play, human activities elevated to a sublime spirituality.

The lines in the following 'shield' stanza describe primarily what
cannot be on the shield. It is certainly possible to show a ragged
urchin alone in a weed-choked field and a bird in the sky above him:
but how could a shield show 'axioms' in a child's mind, and how
indeed could it show *what he has never heard of*? These notions exist in
an abstract and hypothetical dimension that cannot be made pictorial;
and so, the poem implies, the spiritual cannot be depicted in poetry or
in any work of art. Just as dimensions are missing in the visual arts, a
dimension is missing in language. Why describe in language ('Were
axioms to him, who'd never heard. . .') what cannot possibly be on the
shield, if not to dramatize that the qualities he has never heard of,
commitment and sympathy, can never be in a work of art?

If art is not wish-fulfillment, as Thetis assumes, what is it? Auden
in the 1950s would say, a means of disenchantment, through which
our expectations for the absolute are answered with the contingent
and derivative. If art's subject is always its own incapacities, then it
will always disenchant those who come to it seeking the fulfillment of
their wishes. The notion of disenchantment is built into an art that
dramatizes what it cannot do. . . .

. . . The central idea of undepictability exists throughout the poem.

In the poem's opening stanza, Thetis expresses the naive audience's wish to see 'Marble well-governed cities,' that is, scenes in which moral values (well-governed) are signified by aesthetic qualities (marble). Thetis wants art to be artistic and 'literary'; her expectations are voiced in pseudo-Homeric formulas, 'ships upon untamed seas.' What Thetis has created in her imagination, the poem uncreates, describing not what *is* on the shield but what is not on it: 'A plain *without* a feature. . . . No blade of grass, no sign of neighborhood,/*Nothing* to eat and *nowhere* to sit down' (emphasis added). An absence – like the compassion the urchin *has never heard* of – is undepictable.

The [third] stanza . . . dramatizes qualities that could not be forged on a shield: the 'voice' without a face and its 'dry and level' tones as well as the *absence* of cheering and discussion. The final lines of this set are reminiscent of Keats's little town: 'They marched away enduring a belief/Whose logic brought them, somewhere else, to grief.' How can this vague 'somewhere else,' the doom to which the five hundred thousand people are marching, be part of the shield? How can a visual art show people marching away 'enduring a belief'? Or how show the logical (though not-yet-existing) outcome of that belief? The absent visual dimension on the shield signifies the absent spiritual dimension of art, which, 'The Shield of Achilles' implies, is limited to telling you by means of *praeteritio* [something mentioned while professing not to be able to mention it] what it cannot tell you.

Thetis's naiveté is not necessarily about 'life'; we do not know what she thinks about that. We only know what she expects art to be, what she 'looked over' Hephaistos's shoulder to see. Thetis expects that art will be aesthetically pleasing, and that some form of moral and spiritual value will be somehow 'built in' to its beauty; that 'marble' and 'well-governed' will be synonymous. . . .

The shield's answer is, again, a comment on art: what you want, it implies, would be empty of spiritual significance. Art is not the same as religion. The 'rites' depicted in art would be without significance. Anything in art is arbitrary: hence the 'arbitrary' spot enclosed by the barbed wire. What you are expecting, the shield suggests, implies that there is no difference between art's version of a 'ritual piety' and the actual ritual. The location of a ceremony in art would not be traditional and sacred. Art would not care whether it was white heifers or pale people who were being sacrificed. *Art has no feelings.* The people in charge of such a fabricated ritual piety might as well be 'bored,' because they do not have insides. You would have a ritual on the surface only, a ritual drained of value.

What is truly significant in any ritual piety is undepictable, a spirituality beyond the capabilities of art. Auden deliberately comments on the shield's own 'anti-ritual' in ways that the shield could not possibly

comment. How could a design on metal say that people about to be executed 'could not hope for help' and that they 'lost their pride/And died as men before their bodies died'? This is an area art cannot touch, cannot talk about, yet this is precisely the area of spiritual significance. Auden creates a scene so obviously undepictable visually in order to dramatize what art cannot do. Art cannot express sympathy: the most it can do is imply that it is unable to express sympathy. . . . . . .
     In the last stanza of 'The Shield of Achilles,' the artist himself appears for the first time. He is 'thin-lipped': he has nothing to say. His work of art says it all for him: why should he talk? He hobbles away because he is finished: he has made his shield and that is all he can do. He cannot stand around chatting with the audience he has just disappointed. After he hobbles off Thetis 'Cried out in dismay,' but the audience's reaction is beyond the concern of the artist. His role is not to comfort her but to create. His creations speak. And what business has Thetis anyway to expect spiritual niceties to please her 'Iron-hearted man-slaying' son? A naive attitude to art betrays an unexamined attitude to the part of the world that is not art also. But the artist does not know that and does not interfere with the realities of her world. Teasingly, defiantly, he embodies in his art his inability to talk about the spiritually significant.[8] □

'In Praise of Limestone' uses the limestone landscape to consider differences and contrasts. While Fuller sees a succession of contrasts between human beings and animals, artists and non-artists, English and Italians, lovers and 'seekers of immoderate soils', and human beings and statues,[9] McDiarmid suggests that the poem 'divides the world into two parts, limestone and everything else':

■ Toward the end of 'In Praise of Limestone' the poet, as such, makes his appearance. Just at the moment when the poem suggests that limestone may not be childishly innocent but 'backward and dilapidated' and seedy, a place to outgrow, limestone begins to show its strength. It

> . . . calls into question
> All the Great Powers assume; it disturbs our rights. The poet,
>   Admired for his earnest habit of calling
> The sun the sun, his mind Puzzle, is made uneasy
> By these solid statues which so obviously doubt
>   His antimythological myth. (*C.P.*, p. 542)

This is the first of those occasions, so prevalent in Auden's later poetry, when the worshipper introduces himself *as poet* in order to denigrate himself and praise a divinity. The two judgments are simultaneous and inseparable: the very moment that first shows limestone's moral authority reveals the poet as shamefaced, silly, undignified. . . . . . .

'In Praise of Limestone' divides the world into two parts, limestone and everything else. The two terms are equivalent to 'Nature' and 'History' as Auden defines them in his later essays and in most of his later poems, particularly those in the volume *Homage to Clio*.[10] Limestone encompasses the entire created world, rocks, water, what is before *homo faber* fabricates anything; the poem's even, regular movements, alternating lines of eleven and thirteen syllables, are a tribute to the regularity of natural rhythms, like breathing or the seasons. As civilization evolves gradually from nature, so child is differentiated from mother. With each line of 'In Praise of Limestone' the process of differentiation is accomplished: each line signifies a new stage of development, as the poem reenacts the development of self-consciousness, from sensual awareness (touch, rounded slopes; smell, fragrance of thyme; sound, springs chuckling; sight, short distances) to Mother to 'brothers' to 'rivals' to the introspective and alienated 'solitude that asks and promises nothing.'

Parallel to this ontogenetic [ontogenesis: history of the individual development of an organised being] development is the evolution of culture, as it rises out of limestone gradually:

> From weathered outcrop
> To hill-top temple, from appearing waters to
> Conspicuous fountains, from a wild to a formal vineyard,
> Are ingenious but short steps that a child's wish
> To receive more attention than his brothers, whether
> By pleasing or teasing, can easily take. (*C.P.*, p.540)

The child's 'works are but/Extensions of his power to charm,' artistic efforts designed to get attention: thus a later, more self-conscious version, the impulse to 'ruin a fine tenor voice/For effects that bring down the house.'

Art, then, is a form of pleasing and teasing and naughtiness, a sign of individuation and separation from loving Mother limestone. Grown up, the naughty children leave limestone and its affectionate embrace for lonelier lives, as saints, Caesars, or isolated romantic voyagers. Out in the big busy world, they look back on limestone as backward and seedy.

It is at this point in the poem that limestone begins to acquire spiritual authority, changing from a warm loving Mommy to a more theological Love. The poet himself is caught in all his pride, deifying himself ('calling . . . his mind Puzzle'), as the capital letter suggests, and depriving nature of any divine power: he calls the sun 'the sun,' not Apollo. His myth is 'antimythological' because he is too knowing and sophisticated to believe in Naiads and Dryads and Daphne and Syrinx. Statues make him uneasy because they are so physical; if, as the poem suggests several lines later, they are 'Innocent athletes,' their nakedness disturbs his intellectuality.

In one of the most complex instances of self-deprecation in all his poetry, Auden humbles the first-person speaker of 'In Praise of Limestone' for his failure to worship limestone, the natural world that the God of Genesis saw and called 'good.'

> I, too, am reproached, for what
> And how much you know. Not to lose time, not to get caught,
> Not to be left behind, not, please! to resemble
> The beasts who repeat themselves, or a thing like water
> Or stone whose conduct can be predicted, these
> Are our Common Prayer, whose greatest comfort is music
> Which can be made anywhere, is invisible,
> And does not smell. (*C.P.*, p. 542)

The capital letters are now attached to the true divinity; 'Common Prayer' introduces a worshipful stance and ritual note as the poem reveals itself to be a 'rite of homage.' It undermines its own spiritual significance: poets are self-centered, solipsistic beings, who deny, reject, and ignore innocent nature for the sake of their own little pleasures. Poetry is not evil; it is just the grown-up version of the teasing playfulness that gets Mommy's attention, the 'incorrigible staginess' acknowledged by Auden's Caliban.

'In Praise of Limestone' turns almost literally into a rite as it invokes the Apostles' Creed: 'if Sins can be forgiven, if bodies rise from the dead' and 'the life to come' echo 'I believe in . . . The Forgiveness of sins . . . The Resurrection of the body: And the Life everlasting.' It closes on a note of self-forgetfulness:

> Dear, I know nothing of
> Either, but when I try to imagine a faultless love
> Or the life to come, what I hear is the murmur
> Of underground streams, what I see is a limestone landscape.
>
> (*C.P.*, p. 542)

In this aetiological narrative [aetiology: inquiry into the origin] the poet defines himself and his art and all art in terms of limestone: poetry is not-limestone, and limestone is not-text, the pure world unsullied by ink, untainted by thought. 'In Praise of Limestone' is a poem of *Sehnsucht*, of longing for what is not itself. My own existence, it says, is derivative, and the not-me comprehends all value. I know there is something outside this poem, and I long for it. It is something I am homesick for, and something I 'try to imagine': it can only be described by my feelings of longing for it. It is a power I am disturbed, reproached, and loved by.

'In Praise of Limestone' describes its own spiritual failures, but not despairingly. They are acknowledged, accepted, lived with, and even loved. (The more adult version of 'displaying his dildo' may be the poet's pleasure in his own naughty and not very significant art.) The mild castigations of limestone, as the poet imagines them, are not a sign of utter and absolute separation from what is spiritually valuable, not a cause for self-flagellation. The poet finds pleasure in imagining a connection with limestone, and in cheerfully, charmingly, winningly writing his good-natured poem. He is still singing 'for effects that bring down the house,' and in fact Auden did bring down a house of sorts, winning (in this period alone) a Pulitzer Prize in 1948, the Bollingen Prize in 1952, and a National Book Award in 1956. To describe the origin of poetry is both to advertise its triviality and to pay homage to the untrivial substance from which it derives. The tone of apology modulates into the tone of worship.[11] □

Fuller expands upon the lines which portray a 'nude young male . . ./. . . displaying his dildo' and remarks that 'The dildo is a symbol of the Freudian sublimation of sex into art'.[12] John R. Boly ends his book on Auden with a discussion of the importance of the 'dildo' in this poem. His use of the term 'prosthetic' (the prosthetic is an addition or replacement, an artificial part fitted to the body) brings Boly's analysis into a playful ('ludic') post-structuralist encounter with Auden's poem in which art and culture find themselves aligned with the young man's dildo:

■ As with all of Auden's most effective voices, it is tempting to take 'In Praise of Limestone' as the expression of the poet, especially when the voice is so accomplished, at the height of its powers. Yet in the case of a ludic voice, its distinctive task is to hold the text within bounds only long enough so that its assembled inscriptions may begin their response. Even magisterial ease can practice forms of play. The syntactic movements of the poem, in contrast to those of 'On this Island,' suggest Caliban's other nostalgic form, an incestuous rapture. Rather than drifting toward a serene horizon, the syntactic body more wondrously sinks upon itself, but without achieving a final collapse. On the contrary, its decline becomes a successive event, a continuous infolding that approaches the deepest center, a neglected origin that is always there, as the source of whatever is indestructible and sustaining. This trustful reliance accepts a Mediterranean indulgence in which usual prescriptions are lifted.

What could be more like Mother or a fitter background
For her son, for the nude young male who lounges
Against a rock displaying his dildo, never doubting
That for all his faults he is loved, whose works are but
Extensions of his power to charm?[13]

The image is startling mainly because it turns the licentious into the commonplace: so capably is the Book of Nature invoked that anything appearing within its bounds is encoded as natural, pure, and thus utterly acceptable. In this rapturous interlude, the usual scruples, as well as their even more tyrannical aesthetic surrogates, are momentarily suspended.

The lascivious vignette repeats the basic meditative design of supportive mother, errant son, and futile works, but in a deliberately disruptive fashion. Each is renamed so that it becomes both an archetype and a caricature: mother as impervious rock (foundation, origin, center); son as indolent nude (shameless, irresponsible); civilized achievement as ludicrous dildo (admission, prop). In this wanton manner, the ludic voice happily endorses what is awkward, inadmissible, unspeakable. Yet its wantonness is also a deliberate pose, a means of playing the text. For the poem's meditative pattern to work, the errant offspring must shuttle between the extremes of an authentic origin and a tempting array of destructive substitutes.

[Cites: "'Come!' cried the granite wastes . . . the various envies, all of them sad' (C.P., pp. 541–2)]

The son may use the rock, or even its absence, to fashion a deviant prosthesis, the works of a culture. But the results must have no bearing on their origin. It is this separation, however, that the licentious namings put at risk. The dildo is the ultimate substitute: the comic prop in which the actual concedes its frailty long enough to summon the makeshift, sterile but useful, as a reminder not only of a lack but of the capacity to lighten it through mimicry. Yet the range of that mimicry is too extensive. The sterile prosthesis can dissemble a plenipotent dick, remnant of the dictionary, a maze of illicit, tricky, and occasionally necessary substitutions. Perhaps such deceit might be tolerated were its outrageous metonymics confined within the regions of their own play. But the energies of the prosthesis are enough to reverse the irreversible, so that they invade even the impervious mass of the precious origin, the center as rock, *petre*, the solid ground on which to put that which shall withstand the ages. The rock is also the punned Peter, a further emblem of evasive motility, of what is alternately irascible, treacherous, intransigent, sanctified. Blissfully unsupervised, licentiously named, the nude young male wields the substitute whose returns come back to haunt even the inviolable rock.

Yet the torment becomes generative as it meets a tacit with an out-right violence. Power, as the preservation of an assured meaning, emanates from a virgin birth: an origin presumed to be pure. But that purity is what the ludic voice refuses to allow. It upsets the clear dichotomy of imagination and reality, univocal origins set against his-torical contingency, if only because the origins always prove to be riddled with dissent.

> The poet
> Admired for his earnest habit of calling
> The sun the sun, his mind Puzzle, is made uneasy
> By these marble statues which so obviously doubt
> His antimythological myth. (*C.P.*, p. 542)

In contrast to that 'earnest habit,' the text's inscriptions propose another scene of origins, licentious, ungovernable, obscene. The drive to find the ultimate source seeks an irreducible genesis, that before which nothing further might occur, and from which nothing different might evolve, 'the historical calm of a site/Where something was settled once and for all'. But the search can never go back far enough. It can attain only 'A backward/And dilapidated province, connected/To the big busy world by a tunnel, with a certain/Seedy appeal'. The authorita-tive forms are already in ruins, mere shadows of a power whose previous grandeur is strangely unwitnessed. And the scene itself is neither pure nor complete, and bears the scattered traces of possibility, the rem-nants of a departed impulse. Yet it is this disreputable passageway that offers the only attainable origin, the farthest point that may be reached, which as always turns out to be a point of further departure.

What ensues from the Book of Nature's nonvirgin birth? The textual reply, 'a stone that responds,' is the otherwise silent resistance that accompanies any voice.

> Dear, I know nothing of
> Either, but when I try to imagine a faultless love
> Or the life to come, what I hear is the murmur
> Of underground streams, what I see is a limestone landscape.
> (*C.P.*, p. 542)

The faultless love of the perfected future is fissured, riddled with devious passages that constantly shift as the limestone dissolves exist-ing solidities and precipitates different ones. To fix or specify this future – the nascent forms waiting within an existing discourse – is out of the question. All that can be known for sure is that the inscriptions of a text, its unvoiced yet discernible memories, will arrange a responsive tumult for them as well, in the surreptitious streams that 'spurt,' 'chuckle,' 'entertain,' and 'murmur,' with accents that are both a complaint and an invitation, a surprise and a renewal.

* * *

To take up the initial question, then, a voice can at least arrest its native violence, though this may be the most intricate task it is asked to perform. For this play cannot be approached directly, nor does it attend upon any of the ordinary resources of the speaking voice, whose effect would be to augment a securely conveyed sense. Rather, a ludic voice must pursue its play through a syntactic mime. By means of its performed gestures, it has the capacity not to enunciate (for that can never be done) but to provoke the response of textual inscriptions. These gestures may involve either an instrumental blitheness or a trustful reliance, though these specific provocations in no way serve as a limit. There can be no official grammar of the textual body or its ludic poses, only the different histories of its continuous play.[14] □

As a coda to this discussion of 'In Praise of Limestone', Donald Davie considers the later poem 'Amor Loci' (1965) as a response to the earlier. Significant here is the repetition of patterns and influences. As the story of Auden's life draws to an end, so the figures return – in this case, Hardy. Davie's description of an 'intense', 'savage' and 'grim' side to Auden's poetry comes as a shock after considering the *ludic* aspects of his work, but the brief and serious encounter with the fact of one's faith seems entirely apt here, and Davie describes it well.

■ 'In Praise of Limestone' contrives, by what is really sleight of hand, to superimpose landscapes of Ischia and even perhaps of Greece on the limestone landscapes of Craven; in 'Amor Loci' the landscapes are those native Pennine landscapes which, as we have seen, were the natural habitation for Auden's imagination from his earliest youth. With this change goes another; whereas the earlier, more expansive poem set up a 'we' against a 'they' (and John Fuller interestingly identifies the 'we' with 'intellectuals'), in 'Amor Loci' there is only an 'I.' 'We' were called 'The Inconstant Ones,' and it was said in the earlier poem that we responded to a limestone landscape because of the treacherous inconstancy of that kind of rock. In 'Amor Loci' that treachery is registered altogether more blankly and fiercely in the astonishing phrase 'the Jew Limestone.' This expression must certainly give offense. For Auden to use it at a time when for instance Eliot is on every side being censured for his use of 'the Jew' in 'Gerontion,' is an act of brutal defiance. And Auden, though in the past he has been often foolhardy and consistently impudent, has never up to this point been defiant. Auden here confronts his reader bleakly and boldly. If we compare these taut syllables with the indulgent inclusiveness of the looping accentual lines of 'In Praise of Limestone,' we are compelled to realize that Auden is being graceful no longer, but intense and savage. And for this reason the modulation into the expression of Christian faith at the end of 'Amor Loci' cannot help but strike us as altogether more in earnest than the corresponding modulation at the end of 'In Praise of Limestone.'

It is against this background of sweeping and violent change in Auden's stance and tone of voice that we must account for an unusually pointed allusion to Hardy in this poem. For such I take to be the phrase, 'in days preterite.' It is a phrase that I can persuade myself I have read in Hardy's *Collected Poetry* (perhaps I have). At all events, it is – in its uncompromising inversion of noun and adjective and in the exact Latinate pedantry of 'preterite' – unmistakably Hardyesque. In a rhetorician so adept as Auden, this does not happen by accident. And we have seen why, from Auden's point of view, a grim brief bow in Hardy's direction would seem appropriate in a poem like this which after so long reverts without equivocation to the Pennine landscape, and looks at it moreover from a height where its contours, strata, and vegetation are laid out before the poet's eye as on a map. Seen from that height, the inhabitants of the landscape are inevitably 'faceless as heather or grass.' And so the poem has no political implications. Though it acknowledges historical perspectives (for the mining captains were gone, the Pennine slopes had reverted from heavy industry to marginal farming, already 'in my time,' in the bicycle age, the poet's boyhood), the poem is set outside history; because it is not concerned to make sense of historical change, it can have no political dimension – as indeed the last stanza makes clear, by insisting that the experience makes emblematic meaning only in a religious perspective.[15] ☐

If 'Amor Loci' was a poem 'set outside history', then this only sets in contrast Auden's relation to history which is explored at length in Mendelson's *Early Auden* in the chapter 'History to the Defeated'. Here the distinction between a determined and purposive *History* 'that will bring mankind to its ultimate fulfilment' is for a short time (in the late thirties) proposed in place of the seemingly more passive *history* which is made up of 'the set of personal and collective acts done in the past that shape the present'.[16] The next piece, taken from Stan Smith's accessible book *W.H. Auden* contains his reading of selected Auden poems from *Nones* through to *Homage to Clio*. This is an important piece of criticism, laying emphasis on Auden's continued *political* interventions in the post-war scene, even if these interventions are couched in poems as seemingly religious in character as the 'Horae Canonicae' sequence. The key term here is *history* and it is Smith's emphasis on the relation between recorded and experienced history that allows him to claim that 'Horae Canonicae' is one of Auden's most deeply political poems. Smith emphasises the discursive power of the 'Serious historians' rather than their passivity, arguing that those who interpret past events, 'the clerks, even, who, in the absence of an actual historical instance' can, in the words of Auden 'compose a model/As manly as any of whom schoolmasters tell'. Smith points to the discursive aspects of a history that, while it creates and praises 'great men' such as Tamburlaine, refuses to let them re-enter history again as active agents, for when their hour is past they can only be passive food for historical discourses. The fact that a figure that was once 'A synonym in a whole armful/Of languages for what is harmful' can be reduced to a crossword anagram makes the point that the earlier elegy to Yeats was making. The dead poet is transformed into 'his admirers' – death takes over that 'last afternoon as himself', the identity of the poet slips away to be replaced and 'modified in the guts of the living' (*C. P.*, p. 247). Smith begins by usefully reading 'Spain, 1937' and 'Homage to Clio' side by side.

■ Auden's attitude towards the social function of art is a problematic one in the three fifties collections, *Nones* (1951), *The Shield of Achilles* (1955) and *Homage to Clio* (1960), but it merely extends that fretting about its irresponsibility which began to emerge towards the end of the thirties, and found its first coherent expression in the poems about art and artists in *Another Time*. In *Secondary Worlds* Auden tried to resolve this by the traditional Christian trope of paradox: 'One might say that for Truth the word *silence* is the least inadequate metaphor, and that words can only bear witness to silence as shadows bear witness to light.' . . . . . .[17]

In *Secondary Worlds* Auden was to write that: 'To write a play, that is to construct a secondary world, about Auschwitz, for example, is wicked: author and audience may try to pretend that they are morally horrified, but in fact they are passing an entertaining evening together, in the aesthetic enjoyment of horrors.' This has generally been taken, somewhat smugly, as a condemnation of politically motivated art, *à la* Brecht. But it is in fact a much larger indictment of the whole frivolous distraction of art in a historical world of suffering. This is why, in 'Homage to Clio', the arts have no icon for the Muse of History, 'who look[s] like any/Girl one has not noticed' (*C.P.*, p. 612). Clio inhabits that realm of silence Prospero had to confront, that historical world where everyone dies in particular and the innocent always have to suffer. Only the newspaper photograph, provisional, instant, unrepeatable, can represent a world of unique historical facts. . . . .

'Homage to Clio' is composed of twenty-three four-line stanzas –

like the version of *Spain, 1937* Auden decided not to reprint in his 1965 *Collected Poems*. In some senses it is a response to *Spain*, its stanzas echoing in image and motif corresponding moments in that poem. . . . . Yet for all the sense that 'Homage to Clio' sets out to refute *Spain*'s 'inexcusable' rhetoric, what both poems share is an idea of history's doubleness as at once a pattern of unique events and the generalizing discourse within which those events are interpreted.

Whereas the opening stanzas of *Spain* tell us of the importunate world of history where it is 'Today the struggle', 'Homage' opens with the poet quietly reading in a spring garden, and reserves the language of combat for nature. Yet by the end that reading has become a more serious matter. *Spain* ends with the lines Auden regretted in 1965 as 'wicked doctrine':

> The stars are dead; the animals will not look:
> We are left alone with our day, and the time is short and
>   History to the defeated
> May say alas but cannot help or pardon.
>   (*The English Auden*, p.212)

In 'Homage', the poet on whom the animals 'Keep watch' finds himself, by the end, wondering just what opinion *History* might form of him. That 'pardon' or 'alas' are both in his mind is indicated by the remark that according to Aphrodite 'to throw away/The tiniest fault of someone we love/Is out of the question.' Nature gives up nothing. But History is a matter of what is preserved and what deleted from the scribal record, what is read or left unread. The urgencies of history return in the poem's closing lines in self-effacing anxiety about the poet's place:

>   Approachable as you seem,
>   I dare not ask you if you bless the poets,
> For you do not look as if you ever read them.
> Nor can I see a reason why you should. (*C.P.*, p.613)

At issue in both poems is the sense of a history made up of changing and unrepeatable human subjects. Central to both is that concern about the writer's responsibility, as a citizen, for a world where people die in earnest. Each too envisages an imaginary dialogue its very assumptions deny. And the deepest distress they share, for all the po-faced earnestness of one and the louche playfulness of the other, issues from a sense of the essential frivolity of art, in a primary World where the first step would always be murder. . . . .

In 'Homage' the power-brokers are relegated to the realm of nature, categorized as the Big who rarely listen, and listed only under the generic epithets that distinguish one species of despot from another, 'The Short, The Bald, The Pious, The Stammerer'. Imagining themselves world-historical individuals, they are reduced in fact to genotypes, in the realm of Clio registered only in their effects on that larger, processive and anonymous history, creating that 'great host/Of superfluous screams' she has to care for. Like Tamburlaine in the poem 'T the Great', whose name was once 'A synonym in a whole armful/Of languages for what is harmful' (*C.P.*, p.602), each despot in time recedes to a nursery-tale bogey-man, ousted from his eminence by successive challengers. He finds his final niche filling the merely verbal space provided by the secondary world of an absurd crossword anagram 'A NUBILE TRAM'. Skulking in the corner of a newspaper where today's history and tyrants roar loudly, to be superseded in turn by tomorrow's, 'T cannot win Clio's cup again.'

The real 'Makers of History', the poem of that name insists, are not the commanders whose names and faces appear on the coinage, but the 'Serious historians' who interpret them, the clerks, even, who, in the absence of an actual historical instance, could and easily did 'compose a model/As manly as any of whom schoolmasters tell'. The 'reiterations of one self-importance' on the coins are discredited by each successive new coinage. The Emperors are as exchangeable as the coins on which they figure, and, in the melting-pot of legend, are turned into 'one/Composite demi-god', attributed with prodigious feats and achievements, but also the subject of moralistic exegesis, gossip, prurience, etc. Clio's real favourites, by contrast, are those anonymous benefactors who improved their horses, supplied answers to their questions, made their things, even the 'fulsome/Bards they boarded'. Great men, whether historical or legendary, depend upon the labours of others – labours which are both productive and fictive, making history by supplying both the raw materials and the ideological means by which it is embodied. . . . . . .

The light ironies of 'Fleet Visit' (its very title a pun) in *Shield* hint at the political order which sustains this world. The sailors of the US Sixth Fleet come ashore in an innocently 'unamerican place' (*C.P.*, p.549). But it is 1951: 'unamerican' is a highly charged adjective, synonymous with 'traitorous' on the lips of a McCarthy. They are ostensibly here to protect not repress, not 'because/But only just-in-case'; yet, like the Greek raiders at Troy, they come ashore from hollow ships. They are 'mild-looking middle-class boys'; but they are not as mild as they look, any more than the ships which 'Without a human will/To tell them whom to kill' *look* 'humane', 'as if they were meant/To be pure abstract design/By some master of pattern and line', worth every cent of the billions they cost. The boys 'look a bit lost' and the ships are 'hollow', in a moral sense, for they are both instruments of destruction. The order they sustain is in the end a predatory and imperial one, where the 'master of pattern and line' exploits the mass culture of boys who read the comic strips, not Homer, for whom 'One baseball game is more/ . . . than fifty Troys', and who would be prepared to wipe out fifty Troys to defend those all-american games. The disparity between how things 'look' (used four times) and how they are is that between art and history too: Homer's poetry made the violence of history look good. The tone of all these poems is a profound ambivalence: the price we pay for an affluent society is our own collusion in repression elsewhere, banality at home.

The poems in *Nones* repeatedly return to those moments of late Imperial decline in which an order, crumbling from within, awaits, yearns for and fears its supersession. The most evocative of these is 'The Fall of Rome' (*C.P.*, p.332), where it is not external threat but internal disintegration which brings about collapse – an inflationary economy expressed in an inflated culture. Everywhere a crisis of legitimacy infects a world eyed by creatures 'Unendowed with wealth or pity'. The poem ends with a typical Auden decentring of the Imperial ideal by cutting to that elsewhere from which Rome's despatch will finally be delivered:

> Altogether elsewhere, vast
> Herds of reindeer move across
> Miles and miles of golden moss,
> Silently and very fast. (*C.P.*, p.333)

. . . . . . 1948 was a year in which the post-war rivalries between US and Soviet dominated blocs came to a head, but it is not necessary to be specific to catch the generalized anxiety of this whole volume. The immanence of supersession, at the height of imperial middle-age, is what lurks behind all these poems, but it's not the clash of one power-bloc with another which animates them – rather it is the contrast between power and an alternative way of defining human life which is at issue.

Auden is not taking sides in the immediate political confrontation. In the 1954 'Ode to Gaea' (*C.P.*, p.553), viewed from an aeroplane, the various 'sub-species of folly' specific to each national territory below seem arbitrary and unreal, embarrassing the tired old diplomat who cannot decide whether he should 'smile for "our great good ally", scowl/at "that vast and detestable empire" or choose/the sneer reserved for certain Southern countries'. Here too, 'on this eve of whispers and tapped telephones/before the Ninth Catastrophe', the real distinction is between the systems of power, 'the Greater Engines . . .

and the police/who go with them', 'the tormentor's/fondling finger' and the orators' lies, on the one hand, and a natural beneficence represented on the other by an Earth which in its plenitude can be equated with natural justice. So, in 'Memorial for the City' (*C.P.*, p.591), Auden's real frontier cuts across the East – West divide, bisecting them laterally between what his 1948 essay on Yeats called 'the social person and the impersonal state'.

Augustine's two cities here are not an otherworldly and a worldly one, perpetually estranged. Rather they are two ways of viewing the same reality. The eye of the camera and the eye of the crow see the real in terms which record only its surface, 'a space where time has no place', reduced to one-dimensionality. The 'hard bright light composes/ A meaningless moment into an eternal fact.' But such candour lies, for 'The crime of life is not time.' Time, on the contrary, is the dimension in which redemption becomes possible. Where we are now, after all, is 'Among the ruins of the Post-Vergilian City/Where our past is a chaos of graves and the barbed-wire stretches ahead/Into our future till it is lost to sight' (*C.P.*, p. 592). For it is precisely in being 'lost to sight' that such redemption lurks, that *beyond* which the eye confined to the present cannot encompass. The world has been divided before, between, for example, Church and State. The New City 'rose/Upon their opposition, the yes and no/Of a rival allegiance', and section II of the poem rehearses some of those changing divided cities in a familiar Audenish potted history.

Immediately after section III, with its vision of the barbed-wire running through all things, the appeal to *'Let Our Weakness speak'* introduces that alternative voice to the discourse of Power, first enunciated by Auden in his doctrine of the Truly Strong, and now embodied in that second Adam who speaks of redemption amidst all acts of dereliction, from the first Adam onwards through a whole gamut of mythical and historic archetypes.

Christ, this surplus, is the perpetual otherness of history, in which 'Metropolis, that too-great city' will be judged. To 'all who dwell on the public side of her mirrors' there will be no peace. 'Our grief is not Greek', the poem had said, the arbitrary change of phoneme opening up a world of difference and revealing the historical exchangeability of the signifier. Another play on words, 'The facts, the acts of the City bore a double meaning:/Limbs became hymns', embodies in the supersessions of language the model of a historic conversion. So, at the end of the poem, the suffering turns round on those who refuse to apportion or accept blame for suffering, turning the photographs into evidence and the photographers into culprits, their disinterestedness complicity:

> At the place of my passion her photographers are
> gathered together;
> but I shall rise again to hear her judged. (*C.P.*, p.596)

In *A Certain World* Auden adds a small twist to the observation about art and Auschwitz in *Secondary Worlds*. 'Christmas and Easter', he observes, 'can be subjects for poetry, but Good Friday, like Auschwitz, cannot. The reality is so horrible it is not surprising that people should have found it a stumbling block to faith.'[18] Yet Auden not only made a poem about the hour of the crucifixion the title poem of *Nones*, and opened that volume with a poem about Good Friday, he also took both poems and made them part of a long sequence, 'Horae Canonicae' (*C.P.*, p.627), which is at the centre of his next volume, *The Shield of Achilles*. This fretful return to the scene of the primal crime has about it both the ambiguous penitence of the culprit and the obsessive compulsion to know of the detective in a Whodunit. 'Just as we were all, potentially, in Adam when he fell,' Auden says in *A Certain World*, 'so we were all, potentially, in Jerusalem on that first Good Friday before there was an Easter, a Pentecost, a Christian, or a Church.' This moment of supersession must have appeared to its participants as merely an everyday, minor episode in a marginal colony. Imagining who he himself might have been, Auden suggests a Hellenized Jew from Alexandria, absorbed in intellectual argument and reacting with prim distaste to the all-too-familiar sight of the crucifixion, 'averting my eyes from the disagreeable spectacle'. This averting of the gaze links the Madonnas of 'Nones' with the Clio of 'Homage', and it implicates, too, that Thetis with whom we identify in 'The Shield of Achilles', binding together the three volumes into a meditation on the evasions and sudden revelations of history, those moments when we have lost control and turn for recognition and forgiveness. . . . . . .

'Horae Canonicae' then is not finally a blasphemous religious poem about 'Good Friday' but a secular poem about 'our dear old bag of democracy'. It uses the Christian fable as a vehicle, not because it does not credit it – it clearly does – but because the very meaning of that crucifixion, within Christian belief, is that Christ offered himself to be used, to become the sacrificial vehicle of meanings other than himself, incarnate in him. The poem itself, that is, shares in the guilty doubleness of which it speaks, proclaiming a secret it would half like to forget, that its innocence is founded in blood, and that under all the arcadias and utopias of art lies that historical share of care symbolized by the victim – '(call him Abel, Remus, whom you will, it is one Sin Offering)' – without whom 'no secular wall will safely stand'. 'Horae Canonicae' is one of the most insistently political of all Auden's poems, not just in its incidental imagery, but in its attempt to address that crisis on the site of modern history compacted into the contradictions of a single line in *Spain*: 'today the/Fumbled and unsatisfactory embrace before hurting'. What it calls for is in fact 'The conscious acceptance of guilt in the fact of murder'.

. . . . . . 'Horae Canonicae' begins with an image of an aristocratic French rebellion, the Fronde, as a metaphor for that which is repressed into the unconscious, 'Disenfranchised, widowed and orphaned/By an historical mistake', to emerge again in dream. 'Bucolics' (*C.P.*, p.556) ends with a dream-vision which is simultaneously arcadian and utopian, which distracts us away from that Paris in which the ghost of a proletarian revolution stalks abroad, haunting Europe. It is as if, slipping off into dream here as at the same moment in 'Compline', Auden cannot remember a thing that happened between noon and three, cannot remember that 'cement of blood (it must be human, it must be innocent)' on which his and Gaston Paris's international community of scholars, 'arcadias, utopias, our dear old bag of democracy are alike founded'. In 'Sext', we recall, first manual and then intellectual labour are seen as the foundations of culture and crime alike. For *Homo Ludens*, the playing poet, still relies on *Homo Laborans*, the working man and woman, without whom 'no secular wall will safely stand'. Clio and Caesar alike rely on a third power, that worker, artificer, artisan figured, in the title poem of *The Shield of Achilles* (*C.P.*, p.596), by the lame and sweating smith, Hephaestos, a heavenly proletarian who is as silent as Clio, and also turns away from what his hands have wrought.

The double stanza pattern of 'The Shield' would suggest that this poem juxtaposes Ariel and Prospero, beauty and truth. And indeed Thetis, looking over Hephaestos' shoulder as he makes the shield for Achilles, does expect to see pastoral scenes like those on Keats's Urn. Her wish to see idyllic images on an instrument of war suggests a contradiction. For her, the shield is also an instrument of propaganda, offering she hopes images of that *patria* for which it is sweet to die, as her son will. Instead, the shield depicts not the simple antithesis of a world easily divided between order and violence, culture and nature – 'Marble well-governed cities/And ships upon untamed seas' – but one in which they are inextricably confounded, 'An artificial wilderness/And a sky like lead' – the oxymoron indicating not only the artifice of the smith's craft, but also the man-made nature of the desolation it depicts. Callan sees Hephaestos as 'the aesthetic god', depicting 'not the ideal Thetis envisioned . . . but the utopian reality', something Callan equates with 'Hitler's dream of a racially pure Nordic state . . . apartheid . . . and the Marxist dream of pure Communism' – which is rather unfair to Hephaestos and to Marx.[19] For what this sweaty armourer produces is a true picture of war and what it brings in its wake, as opposed to ennobling propaganda. When Callan quotes Auden's comment from *The Dyer's Hand* that 'A society which was really like a good poem, embodying the aesthetic virtues of beauty, order, economy and subordination of detail to the whole, would be a nightmare of horror',[20] his quotation turns back upon the all-American Mom Thetis, for it is her wish that this describes, not Hephaestos' reality.

But Hephaestos himself cannot escape contradiction. For this work in heavy metal, exhaustingly produced by hard labour, and depicting an ugly and problematic world, manages to achieve the transformation of pain and disorder into art. Poem and shield both force open a division between the beauty of the representation and the ugliness it represents, translating 'shining metal' into 'a sky like lead' in a way which both affirms and conceals its artifice under the success of its illusion.

As Callan's comments reveal, the role of the reader is crucial in this poem, for what it sets up is a potentially infinite regress of perspectives in which the hermeneutic circle is never closed. You, gentle reader, look over my shoulder as I look over the speaker's shoulder as he looks over Thetis' shoulder as she looks over Hephaestos', who in turn looks at a world in which 'A crowd of ordinary decent folk' (like you, me and Mr Callan) look on as three pale figures are led forth and shot – which is where all looking ceases. The crowds do nothing, the officials are bored, the sentries sweat:

> The mass and majesty of this world, all
>   That carries weight and always weighs the same
> Lay in the hands of others; they were small
>   And could not hope for help and no help came:
>   What their foes liked to do was done . . . (*C.P.*, p.597)

But it is all all right. For these are only 'figures' on a shield. The hands we are in are Hephaestos' own, or Auden's; and we can here wash our own of complicity in that crime, just like the crowd, the sentries and the officials. Words have no weight. We are in fact 'passing an entertaining evening together, in the aesthetic enjoyment of horrors'. Richard Johnson, in *Man's Place*, even sees Thetis' pastoral stanzas offering a 'positive image of possibility' which refutes Hephaestos' ultimately insufficient realism with a vision of redemption. There is no cause for alarm.[21]

But there is cause for alarm. The last stanza should be one of Thetis' pastoral pieties. Instead, in a movement in which the three parties to the shield's making – commissioner, producer, user – are named for the first time, the figures and voices momentarily gathered here disperse, Hephaestos hobbling away in thin-lipped silence, Thetis crying out in dismay 'At what the god had wrought/To please her son', rather than at the fact he is a man-slayer or that he too will not live long. The representation has more effect than the reality. We too, poet and reader alike, go our separate ways, moved more by the rhetoric of suffering than the knowledge that such things are actually happening out there, at this moment as we read or write – today in El Salvador, yesterday in Teruel, Nanking, Dachau. Is it Achilles who is 'Iron-hearted, man-slaying', or is it us? The look we see reflected back from the shining metal is our own. What stares out of the mirror of the poem is still

Imperialism's face
And the international wrong.
(*The English Auden*, p. 245)[22] ☐

As Smith takes pains to argue, Auden's poetry often produced the 'sense of a history made up of changing and unrepeatable human subjects' and it is therefore ironic that one of the most consistent criticisms of Auden's later work has been of his attention to the more mundane details of everyday life. These details, mundane or not, nevertheless mark the very place where the events of history are recorded, and their effects felt. I have included a piece from Edward Callan's book *Auden: A Carnival of Intellect* (1983) as it brings out the power and the importance of the apparently trivial 'domestic' poems in *About the House* (1965).

Callan earlier describes *The Shield of Achilles* as one of Auden's 'best single volumes', adding that

■ The poems in it are distinguished by a sense of place that sets them apart from his poetry of any other period. Individual poems are frequently meditative. They begin in the world of the everyday – the thinker's body, house, or garden – and then move outward in space or in memory.[23] ☐

The sense of place that the poems in *About the House* deals with is even more 'everyday' in scope, but Callan captures the way that these poems 'move outward' from their domestic frame and engage with wider concerns – while at the same time, saying some important things about the domestic setting.

It may be useful to think of how Auden gets subtly gendered in the criticism of his late poetry, facing accusations that would not seem out of place in Virginia Woolf's *A Room of One's Own* (1928) where the 'important' world of historical events always takes precedence over the 'triviality' of domestic detail.[24] The anonymous reviewer in the *TLS* for example declared that *About the House* was a 'disappointing, trivial volume'[25] whereas C. B. Cox in *The New Statesman* realised the important undercurrent that flowed below an apparently unserious facade:

■ Because modern science has destroyed our faith in the naive observations of our senses, telling us that we cannot know what the
physical universe is *really* like, art can no longer be a completely adequate representation of either religious truth or 'the baffle of life'. The
poet, therefore, must 'wink', must keep his readers conscious that his
words are part of a game.[26] □

The significance of Blair's comments on Auden's light verse (see chapter
two) becomes apparent when we consider the poet's relation to this
game. Auden's later poetry, and the poems in *About the House* in particular, offer themselves to be read *across* these distinctions between serious
and unserious, between fiction and reality, and between the weighty law
of the statement and the ambiguous status of the game.

   Callan begins by referring to the house in Kirchstetten where Auden
spent the remaining years of his life. It is to this special place (a 'Good
Place') that Auden addresses these deceptively homely poems. And yet,
as Callan makes clear, a religious element shines luminously through the
secular materiality of poems such as 'Down There' (*C.P.*, p.696) or
'Tonight at Seven-Thirty' (*C.P.*, p.708) in which contemporary theological debates and religious symbolism are apparent. In 'The Cave of
Making' (*C.P.*, p.691) Auden muses on the diminishing role of the poet
in modern times where poetry is an 'unpopular art' which 'stubbornly
still insists upon/being read or ignored'. Auden's playful dismissal of
serious critical attention also surfaces here as he remembers a
'Symposium' attended with MacNeice at which they 'exchanged winks
as a juggins/went on about Alienation' (*C.P.*, p.693). Irreverent perhaps,
but the careful selection of the word 'juggins' (simpleton) leads us back
into the world of the early poetry where the select group bolstered each
other with private codes and messages. Here, the mature Auden delivers
a poet's insult, and at the same time shows us that maybe, while we can
still 'wink' something is being preserved that is not alienated and that lies
out of reach of the 'juggins" analysis.

■ The cycle 'Thanksgiving for a Habitat' consists of twelve poems celebrating the Kirchstetten house and its rooms – kitchen, living room,
dining room, bathroom, toilet, cellar, attic, and so on. The house and
rooms serve practical functions, but as the occasion for a poem in the
cycle each room provides a locus for expanding circles of analogy
reaching ultimately toward some spiritual horizon. In celebrating the
artist in the bath, at stool, in bed, presiding at a feast, or composing an
elegy on a friend, Auden is engaged in the quite unromantic pursuit
that Martin Buber calls 'the hallowing of the everyday.'
   ...... The house at Kirchstetten – the only 'home' he ever owned
– with its appurtenances within and without provides the poet with a

symbolic center for celebrating, like the Psalmist, his providential circumstances, his heritage in nature, history, art, and belief. . . . . . .
Auden's Thanksgiving is a carnival rite rather than a solemn memorial, and the poems in the cycle achieve much of their impact through humor and ironic understatement. The language has an astonishing lexical range and evocative overtones reflecting Auden's aspiration that every poem of his should be a hymn in praise of the English language.

The twelve self-reflective poems of the cycle permit a complex view of the world-about-me contained within the horizon of the self – not a morbidly confessional self; but one capable of affirming the potentialities of the imagination, the intellect, and the flesh. The poet at the center is *Homo viator*, preferring the Pilgrim's Way to the War Path, reflecting on his relationship to space and time, to things given by nature, and to things that are man-made, and taking particular delight in contemplating the shell man constructs for himself as an expression of what he imagines his ideal *self* to be. . . . . . .

The cycle's Prologue, 'The Birth of Architecture,' (*C.P.*, p. 687) places the poet in his own historical setting with a rapid sweep through time from gallery-grave (Hetty Pegler's Tump is named in the next poem) to his own first bicycle at about age seven – the traditional 'age of reason':

> From gallery-grave and the hunt of a wren-king
>   to Low Mass and trailer camp
> is hardly a tick by the carbon clock, but I
>   don't count that way, nor do you:
> already it is millions of heartbeats ago
>   back to the Bicycle Age,
> before which is no *After* for me to measure,
>   just a still prehistoric *Once*
> where anything could happen. (*C.P.*, p. 687)

This Prologue touches in small space on all the major concerns of the cycle: the human imagination, its products, and their relation to time and to nature. Architecture, whose changing styles embody a changing human vision of the self, provides the appropriate instances of the human faculty, the realistic imagination that distinguishes man from other creatures in Mother Nature's Commonwealth:

>   Among its populations
> are masons and carpenters
>   who build the most exquisite shelters and safes,
> but no architects, any more

> than there are heretics or bounders: to take
> umbrage at death, to construct
> a second nature of tomb and temple, lives
> must know the meaning of *If*. (*C.P.*, pp. 687–8)

To emphasize the significance of the final phrase – that each life must exercise its own imaginative powers – Auden added a blunt, disenchanting 'Postscript' in octosyllabic couplets, deflating the contemplative mood of this poem through an unpleasant contrast in both style and attitude. This 'Postscript,' like the voice of Caliban in Ariel's domain, warns against the Romantic tendency to regard the poet in the flesh as the heroic possessor of a creative imagination.

The Romantic tendency to idealize either art or the artist is a target that Auden frequently belabors with his later vocabulary of heresies, particularly his characterization of outlooks or attitudes as Manichaean or Gnostic. *About the House* constantly warns against the undervaluing of the creaturely and mocks at a fastidiousness that seeks detachment from material things. His poem celebrating the water-closet, while attacking such fastidiousness exuberantly, finds room for an aside on its heretical roots:

> (Orthodoxy ought to
> Bless our modern plumbing:
> Swift and St. Augustine
> Lived in centuries
> When a stench of sewage
> Ever in the nostrils
> Made a strong debating
> Point for Manichees.)
> (*C.P.*, p. 700)

Auden's mockery of those who prefer their humanity idealized is aimed ultimately at the misuse of imagination by political systems idealizing a class or a race, or proposing to build future Utopias on the sufferings of those living now. In the realm of imagination he is more tolerant of Edens than of Utopias. Both are imaginatively possible; but while Edens are immediately recognizable as fanciful and are therefore innocent or harmless fun, Utopias can cause endless suffering if their agents attempt to impose them on present reality. . . . . . .

If 'Encomium Balnei' offers a fanciful Eden to be enjoyed as a respite from the daily tensions of the Pilgrim's Way, 'Up There' suggests that the attic, with its motley souvenirs, may be visited safely only by children 'who conjure in its plenum,/. . . /Now a schooner on which a lonely only/Boy sails north or approaches coral islands' (*C.P.*, p.698). For adults it encourages the false day-dream of innocence, and that sentimentality of disoriented feeling of which Rosetta in *The Age of Anxiety* supplies the representative Jungian type. It is in this Jungian context, which distinguishes consciousness as masculine and the unconscious as feminine, that the words men and women are used in the opening stanza of 'Up There':

> Men would never have come to need an attic.
> Keen collectors of glass or Roman coins build
> Special cabinets for them, dote on, index
> Each new specimen: only women cling to
> Items out of their past they have no use for,
> Can't name now what they couldn't bear to part with.
>
> *(C.P., p.697)*

The cellar on the other hand, 'deep in Mother Earth beneath her key-cold cloak,' leads through the more difficult route of the instinctive and the natural to the core of the unconscious – a route which, if braved, can be realistically fruitful.

> sometimes, to test their male courage,
> A father sends the younger boys to fetch something
> For Mother from down there; ashamed to whimper, hearts pounding,
> They dare the dank steps, re-emerge with proud faces.
>
> *(C.P., p.697)*

Approached solely at the psychological level 'Up There' and 'Down There' may be seen as minor pieces helping to fill out the cycle while permitting oblique glances at the imagination feeding on useless day-dream, or manfully accepting the realities of flesh and instinct. But their humor is more readily apparent when they are read in the light of contemporary theological discussion. The titles 'Up There' and 'Down There' are drawn from the technical vocabulary of existentialist theologians (as was the term 'out there' in 'Prime') and reflect ideas to be found in Heidegger and Tillich that were given popular currency in Bishop John Robinson's *Honest to God* (1963) at about the time Auden was composing the cycle. One theme of Robinson's book was that the traditional image of God as 'up there' or 'out there' must be abandoned in favor of a concept of God 'down there' as the depth and ground of being. *Honest to God* caused an immediate flurry of controversy in England in both press and television that drew in even the Archbishop of Canterbury.[27] Auden, who shared Tillich's view that religious thought should recognize depth psychology, would have enjoyed the controversy both for its serious and humorous aspects – so much so that if his house lacked either cellar or attic he would have felt the need to invent them to accommodate a contemporary concern. In the light of these theological concerns the final stanza of 'Down There' culminates in a parable of human and divine love:

> ... a cellar never takes umbrage;
> It takes us as we are, explorers, homebodies,
> Who seldom visit others when we don't need them.
>
> (*C.P.*, p.697)

But however close to God, a cellar may not be an ideal place for the work of the imagination in transforming insights into lasting objects. For this a 'Cave of Making,' designed to shut out the attic's daydream and the cellar's natural life and so to heighten consciousness, is essential:

> from the Olivetti portable,
> the dictionaries (the very
> best money can buy), the heaps of paper, it is evident
> what must go on. Devoid of
> flowers and family photographs, all is subordinate
> here to a function, designed to
> discourage daydreams – hence windows averted from plausible
> videnda but admitting a light one
> could mend a watch by. . . . (*C.P.*, p.691)

'The Cave of Making' becomes an elegiac monologue addressed to the shade of Louis MacNeice, with confidential asides on the present status of the poet's craft. 'This unpopular art which cannot be turned into/background noise for study/or hung as a status trophy by rising executives.' In tone, it preserves a fine balance between the understatement that characterizes all the poems in the cycle and an elegiac strain tinged with nostalgia. The movement of rhythm and syntax is masterful, except for one passage where the involutions of the syntax become too much for the speaking voice to carry effectively, and the tone, in 're the Cross,' skirts bathos – possibly for the sake of strict syllable count:

> I should like to become, if possible,
> a minor atlantic Goethe,
> with his passion for weather and stones but without his silliness
> re the Cross: at times a bore, but,
> while knowing Speech can at best, a shadow echoing
> the silent light, bear witness
> to the Truth it is not, he wished it were, as the Francophile
> gaggle of pure songsters are too vain to. (*C.P.*, p.693)

No such awkwardness mars 'Tonight at Seven-Thirty,' the poem most successful in combining the themes of the flesh, the imagination, and the spirit. . . . Although its overtones imply the ritual of a sacred meal, the literal subject of 'Tonight at Seven-Thirty' is a dinner party of our times. The poem begins with a typical sweep through evolutionary time to reach man who shares a common need for food with other creatures but who differs from them in his potentiality for gratuitous acts. Food may be necessary, but a feast is gratuitous, and is, like art, an expression of man's uniqueness. . . . . . .
The guests are '. . . men/and women who enjoy the cloop of corks, appreciate/dapatical fare, yet can see in swallowing/a sign act of reverence,/in speech a work of re-presenting/the true olamic silence' (*C.P.*, p.710). The poem itself becomes a work of re-presenting this vision of order. As an object it represents a playful order composed by *Homo Ludens*, related by analogy to the social harmony of the dinner party which is a microcosm of the ideal society, and related allegorically to the harmony of the olamic Sabbath 'when at God's board/the saints chew pickled Leviathan.' Apart from its spiritual analogies, this poem draws much of its detail from M.F.K. Fisher's 'The Perfect Dinner' in *The Art of Eating* (for which Auden provided an introduction in 1963), and it is appropriately dedicated to her.[28]
Few poets would risk 'the hallowing of the everyday' on so extensive a scale as Auden does in this cycle. Simply to carry such a scheme through without pratfall would be an accomplishment. But Auden does not merely squeeze by. He invents a style that is formally appropriate and musically compelling and that can bear repeated reading.[29] □

Written at the publication of Auden's collection *Epistle to a Godson* (1972), the next extract from Clive James's assessment of Auden's life and work is fired with enthusiasm, arguing not that his talent dwindled, but for a continuous and consistent *abundance* which, from the very start, Auden had to keep in check. Auden was a rare poet, he says: 'that most disciplined of all artistic adventurers, the man who gets sick of his own winning streak'. James basically argues that Auden was boring and outrageous, pedantic and mawkish, homely and conservative, but *on purpose*, and while it might at first seem like a commonplace description of a poet self-fashioning his personae in his poetry, James gives his argument a subtle twist. For Auden never gained kudos or critical points for his position – on the contrary, he was forever being written off and recreated by a criticism that didn't know quite what to do with him. More than a touch of exasperation enters into the tone of many reviewers as they deplore the mannerisms of the later Auden, but I think that James offers a comprehensible and useful answer which not only lets us revaluate Auden as an *historical* poet, critically aware of his own place in present and future historical and literary discourses, but also rekindles the discussion of Auden's personae by critics such as Replogle.[30] James lets us map onto Auden's life the pattern that was set up by long poems such as *The Sea and the Mirror* in the early forties, where the poet, although a dealer in words and music, was also taking a way of *silence* about which he could not, by definition, speak, but which we, through careful listening to what the poet is telling us, may detect at the heart of his work.

■ 'You don't need me to tell you what's going on,' writes W.H. Auden in his latest book's first piece, 'the ochlocratic media, joint with under-the-dryer gossip, process and vent without intermission all to-day's ugly secrets. Imageable no longer, a featureless anonymous threat from behind, to-morrow has us gallowed shitless: if what is to happen occurs according to what Thucydides defined as "human", we've had it, are in for a disaster that no four-letter words will tardy.'

This passage is highly interesting prose, detectable only in its lexical intensity as the work of a poet: Hazlitt, right on this point as on so many others, long ago laid down the word about the giveaway proneness to local effect. An ochlocracy is mob rule; the 'OED' last noticed 'joint' being used that way in 1727; to gallow is an obsolete form of to gally, which is itself a way of saying to frighten that hasn't been heard for a long time anywhere except in a whaling station; 'tardy' as a verb staggered on a few years past its moment of glory in 'A Winter's Tale' to disappear in 1623. But let's start again.

In the title poem of his latest book, W.H. Auden writes:

> . . . You don't need me to tell you what's
> going on: the ochlocratic media,
>   joint with under-the-dryer gossip,
>   process and vent without intermission
>
> all to-day's ugly secrets. Imageable
> no longer, a featureless anonymous
>   threat from behind, tomorrow has us
>   gallowed shitless: if what is to happen
>
> occurs according to what Thucydides
> defined as 'human', we've had it, are in for
>   a disaster that no four-letter
>   words will tardy. (*C.P.*, p.833)

This passage is highly interesting poetry, but only within the confines of Auden's strictly prosaic later manner. Sentences wriggle intricately and at length down the syllabic grid.

Blessed be all metrical rules that forbid automatic responses,
force us to have second thoughts, free from the fetters of Self,

(C.P., p.856)

The greatest modern verse technician, Auden long ago ran out of metrical rules needing more than a moment's effort to conform to.
Technically, his later manner – which involves setting up a felt rhythmic progress inside an arbitrary syllabic convention – is really a way
of restoring to the medium some of the resistance his virtuosity earlier
wiped out. This technical mortification is closely allied with the ethical stand forbidding any irrationalities, all happy accidents. No
automatic responses, no first thoughts. Helping to explain the omission of certain poems from his 'Collected Shorter Poems 1927–1957',
Auden wrote in 1966:

A dishonest poem is one which expresses, no matter how well,
feelings or beliefs which its author never felt or entertained. For
example, I once expressed a desire for 'New styles of architecture';
but I have never liked modern architecture. I prefer old styles, and
one must be honest even about one's prejudices. Again, and much
more shamefully, I once wrote:

History to the defeated
may say alas but cannot help nor pardon.

(The English Auden, p.212)

To say this is to equate goodness with success. It would have been
bad enough if I had ever held this wicked doctrine, but that I
should have stated it simply because it sounded to me rhetorically
effective is quite inexcusable.[31]

Glumly reconciling themselves to the loss of 'September 1, 1939' in its
entirety and favourite fragments from other poems engraved in the
consciousness of a generation, critics respectfully conceded Auden's
right to take back what he had so freely given. It was interesting,
though, that no strong movement arose to challenge Auden's assumption that these youthful poetic crimes were committed by the same self
being dishonest, rather than a different self being honest. Auden was
denying the pluralism of his own personality. It was his privilege to
do so if he wanted to, but it was remarkable how tamely this crankily
simplistic reinterpretation of his own creative self-hood was accepted.
    More remarkable still, however, was the virtual silence which
greeted the spectacle of a great modern talent disallowing the automatic response, proclaiming the virtues of knowing exactly what you

mean against the vices of letting the poem find out what it wants to mean. Auden had apparently worked his way through to the last sentence of the *Tractatus Logico-Philosophicus*. 'Wovon man nicht sprechen kann', Wittgenstein had written, 'darüber muss man schweigen'. What we cannot speak about we must pass over in silence. It was piquant to find the poet who above all others seemed to command the secret of modern magic occupying this position so very long after the philosopher who thought of it had moved out. Here was a man attacking the validity of his own serendipity, discrediting his own trick of setting up a bewitching resonance. Long before, combining with Louis MacNeice in preparing that seductive lash-up of a book *Letters from Iceland*, Auden had written:

> And the traveller hopes: 'Let me be far from any
> Physician'; And the poets have names for the sea;

But on the way to press this was accidentally transformed into

> And the traveller hopes: 'Let me be far from any
> Physician'; And the ports have names for the sea;
> (*The English Auden*, p. 203)

Noting straight away that 'ports' suggested more than 'poets', Auden let the slip stand. The names that ports have for the sea are likely to be functional as well as mythical, mistrustful as well as admiring, many-rooted rather than casually appropriate – in a word, serious. Or so we guess. Or so the unexpected ring of the word, its unpredictability in that context, leads us to conjecture – gives us *room* to conjecture. And this thinking-space, the parkland of imagination that existed in Auden's earlier manner, was what marked it out – and what he annihilated in forming his later manner. There have been artists who possessed some of Auden's magic and who went on to lose it, but it is hard to think of anyone who deliberately suppressed it. All conscious artists feel the urge to refine what is unique in their work, but few interpret this call to refine as a command to eliminate. Unless we are dealing with a self-destructive enthusiast – and Auden on the face of it can scarcely be categorized as one of those – then we are up against that most disciplined of all artistic adventurers, the man who gets sick of his own winning streak.

Pick up a Photostat of the 1928 *Poems* and read it through[32] (it takes about twenty minutes): was there ever a more capacious young talent? It goes beyond precocity.

We saw in Spring
The frozen buzzard
Flipped down the weir and carried out to sea.
Before the trees threw shadows down in challenge
To snoring midges. Before the autumn came
To focus stars more sharply in the sky
In Spring we saw
The bulb pillow
Raising the skull,
Thrusting a crocus through clenched teeth.

(The English Auden, p.437)

Hindsight lends us prescience, but it is permissible to claim that merely on the basis of this passage's first three lines we would have pronounced the writer capable of virtually anything. The way the turn from the second line into the third kinetically matches the whole stated action is perfect and obviously instinctive – what other men occasionally achieve was all there as a gift.

The sprinkler on the lawn
Weaves a cool vertigo, and stumps are drawn; . . .

(The English Auden, p.437)

Elated by the effortless lyricism of a coup like this, we need to remember not just Auden's age, but the time. Yeats had not yet finished forming the compact musicality of his last phase, and the authoritative clarities of the first of Eliot's Quartets were still years away. Auden got this sonic drive absolutely from out of the blue. The plainest statement he could make seemed to come out as poetry:

Nor was that final, for about that time
Gannets blown over northward, going home . . .

(The English Auden, p.24)

It was a Shakespearean gift, not just in magnitude but in its unsettling – and unsettling especially to its possessor – characteristic of making anything said sound truer than true. In all of English poetry it is difficult to think of any other poet who turned out permanent work so early – and whose work seemed so tense with the obligation to be permanent. In his distinguished essay on Auden, John Bayley penetratingly pointed out that it was not in Auden's creative stance ever to admit to being young. What has not yet sufficiently been noticed is that it was not in the nature of Auden's talent to win sympathy by fumbling towards an effect – to claim the privileges of the not yet weathered, or traffic in the pathos of an art in search of its object. Instant accomplishment denied him a creative adolescence. As always in Auden, ethics and techniques were bound up together. Barely out of his teens, he was already trying to discipline, rather than exploit, the artistic equivalent of a Midas touch. It is for this reason that the 'Scrutiny' group's later limiting judgments and dismissals of Auden were wrong-headed as well as insensitive: they were branding as permanently undergraduate the one major modern gift which had never been content with its own cleverness for a moment. They missed the drama of Auden's career in the 1930s and 1940s, never realizing that the early obscurity and the later bookishness were both ways of distancing, rather than striving after, effect. The moral struggle in Auden was fought out between what was possible to his gift and what he thought allowable to it: the moralists, looking for struggles of a different kind, saw in his work nothing but its declarative self-assurance. The more he worked for ironic poise, the more they detected incorrigible playfulness. Subsequent critical systems, had they been applied, would not have fared much better. Suppose, for example, that our standards of the desirable in poetry are based on the accurate registration of worldly things. We would think, in that case, that a man who had come from the frozen buzzards of 1928 to the etymological fossicking of 1972 had moved from the apex of an art to the base. But suppose the ability to send frozen birds flipping over the mind's weir came too easily to be gone on with? What then?

[Cites: 'Doom is dark and deeper than any sea-dingle . . . an unquiet bird' (*C.P.*, p. 62)]

Quoted from the first public edition of *Poems*, this stanza was the kind of thing which made Auden the hero of the young intelligentsia. Noteworthy, though, is the way in which the enchanting declarative evocation discussed above is painstakingly avoided. The stanza's rhythmic progress is as dazzlingly erratic as a skyrocket toppled from its bottle. The switchback syntax, the Hardyesque hyphenated compounds – they pack things tight, and the reader is never once allowed to draw an inattentive breath. One of the many triumphs of Auden's first public volume was that this difficult verse came to be regarded as equally characteristic with the simpler felicities that were everywhere apparent.

Beams from your car may cross a bedroom wall.
They wake no sleeper; you may hear the wind
Arriving driven from the ignorant sea.
To hurt itself on pane, on bark of elm
Where sap unbaffled rises, being spring. (*C.P.*, p. 33)

Merely to mention the headlight beams crossing the wall was enough to create them for the reader's dazzled eye. But Auden's maturity had already arrived: he was well aware that such moments were not to be thought of as the high points of poetry – rather as the rest points. Take, for example, these lines from 'Prologue', the opening poem of his 1936 collection *Look, Stranger!*

And make us as Newton was, who in his garden watching
The apple falling towards England, became aware
Between himself and her of an eternal tie.
(The English Auden, p. 119)

The apple falling towards England is superb, but poetry which had such effects as a *raison d'être* would be a menace. This very instance has in fact come under critical attack – an accusation of decadence has been levelled. But it should be obvious that Auden had no intention of allowing such facility to become fatal. Set against it were the inhibitors; syntactical, grammatical, lexical. And with them they brought ambiguity, resonance, areas of doubt and discovery – all the things his later poetry was to lose. The suggestiveness of Auden's poetry lay in the tension between his primal lyricism and the means employed to discipline it. The suggestiveness couldn't survive if either term went missing. And eventually it was the lyricism that went.

Looking through the individual collections of Auden's poems, each in succession strikes us as transitional. On each occasion there seems to be a further move towards paraphrasable clarity. Even at the height of his bookish phase (in, say, *New Year Letter*) Auden is still being more narrowly clear than he was before. Gradually, as we read on to the end, we see what kind of progress this has been. It has been a movement away from excitement and towards satisfaction.

Epistle to a Godson is like *About the House* and *City Without Walls* in being utterly without the excitement we recognize as Audenesque. And yet it, like them, gives a peculiar satisfaction: the patriarch grunts, having seen much and come a long way. The book is flat champagne, but it's still champagne. Part of Auden's genius was to know the necessity of chastening his talent, ensuring that his poetry would be something more enduring than mere magic. The resource and energy he devoted to containing and condensing his natural lyricism provide one of the great dramas in modern literary history. Pick up *Look, Stranger!* or *Another Time* – they read like thrillers. Every poem instantly establishes its formal separateness from all the others. Through Auden's work we trace not just themes but different ways of getting something unforgettably said: the poem's workings are in the forefront of attention. Finally the contrast between the early and the late manners is itself part of the drama. To understand Auden fully, we need to understand how a man with the capacity to say anything should want to escape from the oppression of meaning too much. Late Auden is the completion of a technical evolution in which technique has always been thought of as an instrument of self-denial. What Auden means by the fetters of Self is the tyranny of an ungoverned talent, and his late poetry is a completed testament to the self-control which he saw the necessity for from the very start – the most commendable precocity of all.[33] □

James gives us a sense of the precarious task facing critical commentators on Auden. A poet prepared to anticipate and second-guess his critics, or to leave them knotted in the paradoxes of his faith must be treated respectfully, not as a passive object awaiting critical dissection. James's comments must also make us wary of the over-serious approach, and imply that we need to be prepared to enter (like Smith and McDiarmid, for example) into the games that poetry and criticism play with language, identity and history. In the next chapter I consider how criticism of Auden has met the challenge of his poetry.

CHAPTER SEVEN

Summary of Critical Texts

A COLLECTION of criticism presents the views of many people, but by its nature the author or poet (often dead) has little to say and tends to remain passive while his or her work is discussed, analysed, criticised. It seems fitting then, to allow Auden to say a few words about critics and criticism here, as it places a useful frame around what is to follow. In his essay 'Reading' (*The Dyer's Hand*) Auden considers what is at stake in the relation between the poet and the critical statement, setting up a two-way link between poet and critic that should always be kept in mind. His poetry and his prose present a consistent probing challenge to *our* position as reader and critic, a challenge to consider our desires and needs as well as his own and those of his personae.

■ If I were to attempt to write down the names of all the poets and novelists for whose work I am really grateful because I know that if I had not read them my life would be poorer, the list would take up pages. But when I try to think of all the critics for whom I am really grateful, I find myself with a list of thirty-four names. Of these, twelve are German and only two French. Does this indicate a conscious bias? It does.

If good literary critics are rarer than good poets or novelists, one reason is the nature of human egoism. A poet or a novelist has to learn to be humble in the face of his subject matter which is life in general. But the subject matter of a critic, before which he has to learn to be humble, is made up of authors, that is to say, of human individuals, and this kind of humility is much more difficult to acquire. It is far easier to say 'Life is more important than anything I can say about it' – than to say – 'Mr. A's work is more important than anything I can say about it'.

There are people who are too intelligent to become authors, but they do not become critics.

Authors can be stupid enough, God knows, but they are not always quite so stupid as a certain kind of critic seems to think. The kind of critic, I mean, to whom, when he condemns a work or a passage, the possibility never occurs that its author may have foreseen exactly what he is going to say.

What is the function of a critic? So far as I am concerned, he can do me one or more of the following services:

1) Introduce me to authors or works of which I was hitherto unaware.

2) Convince me that I have undervalued an author or a work because I had not read them carefully enough.

3) Show me relations between works of different ages and cultures which I could never have seen for myself because I do not know enough and never shall.

4) Give a 'reading' of a work which increases my understanding of it.

5) Throw light upon the process of artistic 'Making'.

6) Throw light upon the relation of art to life, to science, economics, ethics, religion, etc.[1] □

Auden's criteria are met, off and on, throughout the criticism of his own work, and I will sketch out an overview of some of the key works – this will not mean that they are automatically *good* works, but that they form an important part of the Auden critical canon.

Firstly, a word about John Fuller's *A Reader's Guide to W.H. Auden* that appeared in 1970 and immediately became an invaluable resource for anyone interested in tracing ideas and meanings in Auden's more intractable verse. Fuller arranged the text to be read alongside the *Collected Shorter Poetry* and the *Collected Longer Poetry* and as such had to ignore variants, and some poems are not discussed at all. This is amended in the 1998 *W.H. Auden: A Commentary* in which Fuller revises the earlier text, and says something about practically all the poetry that Auden published. Both of these texts provide the reader with an intelligent companion that offers sensible readings of, and contextual references for, the poetry.

Biographies

A foundation stone of the critical canon is the biography, and all biographers must deal with the awkward fact that Auden specifically asked that a biography should *not* be written after he died. In 1964, Auden wrote that the 'man of action', a statesman or a general, 'is identical with his biography', because, as a 'doer', he has an essentially uncomplicated relationship to the textual representation of his life.

■ In the case of any kind of artist, however, who is a maker not a doer, his biography, the story of his life, and the history of his works are distinct.² □

Auden suggests that the artist is *already* written into other representations (his or her poetry, novels, or paintings for example) and that a biography produces a set of complex doublings too easily conflated or misread. The biographer and his readers must realise, says Auden, that a biography 'throws no light whatsoever upon the artist's work'. He then put the problem back into flux:

■ The relation between his life and his works is at one and the same time too self-evident to require comment – every work of art is, in one sense, a self-disclosure – and too complicated ever to unravel. □

The writer's position is at once too obvious and too complex, the work of art is a 'self-disclosure' that contains a secret that is 'too complicated ever to unravel'. The writer can never be identical with his biography, and this elusive difference serves as the fundamental contradiction that haunts the three major works of biography to date.

The first is Charles Osborne's *W.H. Auden: The Life of a Poet* (1980) which was written from the perspective of one who knew the poet personally. This is a reasonable attempt to deal with the life and the work, and its intimacy often helps the narrative rather than hinders it. The main work is Humphrey Carpenter's *W.H. Auden: A Biography* (1981) which combines the work of a skilled biographer with that of a competent literary critic. Most of the picture of Auden that we have today is due to Carpenter's work, and he will be cited invaluably in critical works that try to get behind the scenes of a poem or a play.

Richard Davenport-Hines's biography *Auden* (1995) introduces the poet into the contemporary critical climate in a text that genuinely extends Carpenter's work and that admits the importance of the earlier biographer to his own project. Davenport-Hines is also aware of his responsibility to Auden's views on biography and wary of reproducing facile anecdotes: 'In this biography I have never tried to vilify or diminish my subject, indeed I think that to do so is decadent and envious.'³ I think that Auden would have approved of such an attitude, and Davenport-Hines maintains a shrewd, critical but respectful stance throughout.

In 1975 Stephen Spender edited an interesting collection of biographical and critical essays which appeared as *W.H. Auden: A Tribute*. These essays are full of useful and idiosyncratic biographical material, as Auden is remembered by those who knew him at all stages of his life. The collection edited by Alan Bold, *W.H. Auden: The Far Interior* (1985) (which contains Walter Perrie's 'Auden's Politics' which is extracted in chapter four), also has an essay by the biographer Charles Osborne on 'Auden as Christian Poet' and an extremely interesting piece by Donald Pearce which remembers Auden as a teacher at Ann Arbor in Michigan in 1941: 'Fortunate Fall: W. H. Auden at Michigan'.

In a poet whose biographical story forms such an integral yet paradoxically distinct part of his work, these texts are extremely useful for building up a picture of Auden's development as a poet, especially the early trips to Berlin where the young man soaked up new ideas at the same time as exploring his sexuality in the gay bars. Here, Norman Page's joint biography, *Auden and Isherwood: The Berlin Years* (1998), which concentrates on the sexual and historical impact of Berlin on the two writers, is particularly useful. The relationship to Chester Kallman is another vital narrative which the biographies describe in some detail. Kallman is implicated in all of Auden's work from 1939 on, and Auden's religious and aesthetic stance is inextricably woven into the story of sexual infidelity and spiritual faith which Kallman represents.

In an entertaining and perceptive essay, 'Auden Askew', Barbara Everett examines the differences between scholar, critic, biographer and historian, and considers the different ways that they deal with the fact and the symbol, and how the over- and under-valuing of one or the other produces anomalies in their works.[4] This is a probing essay that chimes with Auden's own scepticism about the modes of critical discourse to which he was prey. Other entertaining reminiscences include Dorothy Farnan's *Auden in Love* (1984), Thekla Clark's *Wystan and Chester* (1995), Harold Norse's *Memoirs of a Bastard Angel* (1990) and a rather grumpy and disappointed memoir by A. L. Rowse, *The Poet Auden* (1987).

Book Length Studies

Richard Hoggart produced the first full-length book on Auden in 1951; his *Auden: An Introductory Essay* was aimed at the general reader of poetry, who might find

■ that this is a very partial account, that I have not understood some things, and have, no doubt, misinterpreted others[5]. □

But it was a brave attempt at the entire Auden *oeuvre* up to 1950, undertaken without the aid of the guides and scholarship that the modern researcher has to hand. It is interesting to note that Hoggart divides up his study between the 'American' poetry, and the poetry written before Auden left England, as if it were an intrinsically different entity. Michael Wood's comments later in this chapter are pertinent here, pointing out that the division between the English and the American poet is more a matter of critical convenience than a substantial quality of the work. Published in 1957, Joseph Warren Beach's *The Making of the Auden Canon* gives us the first systematic exploration of the changes that the later Auden made to his work up to the late fifties. In the summarising section 'The Question of Identity' Beach demonstrates the difficulties facing later readers who want to assess the political poems of the late thirties, but which Auden altered to conform to the religious context of the mid forties. Beach's criticism rests on an assumption that there is a perceptible, recognisable and consistent *centre* to the early poetry, which is sustained by the conjunction of Auden's thought with the historical moment in which it was written. Beach argues that the later revisions in some ways betray the coherence of the earlier situation, and such a reading remains aware of an awkward and ungainly insertion of a later mode of thinking into poems that were never made to wear such ideas.

■ Even more dismaying was the transformation made in the satirically intended Vicar's Sermon in *The Dog Beneath the Skin* when it was solemnly served up among other edifying dishes in the *Collected Poetry*. The fault in artistry here is in supposing that a piece written in this style, to expose the employment of ecclesiastical rhetoric for morally questionable ends, can, without the slightest change, be made to serve for serious spiritual edification. I suppose the reason why this prodigious sleight of hand has gone unnoticed is that serious readers of 'Depravity: A Sermon' were not acquainted with the play in which it first made its appearance. Or more likely, there have been no devout readers of Auden's poetry who have taken this piece of prose seriously enough, or read it with close enough attention, to have realized its absurdity. In the case of the Vicar's sermon, Auden in reprinting told us in a prefatory note just how he wished the piece to be understood. For the most part, with such questionable work where it is reproduced with little or no revision, he simply leaves it to its new setting to suggest an interpretation conformable to the sounder views of his maturity.[6] □

I am not suggesting Beach as a model for considering the revisions, but as an indication of what was at stake in the critical discourses of the time, when Auden changed and dispersed the apparent coherence of his earlier work. Beach remains sure that the Vicar's Sermon is offered seriously in the *Collected Poetry* of 1945. It is this kind of certainty that Auden disrupts, and the entire act of revision is one that puts the body of his work in crisis. Poems initially headed with austere Roman numerals return in the *Collected Poetry* with camp quips as titles. This tended to compound the temporal disorientation that Auden caused by placing his poems in a delightfully perverse alphabetical order in order to dissuade would-be critics from detecting any false development or falling away in his work.

This is our problem, and one that any student of Auden's work must confront. The material in the innocent looking *Collected Shorter Poems* is full of changes – and the poems are lumped into loose chronological categories, and carry disorienting titles. It is important to go back to the original volumes, if only to get a sense of the immediate context in which the poems were presented (see Appendix for a list of collection titles and dates). This is why Mendelson's *The English Auden* is such an indispensable resource, listing as it does the contents of the collections up to 1940, and placing significant alterations and excisions in an appendix.

Monroe K. Spears wrote *The Poetry of W.H. Auden: The Disenchanted Island* in 1963, and it forms one of the first comprehensive overviews of the poet's work. Spears looks carefully at Auden's religious work as well as providing a clear and cogent introduction to Auden's poetry (see Spears's piece in chapter five of this Guide). Spears's well chosen *Auden: A Collection of Critical Essays* (1964) helped to consolidate the importance and stature of Auden's career. In his Introduction, Spears announces a new era in Auden criticism, noting that the landscape had been too severely dominated by the sceptical opinion of Leavis, and that it was time that new voices began to be heard, voices that would confirm the status of Auden's poetry without relying on assumptions made by this influential critic who remained disappointed by Auden's refusal to 'grow up'. There are some good essays in this collection from Stephen Spender, Edmund Wilson, Edward Callan and Cleanth Brooks. Spears makes a case for a new critical tone which wants to break out of the established frame. Of the negative criticism he says:

■ The cumulative effect of the criticism I have described [Leavis and Jarrell] has been to create the widespread impression that Auden has been 'proved' guilty of immaturity, frivolity, irresponsibility, and other vices, and is therefore not to be taken seriously. Minor critics speak of him with condescension and refer knowingly to his inverted development, his changes of ideology, and his mutilation of his earlier poetry when he deserted politics for religion. It is no wonder that Auden has always been skittish about critics and, though he himself has written a very large amount of criticism and is certainly one of the major critics of our time, has been unwilling until very recently to appear in the role by publishing a volume of selected criticism.[7] □

Spears does not try to be representative in this collection, and therefore there is no 'negative' criticism. Instead, he chose 'only those essays that seem to me both illuminating and likely to retain some permanent value'.

In 1965 John G. Blair argued in his *The Poetic Art of W.H. Auden* that the 'major failing' of criticism has resulted from 'a refusal to look at the art of his poetry as distinguished from the ideas it expresses or implies'. Blair wanted to build 'a sense of the fundamental aesthetic attitudes and practices that have guided his poetry to date' which he claims are 'anti-Romantic'. Blair singled out Beach for criticism, sensing that although the 'demand for wholeness or consistency is appropriate and reasonable' it is not so when the critic 'set[s] the terms within which the poet must be consistent'.[8] Blair takes issue with Beach again in an article in *Shenandoah*, 'W.H. Auden: The Poem as Performance' (1965), which tries to shift critical attention away from articulating a single fixed meaning, towards an understanding of the importance of the performative creation of meanings which occurs each time a poem is read. (See chapter two for Blair's piece on Auden's light verse.)

Blair's book followed his 1962 Ph.D. dissertation on Auden and is one of a series of works that constitute the American academic boom in the Auden industry of the 1960s. Other academic critics such as Edward Callan, Justin Replogle, Herbert Greenberg, Edward Mendelson and Richard Johnson all wrote dissertations on Auden, and when the fruit of their work appeared as books later in the decade, they had established the study of Auden's poetry as a professional academic activity to be taken seriously.

Herbert Greenberg in *Quest for the Necessary: W.H. Auden and the Dilemma of Divided Consciousness* (1968) explores the poetry through what he sees as a key aspect of the poet's work: 'Divided consciousness, I would suggest, is more than a controlling idea in Auden's thought; it is the principal subject matter of his poetry, and it provides the conceptual foundation for his way of looking at things.' Greenberg charts the divided consciousness through Auden's poetry from the early stage of Love as 'a gratification of energies' and thus necessary, through to a Marxist inflection where 'freedom means "consciousness of necessity", a developing knowledge not only of the world but of the self'.[9] Auden's later religious interpretation of necessity is summed up when Greenberg suggests that the poet's 'hopes are no longer informed by a belief in knowledge as our ultimate salvation. He has discovered that to know the good is not necessarily to will it, and in this fact there stands revealed for him our dependence upon God.'

As well as Gerald Nelson's *Changes of Heart: A Study of the Poetry of W.H. Auden*, a book that considers the developing *personae* in Auden's poetry, 1969 saw the publication of Justin Replogle's *Auden's Poetry*. Replogle begins by stating: 'If, as Auden sometimes says, poetry is a kind of game, then criticism is talk about the game.'[10] Replogle explores aspects of the playful, the hidden, and the anti-poet in Auden's poetry, and makes good use of the potential for uncertainty and dialogic exchange in the poems.[11] Two large chapters on 'The Pattern of Ideas' and 'The Pattern of

Personae' open up many possibilities for Auden critics, as well as explain many of the private jokes and associations with which the young Auden peppered his poetry. The tension between the poet and anti-poet, regardless of whether this is simply a critical device constructed to 'talk about the game' of poetry, is nevertheless a useful theme to use in order to break down the sense of monolithic meaning in Auden's poetry, and paves the way for contemporary, post-structuralist readings of Auden's work.

Also in 1969, part of the *Twayne United States Authors Series*, George T. Wright's *W.H. Auden* provides a useful historical overview of the poet's work from all periods, while George W. Bahlke's *The Later Auden: From 'New Year Letter' to 'About the House'* (1970) was the first book to deal exclusively with the later poetry, and provides some detailed analysis of Auden's return to faith and his 'relation to Christian thought'.

In his book *The Case of the Helmeted Airman* (1972) François Duchene considers Auden's work as a process of decline. What is interesting here is the way that Duchene keeps finding exceptions to prove his own argument wrong.

■ Yet such a simple conclusion is not borne out by the quality of the best later poems. They may be different from the earlier ones, riper, less dynamic, but it is impossible to say they are less good. Some poems like 'Vespers', 'Under Which Lyre', 'Woods', 'The Willow-wren and The Stare', 'In Praise of Limestone' and a sizable number of others are as fine as anything Auden has done.[12] □

In 1973 Frederick Buell's *W.H. Auden as a Social Poet* looked carefully at the social and political aspects of Auden's work and career, while Richard A. Johnson's *Man's Place: An Essay on Auden,* published in the same year, examined the poetry from a philosophical position – poems being a 'primary mode of discovering and knowing'.

Auden's literary executor Edward Mendelson has played a major part in shaping the thinking about Auden's poetry, not only by presenting that work to readers through his careful editing of the *Complete Works of W.H. Auden* series which is ongoing, but with two substantial biographical/critical texts: *Early Auden*, and *Later Auden*. In 1981 Mendelson published *Early Auden*, 'a history and interpretation of W.H. Auden's work up to 1939, the year he left England for America'. Mendelson's thorough knowledge of the poetry and his familiarity with the letters and notebooks left behind at the poet's death has lent to his work a precision that results in readings which feel, at times, too close and claustrophobic for comfort, but the integrity and intelligence are obvious. The pattern and mutation of Auden's ideas about history and necessity are looked at in detail, and many poems are explored and explicated. This book provides an excellent immersion into Auden's world in the thirties and helps to unfold many of the mysterious references and allusions in the early work. Mendelson's scholarship is represented in this Guide in chapter five where he discusses Auden's notorious revisions.

1981 also saw the publication of an interesting book by Donald Mitchell, *Britten and Auden in the Thirties: The Year 1936* (originally the 'T. S. Eliot Memorial Lectures' given at the University of Kent). Mitchell discusses the relation between the poet and the composer in an enthusiastic and refreshing tone, admitting when Auden's difficult meanings get the better of him. This slice of the thirties focuses the way that the political encroached onto every aspect of the artists' work, and Mitchell's close reading of settings such as 'Our Hunting Fathers' and the cabaret songs produces an alternative perspective on these poems and songs.

Edward Callan's *Auden: A Carnival of Intellect* (1983) provided a long-awaited exploration of Auden's work in a sound philosophical and religious frame. Callan reads Auden's texts with sympathetic intelligence and provides an important context for the more difficult poems such as *The Age of Anxiety*. Callan argued that it was no longer useful to assess Auden next to the contemporary poets who had been considered as the 'Auden Group' (Spender, Day-Lewis, MacNeice), but that he was 'more aptly classed in the company of Pope and Wren whose names recall an age'.[13] Callan's main representation in this Guide comes in chapter six when he discusses the 1965 collection *About the House*.

Michael Sidnell's extensive survey of Auden's work in the theatre, *Dances of Death: The Group Theatre of London in the Thirties*, appeared in 1984 and provides a detailed and intelligent introduction to Auden's dramatic politics. Sidnell provides a fascinating insight – literally 'behind the scenes' – as Auden and Isherwood are attracted by the lure of the 'West End'. Sidnell also discusses Eliot's involvement in the Group Theatre and it is instructive to read that Auden's *The Dance of Death* was performed on the same programme as Eliot's *Sweeney Agonistes* in 1935, as once again the interaction between Eliot and Auden is shown to be an active one. See Sidnell's discussion of Auden's play *The Dance of Death* in chapter four of this Guide.

Stan Smith introduced the world of post-structuralist theory into Auden's poetry with his important little book, *W.H. Auden* (1985), which was part of the *Re-Reading Literature* series. Auden's poetry, as well as his life, were radically recast as being predominantly *discursive* entities, and as such demanded a different kind of reading, that moved away from discussions of intentionality, and embraced instead *intertextual* ideas and effects that the poetry produced. What this book confirmed was that Auden's poetry had been treated for too long as a passive medium when in fact it had been actively undermining much of the criticism that had been placed around it. Auden's poetry emerges from Smith's book as far more radical and political than a quasi-biographical account of Auden's 'conversion' could produce. Here, the separation of the author from the work is used in a positive (and only occasionally reductive) way, and confirms the value of Auden's work to a post-structuralist critical field. Smith is represented in this Guide in chapters two and six.

Lucy McDiarmid begins her 1990 book *Auden's Apologies for Poetry* with the remark that 'Auden's work is more important than anything I can say about it'.[14] The book looks at the way that Auden addressed the problem of the relation between art and life that his religious beliefs demanded from him. McDiarmid confirms that 'Auden writes against the grain of most people who talk about art' and proceeds to assess the importance of 'frivolity' in Auden: 'Auden's justification of frivolity is not frivolous', thus opening out aspects of what Replogle had earlier acknowledged as the 'game' that gets played out between poetry and its criticism. McDiarmid concludes her Preface with an admission:

■ By reading Auden, who confidently calls poetry frivolous and play-ful, this book can indulge in the elaborate and harmless pleasures of criticism, acknowledging here its separation from the larger extrapoetic world where, as Auden says, heroes roar and die, and the 'lion's mouth whose hunger/No metaphors can fill' waits to be satisfied.[15] □

This is an important work, I think, as it takes the time to look carefully at that self-conscious mirroring that takes place when a poet discusses poetry in a poem. McDiarmid explores Auden's faith in chapter five of this Guide, and two key poems – 'The Shield of Achilles' and 'In Praise of Limestone' – in chapter six.

In 1990 the first of the scholarly *Auden Studies* (OUP) was published. *W.H. Auden: 'The Map of all my Youth', Auden Studies 1*, edited by Katherine Bucknell and Nicholas Jenkins, opens an intelligent series that focuses on different, but themed aspects of Auden's work. Alongside scrupulously edited, previously unpublished material (poems, lectures and letters by Auden, for example) there are symposia on particular poems, and articles on specific topics. Apart from those mentioned throughout this Guide, notable essays include 'Everything Turns Away: Auden's Surrealism' by David Pascoe (*Auden Studies 2*) and Katherine Bucknell's Introduction to Auden's lecture, 'Phantasy and Reality in Poetry', in which she discusses Auden's relation to Freud (*Auden Studies 3*). *Auden Studies* also provides a locus for Mendelson's bibliographic updates.

John R. Boly, in his *Reading Auden: The Returns of Caliban* (1991) adopts a post-structuralist position in the stress on reading that his title implies. Some of his readings are credible, some are more far-fetched (see the extract from his reading of 'In Praise of Limestone' in chapter six of this Guide), but this is precisely the point in a book that begins from the premise that 'W. H. Auden wrote his poetry to help people become more aware of what happens when they read'. When he uses Bakhtin's concept of dialogism (that any utterance, even by a solitary person, involves an implied dialogue and response) he suggests that Auden's poetry resists the 'tyranny of poetic genres' by retaining 'an acute sense of more elusive textual interiors, the realm of an utterance's topography that remain open to poetic dialogism'.[16] Here the earlier work of critics such as Replogle (poet/anti-poet) and Blair (poem as performance) can be rethought through Boly's contemporary frame. Boly's criticism of Randall Jarrell's schematic reading of Auden's work appears in chapter two of this Guide.

The poet Anthony Hecht wrote his *The Hidden Law: The Poetry of W.H. Auden* in 1993 and it remains a substantial work that reads the poetry carefully and with an attention to the many subtexts and intertexts from which Auden produced his work. Hecht views the critic as 'a kind of code-breaker, a *soi disant* Champollion whose sustaining energy derives from the conviction, not always justified, that he has rent the veil and seen to the heart of the mystery'.[17] This is a series of loving and generous readings in which the poems discussed are teased into relevance by an enquiring and committed voice.

Mendelson completed his survey of Auden's work with his *Later Auden* (1999) and again the same careful and detailed attention has been applied to the later works. Here, an extract from Michael Wood's review of *Later Auden* from *The London Review of Books* gives a sense of the questions that Mendelson asks in this work:

■ But the critical question, which Mendelson addresses throughout his book, is really whether Auden had got worse, whether the 'English Auden', a person of glittering, memorable talent, had disappeared without a trace, leaving only a fussy, well-regarded, comfortable 'American Auden' in his place. Auden himself was clear enough. 'If by memorability, you mean a poem like "Sept 1st, 1939", I pray to God that I shall never be memorable again.' But maybe he just decided not to be memorable again, and wasn't. And since he kept insisting he was a minor poet perhaps he was. There is a dangerous moment when Mendelson's defence of the later Auden almost caves in on itself. 'Auden had perfected a technique of writing about the darkest possible subjects in a tone that deceived real or imaginary enemies into thinking him too mild and avuncular to bother contending with.' With a technique like that you could deceive your real and imaginary friends too, but Mendelson goes on to say that Auden had learned this tactic from Frost and the danger is over, or at least diminished. It is possible to sound light about dark subjects, and simple about complicated ones. It's also possible to trivialise important subjects, and Auden was pretty good at that too, but Mendelson is not arguing that he didn't trivialise, only that he didn't always trivialise once he was in America. I don't think the critical argument really pits the English Auden against the American, the early against the later. It pits the English Auden and the early American one, say up to 1948, against the Auden after that and it asks how many good poems he wrote in his last 25 years. This means we don't have to argue about the elegies for Yeats and Freud (1939), *New Year Letter* (1940), *The Sea and the Mirror* (1944), 'In Praise of Limestone' (1948), and much else. But we do have to look at 'The Shield of Achilles' (1952) and 'Horae Canonicae' (1949–1954), and Mendelson makes large claims for 'First Things First' (1957) and 'River Profile' (1966). 'Horae Canonicae', he says is 'arguably' Auden's greatest work, 'the richest and deepest of his poems about the fatal irreversible acts of the human will'. 'First Things First' is an 'imposingly great poem'; 'River Profile' is 'the greatest poem of his last years, and one of the greatest and strangest poems of its century'.[18] □

Once more we see the difficulty faced by Auden's critics in assessing his tone. As Wood notes, Mendelson skirts a 'dangerous moment' when his argument nearly 'caves in on itself'. Why does this happen? Because over the years, Auden had constructed a series of ambiguous personae that made it almost impossible to be sure not only if he was a major or a minor poet, or if he was talking seriously or flippantly, but whether he was defending himself against his enemies, or preventing the over-quick comprehension of his friends.

Collections of Essays and Articles in Journals

Refer to the bibliography for a listing of essay collections, articles, introductory books and other related texts that discuss Auden's work.

* * *

Despite the slow sedimentation of critical material that has built up over Auden's poetry from the earliest privately published *Poems* (1928) to the posthumous *Thank You Fog* (1974), his work remains peculiarly resistant to grand explanatory schemes and final judgements. In part this is due to the playful, protean nature of many of his poems and critical statements, and in part because Auden took the trouble to build into his work a rigorous questioning of the way the world works – a questioning that would include the very criticism applied to his work. In his 1935 essay 'Psychology and Art To-Day', Auden claimed that 'To a situation of danger and difficulty there are five solutions', and listed them thus:

■ **(1) To sham dead: The idiot.**
(2) To retire into a life of phantasy: The schizophrene.
(3) To panic, i.e., to wreak one's grudge upon society: The criminal.
(4) To excite pity, to become ill: The invalid.
(5) To understand the mechanism of the trap: The scientist and the artist. (*The English Auden*, p. 335) □

I like to think that when Auden left his poetry to take its chance in the world after his death, he had left it with the skills of the scientist and artist – to 'understand the mechanism of the trap', a trap of which it was at once the maker and the bait.

CHAPTER EIGHT

Conclusion

THE CRITICAL material represented in this Guide bears out Stan Smith's argument in chapter two that 'The Auden we perceive as a historical figure is also the product of discourses which run through and beyond him'.[1] To describe Auden as such a 'product' does no disservice to a poet who maintained a self-conscious awareness of the power that circulated between the critical, biographical and aesthetic discourses from which he was made. Auden was also aware that 'The words of a dead man/Are modified in the guts of the living' in increasingly complex ways when, after his death, the poet is transformed into an historical *object* and banished to the margins of his own work. Auden's resistance to this kind of historical treatment makes him an exciting poet to study in our contemporary critical context.

There can be no definitive Auden, he made sure of that himself by revising and scrapping poems that left his *ouevre* peppered with important strategic omissions. But the poems are still available, and the fact that they could never be *physically* suppressed suggests that the censorship of the older poet retains a *performative*[2] aspect which leaves the meanings of their revision in flux.

A poet whose work presents such an 'open architecture' to the reader will offer plenty of opportunities to explore contemporary critical concerns. Auden's homosexuality, for example, has a healthy life in many biographically oriented critical accounts of the poetry, and the relation between Auden's sexuality and his language and diction is still relatively unexplored. From Janet Montefiore's account of Auden and Isherwood's plays in chapter four we can infer that there is scope for further gender-sensitive readings of the poetry as well as the dramatic work.

As a poet who spoke often of the need to build a 'New Country', Auden's work allows us to think about changing ideas about England and Englishness in the thirties. In chapter three Steve Ellis described how in Auden's poetry a 'unitary England is indeed often set up . . . only to be subsequently challenged'. Growing up in an age that was witnessing the 'end of Empire' and the death of liberal England, Auden was part of a generation that began, in Trotter's phrase, by 'Finding things to say good-bye to', only to find that they were expected to usher in the 'birth of a new social order':

■ Always the following wind of history
   Of others' wisdom makes a buoyant air
   Till we come suddenly on pockets where
   Is nothing loud but us . . . (*C.P.*, p. 11) □

Auden's reappropriation of late colonial discourses in texts such as *The Orators* not only parodies the ideology of the scoutmaster or the retired colonel, but allows us to think of Auden's ambiguous and deliberate mimicry of these discourses as prefiguring a postmodern strategy of subversion. Also, Auden's sensitivity to the political effects of power on the individual invites readings informed by thinkers on institutional power such as Michel Foucault, or the more language based work of Mikhail Bakhtin.

Auden was a playwright, librettist, critic and translator as well as a poet, and the variety of his work, combined with the open and unfinished nature of his critical status, presents the student with a challenging subject to explore. It is likely too that in following one of the many paths into Auden's work, one finds an unfamiliar path that leads back to oneself.

APPENDIX

Chronology of main works discussed in this text:

1928 – *Poems* (1928) printed by Spender
1930 – *Poems* (1930) includes *Paid on Both Sides*
1932 – *The Orators*
1933 – 'A Summer Night'
       The Dance of Death
1935 – *The Dog Beneath the Skin* (with Christopher Isherwood)
       Work with the GPO Film Unit
1936 – *The Ascent of F6* (with Christopher Isherwood)
       Look, Stranger!
1937 – *Spain*
       Letters from Iceland (with Louis MacNeice)
1938 – *On the Frontier* (with Christopher Isherwood)
1939 – *Journey to a War* (with Christopher Isherwood)
       Moves to America
1940 – *Another Time*
1941 – *New Year Letter* (*The Double Man*)
       Paul Bunyan (operetta with Benjamin Britten)
1944 – *For the Time Being* (includes *The Sea and the Mirror*)
1945 – *The Collected Poetry* (poetry placed in alphabetical order)
1947 – *The Age of Anxiety*
1950 – *The Enchafèd Flood* (lectures on Romanticism)
1951 – *Nones*
1955 – *The Shield of Achilles*
1960 – *Homage to Clio*
1962 – *The Dyer's Hand* (prose)
1965 – *About the House*
1966 – *Collected Shorter Poems 1927–1957*
1968 – *Collected Longer Poems*
1969 – *City Without Walls*
       Secondary Worlds (lectures)
1971 – *Academic Graffiti*
1972 – *Epistle to a Godson*
1973 – *Forewords and Afterwords* (prose)
1974 – *Thank You Fog* (posthumous poems)

NOTES

INTRODUCTION

1 F.R. Leavis cited in John Haffenden, ed., *W.H. Auden: The Critical Heritage, (London:* Routledge, 1983), p.101.
2 D.S. Savage, 'The Strange Case of W.H. Auden', in *The Personal Principle*, (London: Routledge, 1944), pp.179–80.

CHAPTER ONE

1 For a plausible reason for Auden's result see V.M. Allom's letter in Humphrey Carpenter, *W.H. Auden: A Biography* (Hemel Hempstead: Unwin, 1983), p.81. Allom claims that 'Auden had nothing of the true scholar in his composition. He was primarily interested in literature as an art, and not as a subject for analytical dissection'.
2 See *Poems* (1928). Facsimile. (Ilkley: Janus Press, 1973.) Moira Megaw, 'Auden's First Poems' in *Essays in Criticism* 25, iii, pp.378–82, discusses the early poetry; also see the *Introduction to Katherine Bucknell*, ed., *W.H. Auden: Juvenilia. Poems 1922–1928* (London: Faber, 1994) where poems from the 1928 collection are discussed.
3 W.H. Auden, *Collected Poems*, ed. Edward Mendelson (London: Faber, 1994), p.33. Hereafter references will be cited in the body of the text as (*C.P.*, p.x).
4 Carpenter (1983), p.95.
5 From William Empson's review of *Paid on Both Sides*, see note 14, chapter 3.
6 George Orwell, 'Inside the Whale', *Collected Essays, Journalism, Letters. Vol 1. An Age Like This, 1920–1940* (London: Secker and Warburg, 1968), p.507.
7 John Haffenden, ed., *W.H. Auden: The Critical Heritage* (London: Routledge, 1983), p.92. I am indebted to Haffenden's book throughout this section.
8 Carpenter (1983), p.116.
9 Haffenden (1983), p.96.
10 The key text here is Samuel Hynes, *The Auden Generation: Literature and Politics in England in the 1930s* (London: Faber, 1976).
11 Michael Roberts, ed., *New Signatures: Poems by Several Hands*, Preface (London: Hogarth, 1932), p.15.
12 See the 'Symposium' on 'A Communist to Others' in Katherine Bucknell and Nicholas Jenkins, eds., *W.H. Auden: 'The Map*

of All My Youth', *Auden Studies 1* (Oxford: Clarendon, 1990), pp.173–95.
13 This poem is discussed in its political context by Arnold Kettle in his essay 'W.H. Auden: Poetry and Politics in the Thirties', in Jon Clark, Margot Heinemann, David Margolies, Carole Snee, eds., *Culture and Crisis in Britain in the 30s* (London: Lawrence and Wishart, 1979), pp.83–101, and by Frank Gloversmith in part II of his essay 'Changing Things: Orwell and Auden', in Frank Gloversmith, ed., *Class, Culture and Social Change: A New View of the 1930s* (Sussex: Harvester, 1980), pp.123–41.
14 Haffenden (1983), p.230.
15 Edward Mendelson, ed., *The Complete Works of W.H. Auden: Plays 1928–1938* (Princeton: Princeton U.P., 1988). This is the definitive resource when studying the plays of the thirties; Mendelson's careful editorial apparatus provides variants and related critical and biographical material.
16 Cited in Michael Sidnell, *Dances of Death: The Group Theatre of London in the Thirties* (London: Faber, 1984), p.247. Sidnell has written a useful appendix in Mendelson (1988) *Plays 1928–1938*, 'Auden and the Group Theatre', pp.490–502.
17 See notes 13 and 14.
18 W.H. Auden and Louis MacNeice, *Letters from Iceland* (London: Faber, 1985), p.31. *Letters from Iceland* also appears in Edward Mendelson, ed., *The Complete Works of W.H. Auden: Prose, Volume 1, 1926–1938* (Princeton: Princeton University Press, 1996).
19 George Orwell, 'Inside the Whale'. *Collected Essays, Journalism, Letters. Vol 1. An Age Like This, 1920–1940* (London: Secker and Warburg, 1968), p.516.
20 Edward Mendelson, *Early Auden* (London: Faber, 1981), p.323. See pp.321–3 for an analysis of Orwell's criticism in 'Inside the Whale'.
21 Valentine Cunningham, ed., *Spanish Front: Writers on the Civil War* (Oxford: Oxford University Press, 1986).
22 Surveys such as *Authors Take Sides on the Spanish War*, 1937, served to force writers to take a stand and make statements about the Spanish War. See Cunningham (1986), pp.51–7.
23 In the myth Daedalus made wings for himself and his son Icarus, who ignored his father's warning not to fly too near to the sun as it would melt the wax that bound the wings together.

24 'I suddenly found I could really do it, that I could make a fighting demagogic speech and have the audience roaring. I felt just covered with dirt afterwards. . . . Never, never again will I speak at a political meeting.' Carpenter (1983), p.256.

25 *The English Auden*, pp.394–406.

26 Carpenter (1983), p.282.

27 'think about England . . .' from *The Orators* (1932), *The English Auden*, p.62, and 'No doctor in England . . .' from the fragmentary play *The Fronny* (1930–32), Mendelson (1988), *Plays 1928–1938*, p.471.

28 Haffenden (1983), p.37.

29 Re: 'family': 'I felt the situation for me in England was becoming impossible. I couldn't grow up. English life is for me a family life, and I love my family but I don't want to live with them.' Carpenter (1983), p.243.

30 Cited in Charles Osborne, *W.H. Auden: The Life of a Poet* (London and Basingstoke: Macmillan, 1982), p.207.

31 See note 2 in chapter six.

32 Haffenden (1983), p.36.

33 See Carpenter (1983), pp.262–3.

34 For Auden's relation with Britten see Donald Mitchell, *Britten and Auden in the Thirties: The Year 1936 (London: Faber,* 1981). There is also some interesting material in Humphrey Carpenter's biography of Britten: *Benjamin Britten: A Biography* (London: Faber, 1992).

35 D.S. Savage, 'The Strange Case of W.H. Auden', in *The Personal Principle* (London: Routledge, 1944), pp.179–80. See quotation in the Introduction to this book.

36 See Carpenter (1983), p.313.

37 See the Introduction to Haffenden (1983), pp.42–3.

38 W.H. Auden, 'Making, Knowing and Judging', *The Dyer's Hand* (London: Faber, 1987), p.57.

39 Auden uses this phrase, taken from Kierkegaard, to signify the immensity and danger of the leap of faith. See Prospero in *The Sea and the Mirror* on this leap, *C.P.*, p.409, cited at the end of this chapter.

40 Carpenter (1983), p.331.

41 Introduction to Haffenden (1983), p.45.

42 Haffenden (1983), p.376.

43 In 'Letter to Lord Byron' Auden says how D.H. Lawrence and Homer Lane taught him to 'express my deep abhorrence/If I caught anyone preferring Art/To Life and Love . . .' *C.P.*, p.111. These lines sum up much of Auden's early stance, and continue to inform the later discussions of the power of Art.

44 Introduction to Haffenden (1983), p.46.

45 Introduction to Haffenden (1983), p.47.

46 John Bayley, *The Romantic Survival* (London: Constable, 1957), p.156.

47 Haffenden (1983), p.435.

48 W.H. Auden, 'Preface', *Collected Shorter Poems* (London: Faber, 1981), p.16.

49 Introduction to Haffenden (1983), p.49.

50 *Collected Shorter Poems*, p.15.

51 Joseph Warren Beach, *The Making of the Auden Canon* (Minneapolis: The University of Minnesota Press, 1957), p.248.

52 Haffenden (1983), p.462.

53 Haffenden (1983), p.472.

54 Introduction to Haffenden (1983), p.51.

55 Introduction to Haffenden (1983), pp.51–2.

56 Haffenden (1983), p.488.

CHAPTER TWO

1 W.H. Auden, 'Shakespeare's Sonnets', *Forewords and Afterwords* (London: Faber, 1973), p.90.

2 W.H. Auden, *The Dyer's Hand* (London: Faber, 1987), pp.50–51. Hereafter *DH*.

3 Stan Smith, W.H. Auden, (Oxford: Blackwell, 1985), pp.1–6.

4 Cited in John Haffenden, ed., W.H. Auden: *The Critical Heritage* (London: Routledge, 1983), p.342.

5 *DH*, pp.3–12.

6 See Robert Medley, *Drawn from the Life* (London: Faber, 1983) for an interesting portrait of Auden as a young man.

7 Extracts from *The Prolific and the Devourer* are reproduced in Edward Mendelson, ed., *The English Auden* (London: Faber, 1988), pp.394–406, and provide an important insight into Auden's immediate view of his aesthetic and political activities during the 1930s.

8 Geoffrey Grigson, ed., *New Verse*, 'Auden Double Number', 26–27 (Nov. 1937), p.1.

9 Dedication to Christopher Isherwood in *Poems* (1930).

10 Grigson (1937), p.25.

11 Stephen Spender, ed., *W.H. Auden: A Tribute* (London: Weidenfeld and Nicholson, 1975).

12 Grigson (1937), pp.4–9.

13 Haffenden (1983), p.82.

14 Bernard Bergonzi, *Reading the Thirties: Texts and Contexts* (London: Macmillan, 1978), p.43.

15 William Logan, 'Auden's Images', from Alan Bold, ed., *W.H. Auden: The Far Interior* (London: Vision Press, 1985), p.117.

16 Janet Montefiore, 'Goebbels and Goblins: Politics and the Fairy-Tale in Auden's Poems' in Bold, ed., 1985, pp. 73–99. Also see the extract from Montefiore's *Men and Women Writers of the Thirties* (London: Routledge, 1996) in chapter four.

17 Cleanth Brooks, 'Auden's Imagery' in Monroe K. Spears, ed., *Auden: A Collection of Critical Essays* (Englewood Cliffs, N.J.: Prentice-Hall, 1964), pp. 15–25.

18 Ian Samson, '"Flouting Papa": Randall Jarrell and W.H. Auden' in Katherine Bucknell and Nicholas Jenkins, eds., *Auden Studies 3, 'In Solitude, for Company': W. H. Auden After 1940* (Oxford: Clarendon, 1995), p. 275.

19 Bucknell and Jenkins (1995), p. 279.

20 See Mitchison's review in Haffenden (1983), pp. 81–3. Auden's use of Anglo-Saxon forms and extracts from the Mummers Plays in the 'Charade' *Paid on Both Sides* are examples of Auden's redefinition of his literary past, and is interesting to consider alongside Eliot's interest and negotiation of tradition which he explored in essays such as 'Tradition and the Individual Talent' (1919) and his series of lectures collected in *After Strange Gods* (1934). Auden's relation to Eliot's idea of tradition is discussed in Stan Smith's essay 'Remembering Bryden's Bill: Modernism from Eliot to Auden' in Keith Williams and Steven Matthews, eds., *Rewriting the Thirties: Modernism and After* (London: Longman, 1997), pp. 53–70.

21 Jarrell is referring ironically to Auden's line: 'Make action urgent and its nature clear' in 'August for the people. . .' *The English Auden*, p. 157.

22 Jarrell is referring here to Cleanth Brooks, *Modern Poetry and the Tradition* (Chapel Hill: University of North Carolina Press, 1939). Monroe K. Spears has usefully extracted significant passages in his *Auden: A Collection of Critical Essays* (1964). See bibliography.

23 Randall Jarrell, 'Changes of Attitude and Rhetoric in Auden's Poetry' in *The Third Book of Criticism* (London: Faber, 1975), pp. 115–31.

24 See Samson in Bucknell and Jenkins (1995), p. 277.

25 Randall Jarrell, 'Freud to Paul: The Stages of Auden's Ideology', *The Third Book of Criticism* (London: Faber, 1975), pp. 153–61.

26 Jarrell (1975), p. 153.

27 Jarrell (1975), p. 158.

28 These terms may need some comment. The *textual* has emerged as a critical term in recent years to mark a distinction between a criticism that foregrounds the importance of the 'author' and that which gives priority to the text. The argument can be seen in its most raw form in Roland Barthes, 'The Death of the Author' in *Image, Music, Text*, 1977. Trans. Stephen Heath (London: Fontana, 1984), pp. 142–8. An emphasis on the ambiguities and uncertainties of the text has led to attention being focused on the idea of *play*, and the *ludic* is a term which incorporates this interest. The *dialogic* is a term from the thinker Mikhail Bakhtin, and is used to open up difference and contestation within apparently closed and single utterances. The *discursive* refers to the interplay of discourses (institutionally coded modes of speaking and acting) and the power that circulates through and between their utterance.

29 [Boly's Note] Randall Jarrell, 'Freud to Paul: The Stages of Auden's Ideology', *Partisan Review*, 12 (1945): 437–57. When the texts that Boly refers to in this extract are in the bibliography they are not referenced, unless they refer to a specific location in that text.

30 [Boly's Note] W.H. Auden, 'Authority in America', *Griffin* 4 (1955): 5–11.

31 John R. Boly, *Reading Auden: The Returns of Caliban* (Ithaca and London: Cornell University Press, 1991), pp. 40–7.

32 See D.S. Savage, 'The Strange Case of W.H. Auden' in *The Personal Principle* (London: Routledge, 1944), pp. 155–82, for an example of hostile criticism of Auden's light verse.

33 [Blair's Note] 'Poets, Poetry, and Taste', *The Highway*, xxxix (December 1936), 44.

34 [Blair's Note] See 'A Preface to Kierkegaard', *The New Republic*, cx (May 15, 1944), 683–86.

35 [Blair's Note] 'Seriously Unserious', *Poetry* [Chicago] lxxviii (September 1951), 352.

36 John G Blair, *The Poetic Art of W.H. Auden* (Princeton, N.J.: Princeton University Press, 1965), pp. 128–43.

37 Justin Replogle, *Auden's Poetry* (London: Methuen, 1969).

38 John Bayley, *The Romantic Survival* (London: Constable, 1964), pp. 144–56.

CHAPTER THREE

1 [Bucknell's Note] W.H. Auden, 'A Literary Transference', in Albert J. Guerard, ed., *Hardy: A Collection of Critical Essays* (Englewood Cliffs: Prentice-Hall, 1963), p. 136.

2 [Bucknell's Note] Guerard (1965), p. 141.

3 [Bucknell's Note] Guerard (1963), pp.139, 140.

4 [Bucknell's Note] W.H. Auden, *The Oxford Book of Light Verse* (Oxford: Clarendon Press, 1938), p.xv.

5 [Bucknell's Note] See Nevill Coghill, 'Sweeney Agonistes (An Anecdote or two)' in *T.S. Eliot: A Symposium*, ed. Richard March and Tambimuttu (London, 1948), p.82. Coghill is vague on the date when Auden said this, 'towards 1926-7', and he may be mistaken. Auden apparently did not go to him for tutorials until the autumn of 1926, but he had discovered Eliot the previous May, and he had begun to imitate him, in moderation at first, within weeks. Auden probably dramatized his announcement to impress Coghill. Nevertheless, it makes an important point – that his new style of writing came as a decisive, relatively sudden change.

6 Katherine Bucknell, ed., *W.H. Auden: Juvenilia. Poems 1922-1928* (London: Faber, 1994).

7 Re: 'had its day' see Auden's poem 'I have a handsome profile', *The English Auden*, p.123.

8 See Francis Mulhern, *The Moment of 'Scrutiny'* (London: Verso, 1981), for a detailed account of Leavis's project.

9 [Spears's Note] F.R. Leavis, *New Bearings in English Poetry* (New York: George W. Stewart, Publisher, Inc., 1950), p.227.

10 [Spears's Note] *Scrutiny*, XX, 16 (Cambridge: Cambridge University Press, 1963).

11 Monroe K. Spears, ed., *Auden: A Collection of Critical Essays* (Englewood Cliffs, N.J.: Prentice-Hall, 1964), pp.1-3. See the introduction to Haffenden (1983) for further comment on Leavis and Auden.

12 F.R. Leavis, *Times Literary Supplement*, 19 March, 1931, p.221. Cited in Haffenden (1983), pp.89-91.

13 Cited in Humphrey Carpenter, *W.H. Auden: A Biography* (Hemel Hempstead: Unwin, 1983), p.83.

14 William Empson, *Experiment* (Cambridge) vii, Spring 1931, 60-1. Cited in Haffenden (1983), pp.78-80.

15 See Leavis's remarks in Haffenden (1983), pp.140-3.

16 [ed.] This was probably Eliot.

17 F.R. Leavis, in Haffenden (1983), pp.100-1. From an unsigned review in *The Listener*, 22nd June, 1932.

18 Stephen Spender, *The Destructive Element* (London: Jonathan Cape, 1938), pp.268-74.

19 Richard Bozorth, '"Whatever You Do Don't Go to the Wood": Joking, Rhetoric, and Homosexuality in *The Orators*', in Katherine Bucknell and Nicholas Jenkins, eds., *The Language of Learning and the Language of Love* (Oxford: Clarendon, 1994), pp.113-36.

20 Ode 1 of *The Orators*, *The English Auden*, p.94.

21 Justin Replogle, 'The Gang Myth in Auden's Early Poetry', *Journal of English and Germanic Philology*, 61, No.3, (1962), pp.481-95. For *Auden's Poetry* see note 37 in chapter two.

22 Cecil Day-Lewis, *A Hope for Poetry* (Oxford: Basil Blackwell,1934), pp.44-6.

23 [MacNeice's Note] Auden is a journalist poet (I do not mean journalistic). If the Odyssey is the work of a longshore Greek, and *The Winding Stair* is the work of a crank philosopher, Auden's poems are the work of a journalist.

24 Michael Roberts, ed., *New Signatures: Poems by Several Hands* (London: Hogarth, 1934).

25 Louis MacNeice, 'Poetry' in Geoffrey Grigson, ed., *The Arts To-Day* (London: John Lane, Bodley Head, 1935), pp.56-60.

26 While occupying the poetic centre stage in contemporary Britain, Auden was also a teacher in the early thirties. John Garrett was the headmaster of the recently opened Raynes Park Grammar School, whose forward looking education policy led them to employ working artists on the staff and to adopt an active political ethos for the school – including a school song with Marxist overtones written by Auden.

27 The automatic response was studied by I.A. Richards in *Practical Criticism: A Study of Literary Judgement* (1929).

28 W.H. Auden and John Garrett, *The Poet's Tongue* (London: Bell, 1935), pp.v-x. Reprinted in *The English Auden*, pp.327-30.

29 W.H.Auden, 'Postscript: Christianity and Art', *The Dyer's Hand* (London: Faber, 1987), p.458.

30 [Hynes's Note] Montagu Slater, 'The Turning Point', *Left Review*, 2 (Oct. 1935), 19, 20.

31 [Hynes's Note] Auden and Garrett (1935), p.ix.

32 [Hynes's Note] W.H. Auden, 'Psychology and Art To-day', in *The Arts To-day*, ed. Geoffrey Grigson (London: John Lane, The Bodley Head, 1935), p.18. Reprinted in *The English Auden*, pp.340-1. Further references will appear in the body of the extract as *The English Auden*, p.x.

33 Samuel Hynes, *The Auden Generation: Literature and Politics in England in the 1930s* (London: Faber, 1976), pp.165–9.

34 See the 'Symposium' on 'A Communist to Others' in Katherine Bucknell and Nicholas Jenkins, eds., *W.H. Auden: 'The Map of All My Youth'*, Auden Studies 1 (Oxford: Clarendon, 1990), pp.173–95. The poem itself 'Brother, who when the sirens roar' is in *The English Auden*, p.120.

35 [Carter's Note] Michael Roberts, *Critique of Poetry* (London, 1934), p.238.

36 Ronald Carter, ed., *Thirties Poets: 'The Auden Group'*, Casebook Series, Introduction, 'The Auden Group: Some Aspects Of Their Poetry In The Thirties' (London: Macmillan, 1984), pp.12–13.

37 [O'Neill and Reeves's Note] *Seamus Heaney, The Government of the Tongue: The 1986 T.S. Eliot Memorial Lectures and Other Critical Writings* (London: Faber, 1988), p.121.

38 [O'Neill and Reeves's Note] Stan Smith, *W.H. Auden* (Oxford: Blackwell, 1985), p.84.

39 Michael O'Neill and Gareth Reeves, *Auden, MacNeice, Spender: The Thirties Poetry* (Basingstoke and London: Macmillan, 1992), pp.148–52.

40 On the definite article see G. Rostrevor-Hamilton, *The Tell-Tale Article* (London: Heinemann, 1949), and Bergonzi on the Audenesque, see chapter two, note 14.

41 [Ellis's Note] Mendelson (1981), p.336.

42 Steve Ellis, *The English Eliot* (London: Routledge, 1991), pp.158–64.

CHAPTER FOUR

1 [Sidnell's Note] C.H. Waddington, 'Specialisation in Poetry', *Cambridge Review*, vol. 55, 1 December 1933, p.148.

2 [Sidnell's Note] Mendelson (1981), p.270, quotes Auden's inscription in a copy of the play, 'The communists never spotted that this was a nihilistic leg-pull'. This was apparently written after 1940 and so after Auden had radically changed his views about political poetry. It tells us more about that change than about Auden's attitude in writing *DD*.

3 [Sidnell's Note] *TLS*, 15 March 1934, p.190.

4 [Sidnell's Note] Thomas Greenidge, *Socialist Review*, vol. 5, January 1934, pp.58–9.

5 [Sidnell's Note] Edwin Berry Bergum, 'Three English Radical Poets', *Masses*, vol. 2, 3 July 1934, p.33.

6 Michael Sidnell, *Dances of Death: The Group Theatre of London in the Thirties* (London: Faber, 1984), pp.68–75.

7 [Montefiore's Note] Samuel Hynes, *The Auden Generation: Literature and Politics in England in the 1930s* (London: Faber, 1976), pp.140, 186.

8 [Montefiore's Note] Edward Mendelson, ed., *The Complete Works of W.H. Auden: Plays 1928–1938* (Princeton: Princeton U.P., 1988), p.xvi; Auden quoted in Mendelson, p.xv.

9 [Montefiore's Note] Mendelson, *Plays* (1988), p.204.

10 Janet Montefiore, *Men and Women Writers of the 1930s* (London: Routledge, 1996), pp.83–92.

11 Lucy McDiarmid, 'W.H. Auden's 'In the year of my youth. . .', *Review of English Studies*, n.s. XXIX, 115, 1978: 267–312.

12 W.H. Auden and Louis MacNeice, *Letters from Iceland* (London: Faber, 1985), p.32.

13 Stan Smith, *W.H. Auden* (Oxford: Blackwell, 1985), p.95.

14 Anthony Hecht, *The Hidden Law: The Poetry of W.H. Auden* (London and Cambridge, Massachusetts: Harvard University Press, 1993), p.171.

15 Tom Paulin, 'Letters from Iceland: Going North', in John Lucas, ed., *The 1930s: A Challenge to Orthodoxy* (Sussex: Harvester, 1978), pp.59–77.

16 [Trotter's Note] George Orwell, *Collected Essays, Journalism and Letters*, Vol. 2 (Penguin), p.109.

17 [Trotter's Note] Rex Warner, *Poems* (1937), p.39.

18 [Trotter's Note] Cecil Day-Lewis, 'A Reply' in Quentin Bell, ed., *Julian Bell. Essays, Poems and Letters* (1938), p.333.

19 [Trotter's Note] Stephen Spender, *World Within World*, p.118.

20 This is the text in *The English Auden*, pp.210–12, pp.424–5.

21 [Trotter's Note] Hynes (1976), p.252.

22 [Trotter's Note] Bernard Bergonzi, *Reading the Thirties* (London and Basingstoke: Macmillan, 1978), p.73.

23 David Trotter, *The Making of the Reader: Language and Subjectivity in Modern American, English and Irish Poetry* (London: Macmillan, 1984), pp.110–23.

24 *The English Auden*, p.425. The poem published in the pamphlet in 1937 is conventionally entitled *Spain*; subsequent printings of the poem in collections refer to the poem as 'Spain, 1937'.

25 [Kettle's Note] Hynes (1976), pp.253–4.

26 [Kettle's Note] Louis MacNeice, *Collected Poems* (London: Faber, 1966), p.112.

27 Arnold Kettle, 'W.H. Auden: Poetry and

Politics in the Thirties', in Jon Clark, Margot Heinemann, David Margolies, Carole Snee, eds., *Culture and Crisis in Britain in the 30s* (London: Lawrence and Wishart, 1979), pp. 83–101.

28 'To-day words so affect me that a pornographic story, for example, excites me sexually more than a living person can do', *The English Auden*, p. 397.

29 Joseph Brodsky, 'On "September 1, 1939" by W.H. Auden', in *Less Than One: Selected Essays* (Harmondsworth: Penguin-Viking, 1986), pp. 305–11.

30 Reprinted in *The English Auden*, pp. 342–54.

31 [Perrie's Note] W.H. Auden, *A Certain World* (London: Faber, 1971), p. 87.

32 [Perrie's Note] Mendelson, *Early Auden* (1981), p. 359.

33 [Perrie's Note] Mendelson, *Early Auden* (1981), p. 235.

34 [Perrie's Note] Justin Replogle, *Auden's Poetry* (London: Methuen, 1969), p. 50.

35 [Perrie's Note] Replogle (1969), p. 50.

36 [Perrie's Note] Humphrey Carpenter, *W.H. Auden: A Biography* (Hemel Hempstead: Unwin, 1983), pp. 288–9.

37 [Perrie's Note] Replogle (1969), p. 61.

38 [Perrie's Note] Replogle (1969), p. 70.

39 [Perrie's Note] Replogle (1969), p. 99.

40 Walter Perrie, 'Auden's Political Vision' in Alan Bold, ed., *W.H. Auden: The Far Interior* (London: Vision Press, 1985), pp. 49–70.

41 Philip Larkin, 'What's Become of Wystan?' in *Required Writing: Miscellaneous Pieces 1955–1982* (London: Faber, 1983), pp. 123–8.

CHAPTER FIVE

1 [ed.] Compare this with Larkin's complaints in the previous chapter. Hynes is citing from a letter Auden sent to his friend E.R. Dodds on 16th January 1940. Kathleen Bell has edited an illuminating set of six letters to Dodds under the title 'A Change of Heart: Six Letters from Auden to Professor and Mrs. E.R. Dodds Written at the Beginning of World War II', in Katherine Bucknell and Nicholas Jenkins, eds., *W.H. Auden: 'The Map of All My Youth'*, *Auden Studies 1* (Oxford: Clarendon Press, 1990), pp. 95–115.

2 [ed.] 'Romantic or Free'. The commencement address, 17 June 1940, *Smith Alumnae Quarterly*, XXXI, 4 (August 1940), pp. 353–8.

3 [ed.] 'Jacob and the Angel'. Rev. of *Behold this Dreamer*, by Walter de la Mare. *New Republic*. CI.1308 (27 Dec. 1939): 292–3.

4 [ed.] 'Criticism in a Mass Society', in Donald A. Stauffer, ed., *The Intent of the Critic* (Princeton: Princeton University Press, 1941).

5 [ed.] 'Tradition and Value'. Rev. of *The Novel and the Modern World*, by David Daiches. *New Republic*. CII.1311 (15 Jan. 1940): 90–1.

6 [ed.] 'Mimesis and Allegory', *English Institute Annual 1940* (New York: Columbia University Press, 1941), pp. 1–19.

7 Samuel Hynes, 'The Voice of Exile: Auden in 1940', *Sewanee Review* XC.1 (Winter 1982): pp. 32–44.

8 [Spears's Note] Review of *Either/Or*, in *The New Republic*, 1941. 7. Review of *Christianity and Power Politics*, in *The Nation*, 1941. In the same year Auden reviewed Niebuhr's major work, *The Nature and Destiny of Man*, in *The New Republic*.

9 [Spears's Note] Review of translations of Kafka in *The New Republic*, 1941.

10 [Spears's Note] *The Living Thoughts of Kierkegaard*, presented by W.H. Auden (New York, 1952). A paperback reprint has been announced for 1963 (Indiana University Press).

11 [Spears's Note] *The Living Thoughts of Kierkegaard*, p. 5.

12 [Spears's Note] *The Living Thoughts of Kierkegaard*, p. 10.

13 [Spears's Note] *The Living Thoughts of Kierkegaard*, p. 16.

14 [Spears's Note] *The Living Thoughts of Kierkegaard*, pp. 17–8.

15 [Spears's Note] Review of Niebuhr in *The Nation*, 1941.

16 [Spears's Note] Review of Cochrane in *The New Republic*, 1944.

17 Monroe K. Spears, 'The Shift in Perspective', *The Poetry of W.H. Auden: The Disenchanted Island* (New York: Oxford U.P., 1963), pp. 171–85.

18 [McDiarmid's Note] See such reviews as 'The Means of Grace', *New Republic* 104 (2 June 1941): 765–6, and 'Eros and Agape', *Nation* 152.26 (28 June 1941): 756–8. For Auden's own account of the change in his views, see Auden's untitled essay in *Modern Canterbury Pilgrims*, ed. James A. Pike (New York, 1956), 32–43. Carpenter's biography also has an account (273–302).

19 [McDiarmid's Note] Essay in *Modern Canterbury Pilgrims*, p. 41.

20 [McDiarmid's Note] For a discussion of the 'vision of agape' see Edward Mendelson, *Early Auden* (New York, 1981), 159–64, 167–71.

21 [McDiarmid's Note] Essay in *Modern Canterbury Pilgrims*, p. 40.

22 [McDiarmid's Note] See the accounts in Carpenter's biography and in Dorothy Farnan, *Auden in Love* (New York, 1984).

23 [McDiarmid's Note] *Secondary Worlds* (London: Faber,1969), p.12.

24 [McDiarmid's Note] *Secondary Worlds*, p.121.

25 [McDiarmid's Note] *The Dyer's Hand*, pp.456, 458.

26 [McDiarmid's Note] Christopher Isherwood, 'Some Notes on Auden's Early Poetry', *New Verse* 26–27 (November 1937): 4.

27 Lucy McDiarmid, *Auden's Apologies for Poetry* (Princeton, N. J.: Princeton University Press, 1990), pp.8–13.

28 John Fuller, *W.H. Auden: A Commentary* (London: Faber, 1998), p.320.

29 Fuller (1998), p.321.

30 Fuller (1998), p.323.

31 Edward Callan, 'Auden's *New Year Letter*: A New Style of Architecture' in Monroe K. Spears, ed., *Auden: A Collection of Critical Essays* (Englewood Cliffs, N.J.: Prentice-Hall, 1964), pp.152–9.

32 G.S. Fraser, 'The Career of W.H. Auden' in Spears (1964), pp.93–4.

33 [Mendelson's Note] W.H. Auden, 'Squares and Oblongs', in *Poets at Work*, ed. Charles D. Abbot (New York: Harcourt, Brace, 1948).

34 [Mendelson's Note] Auden, *The Prolific and the Devourer* (Hopewell, New Jersey: Ecco Press, 1993), p.24. This work was written in 1939 and published posthumously. [ed. Extracts appear in *The English Auden*, pp.394–406.]

35 [Mendelson's Note] 'Squares and Oblongs', p.178.

36 [Mendelson's Note] Auden, *Collected Shorter Poems 1927–1957* (London: Faber, 1966).

37 [Mendelson's Note] 'Squares and Oblongs', p.180.

38 Edward Mendelson, 'Revision and Power: The Example of W.H. Auden', *Yale French Studies*, no. 89, (1996), pp.103–12.

39 Edward Callan, *Auden: A Carnival of Intellect* (New York: O.U.P., 1983), p.205.

40 Richard Hoggart, *Auden: An Introductory Essay* (London: Chatto and Windus, 1965), p. 194 and p.202.

41 Ian Samson, '"Flouting Papa": Randall Jarrell and W.H. Auden' in Katherine Bucknell and Nicholas Jenkins (eds), *Auden Studies 3, 'In Solitude, for Company': W.H. Auden After 1940* (Oxford: Clarendon, 1995), p.274.

42 Haffenden (1983), p.366.

43 Haffenden (1983), p.369.

44 Haffenden (1983), pp.372–3.

45 Haffenden (1983), p.376.

46 Fuller (1998), p.387.

47 John Bayley, *The Romantic Survival* (London: Constable, 1964), p.133.

CHAPTER SIX

1 Haffenden (1983), p.393.

2 See for example the 'People and Places' section of Auden's *Another Time* (London: Faber, 1940). Poems were written on Rimbaud, Housman, Lear, Yeats, Toller, Melville, Freud, James, Luther and Montaigne.

3 See Auden's essay 'The Public v. the Late Mr. William Butler Yeats' in *The English Auden*, pp.389–93. The piece originally appeared in the *Partisan Review* in 1939.

4 Michel Foucault is particularly acute in his discussion of the relation between the critical text and the object text in his inaugural lecture 'The Order of Discourse' in Robert Young, ed., *Untying the Text* (London: Routledge, 1981).

5 Fuller (1998), p.449.

6 Fuller (1998), p.449.

7 [ed.] John Nower from Auden's 'Charade' *Paid on Both Sides* (1930) and Michael Ransom from the Auden and Isherwood play *The Ascent of F6* (1936).

8 Lucy McDiarmid, *Auden's Apologies for Poetry* (Princeton, N. J.: Princeton University Press, 1990), pp.127–33.

9 Fuller (1998), p.406.

10 [ed.] For a discussion of the 'two worlds' McDiarmid refers the reader to Auden's essay 'The Virgin and the Dynamo', *The Dyer's Hand* (London: Faber, 1987), pp.61–71.

11 McDiarmid (1990), pp.134–7.

12 Fuller (1998), p.407.

13 [ed.] *The Collected Poems* edits this version. See *Nones* (1951), p.11.

14 John R. Boly, *Reading Auden: The Returns of Caliban* (Ithaca and London: Cornell University Press, 1991), pp.228–31.

15 Donald Davie, 'The Hawk's Eye', from *Thomas Hardy and British Poetry* (London: Routledge and Kegan Paul, 1973), pp.126–8.

16 Edward Mendelson, *Early Auden* (London: Faber, 1981), p.304.

17 [Smith's Note] *Secondary Worlds*, p.136.

18 [Smith's Note] *A Certain World*, p.168.

19 [Smith's Note] Edward Callan, *Auden: A Carnival of Intellect* (Oxford and New York:

Oxford University Press, 1983), p.16.
20 [Smith's Note] *The Dyer's Hand*, p.85.
21 [Smith's Note] Richard Johnson, *Man's Place* (Ithaca, N.Y., Cornell University Press, 1973), pp.169–71.
22 Stan Smith, 'Caesar and Clio: Poetry Under a Faffling Flag', *W.H. Auden* (Oxford: Blackwell, 1985), pp.168–94.
23 Edward Callan, *Auden: A Carnival of Intellect* (Oxford and New York: Oxford University Press, 1983), p.219.
24 Virginia Woolf, *A Room of One's Own* (London: Hogarth, 1928).
25 Haffenden (1983), p.438.
26 Haffenden (1983), p.431.
27 [Callan's Note] See David A. Palin, 'Theology', in C.B. Cox and A.E. Dyson, eds., *The Twentieth-Century Mind*, 111 (Oxford University Press, 1972), pp.142–3.
28 [Callan's Note] Auden reviewed the 1958 American edition of *The Art of Eating* in 'The Kitchen of Life', *Griffin* 6 (June 1958), 4–11, and he revised this for his introduction to the Faber edition (London, 1963).
29 Edward Callan, *Auden: A Carnival of Intellect* (Oxford and New York: Oxford University Press, 1983), pp.241–9.
30 See the section 'The Pattern of Personae' in Justin Replogle, *Auden's Poetry* (London: Methuen, 1969).
31 [ed.] *Collected Shorter Poems*, p.15.
32 [ed.] W.H. Auden, *Poems. 1928*. Facsimile. (Ilkley: Janus Press, 1973).
33 Clive James, Unsigned Review, *Times Literary Supplement*, January, 1973, pp.25–6. In Haffenden (1983), pp.473–80.

CHAPTER SEVEN

1 W.H. Auden, 'Reading', *The Dyer's Hand* (London: Faber, 1987), pp.8–9.
2 W.H. Auden, 'Shakespeare's Sonnets', *Forewords and Afterwords* (London: Faber, 1973), p.89.
3 Richard Davenport-Hines, *Auden* (London: Heinemann, 1995), p.4.
4 Barbara Everett, 'Auden Askew' in *Poets in Their Time: Essays on English Poetry from Donne to Larkin* (London: Faber, 1986), pp.209–29.

5 Richard Hoggart, *Auden: An Introductory Essay* (London: Chatto and Windus, 1965), p.10.
6 Joseph Warren Beach, *The Making of the Auden Canon* (Minneapolis: University of Minnesota Press, 1957), p.249.
7 Monroe K. Spears, ed., *Auden: A Collection of Critical Essays* (Englewood Cliffs, N.J.: Prentice-Hall, 1964), p.4.
8 John G. Blair, *The Poetic Art of W.H. Auden* (Princeton, N.J.: Princeton University Press, 1965), pp.4–5.
9 Herbert Greenberg, *Quest for the Necessary: W.H. Auden and the Dilemma of Divided Consciousness* (Cambridge, Massachusetts: Harvard University Press, 1968), pp.1–2, p.11.
10 Justin Replogle, *Auden's Poetry* (London: Methuen, 1969), p.vii.
11 Re: Dialogic. A term from Mikhail Bakhtin which he used to describe the way that a single utterance always contains an ongoing dialogue.
12 François Duchene, *The Case of the Helmeted Airman: A Study of W.H. Auden's Poetry* (London: Chatto and Windus, 1972), p.181.
13 Edward Callan, *Auden: A Carnival of Intellect* (Oxford and New York: Oxford University Press, 1983), p.8.
14 Lucy McDiarmid, *Auden's Apologies for Poetry* (Princeton, N.J.: Princeton University Press, 1990), p.ix.
15 McDiarmid (1990), p.xiii.
16 John R. Boly, *Reading Auden: The Returns of Caliban* (Ithaca and London: Cornell University Press, 1991), p.28.
17 Anthony Hecht, *The Hidden Law: The Poetry of W.H. Auden* (London and Cambridge, Massachusetts: Harvard University Press, 1993), p.viii.
18 Michael Wood, 'What Kind of Guy?', *London Review of Books*, 10 June 1999.

CHAPTER EIGHT

1 Stan Smith, *W.H. Auden* (Oxford: Blackwell, 1985), p.5.
2 That is, the act of suppression itself is as full of meaning as the material suppressed, and can be 'read' as such.

SELECT BIBLIOGRAPHY

Editions of Auden's Poetry and Prose

Bucknell, Katherine, ed., *W.H. Auden: Juvenilia. Poems 1922–1928*. London: Faber, 1994.

Mendelson, Edward, ed., *The English Auden: Poems, Essays and Dramatic Writings 1927–1939* (1977). London: Faber, 1988.

Mendelson, Edward, ed., *Collected Poems*. London: Faber, 1994. (This edition is a completely reset version of the 1976 *Collected Poems* and has different pagination. This is the latest edition and therefore the one used throughout this guide.)

Collected Longer Poems. 1968. London: Faber, 1977.

Collected Shorter Poems. 1966. London: Faber, 1981.

The Collected Poetry of W.H. Auden. New York: Random House, 1945.

Mendelson, Edward, ed., *The Complete Works of W.H. Auden. W.H. Auden and Christopher Isherwood: Plays 1928–1938*. Princeton: Princeton U.P., 1988.

Mendelson, Edward, ed., *The Complete Works of W.H. Auden. Libretti and Other Dramatic Writings, 1939–1973* (with Chester Kallman). Princeton: Princeton U.P., 1993.

Mendelson, Edward, ed., *The Complete Works of W.H. Auden. W.H. Auden: Prose and Travel Books in Prose and Verse. Volume 1, 1926–1938*. Princeton: Princeton U.P., 1996.

The Dyer's Hand (1963). London: Faber, 1987.

Forewords and Afterwords. London: Faber, 1973.

Mendelson, Edward, ed., *Selected Poems*. London: Faber, 1979.

Poems (1928). Facsimile. Ilkley: Janus Press, 1973.

Bibliographies

Bloomfield, B.C., *W.H. Auden: A Bibliography: The Early Years through 1955*. Charlottesville: University Press of Virginia, 1964.

Bloomfield, B.C., and Mendelson, Edward, *W.H. Auden: A Bibliography 1924–1969*. Charlottesville: University Press of Virginia, 1972.

Bucknell, Katherine and Jenkins, Nicholas, eds., *Auden Studies*. Oxford: Clarendon, Vols. 1–3 conclude with bibliographic updates by Edward Mendelson.

'W.H. Auden: A Bibliography', 'The Library', Sixth Series, 4, 1, March 1982, pp.75–9.

Reference Guide and Criticism

Gingerich, Martin E., *W.H. Auden: A Reference Guide*. Boston, Massachusetts: G.K. Hall; London: Prior, 1977. (A useful resource that lists secondary sources – articles and books – on Auden, and briefly summarises every entry. Good cross-referenced index. Ends in 1976.)

Haffenden, John, ed., *W.H. Auden: The Critical Heritage*. London: Routledge,

1983. (An excellent source of reviews with an intelligent and useful introduction.)

University and College libraries have facilities for on-line searching. Databases such as the MLA (Modern Language Association) and BIDS (Bath Information and Data Services) allow students to search for subjects and titles related to their interest. In the case of Auden, where the critical field is fairly extensive, this is a useful way to begin sifting through the available material.

Biographies

Carpenter, Humphrey, *W.H. Auden: A Biography*. London: Allen and Unwin, 1981.

Davenport-Hines, Richard, *Auden*. London: Heinemann, 1995.

Osborne, Charles, *W.H. Auden: The Life of a Poet*. London: Methuen, 1980.

Page, Norman, *Auden and Isherwood: The Berlin Years*. London: Macmillan; New York: St. Martin's Press, 1998.

Spender, Stephen, ed., *W.H. Auden: A Tribute*. London: Weidenfeld and Nicolson, 1975.

Books on Auden

Bahlke, George W., *The Later Auden: From 'New Year Letter' to 'About the House'*. New Brunswick: Rutgers University Press, 1970.

Beach, Joseph Warren, *The Making of the Auden Canon*. Minneapolis: University of Minnesota Press, 1957.

Blair, John G., *The Poetic Art of W.H. Auden*. Princeton, N.J.: Princeton University Press, 1965.

Boly, John, R., *Reading Auden: The Returns of Caliban*. Ithaca and London: Cornell University Press, 1991.

Bucknell, Katherine, and Jenkins, Nicholas, eds., *Auden Studies 1, W.H. Auden: 'The Map of All My Youth': Early Works, Friends and Influences*. Oxford: Clarendon, 1990.

Bucknell, Katherine, and Jenkins, Nicholas, eds., *Auden Studies 2, 'The Language of Learning and the Language of Love'*. Oxford: Clarendon, 1994.

Bucknell, Katherine, and Jenkins, Nicholas, eds., *Auden Studies 3, 'In Solitude, for Company': W.H. Auden After 1940*. Oxford: Clarendon, 1995.

Buell, F., *W.H. Auden as a Social Poet*. New York: Cornell U.P., 1973.

Callan, Edward, *Auden: A Carnival of Intellect*. New York: Oxford U.P., 1983.

Carter, Ronald, *W.H. Auden*. Milton Keynes: Open University Press, 1975.

Davison, Dennis, *W.H. Auden*. London: Evans Brothers, 1970.

Duchene, François, *The Case of the Helmeted Airman: A Study of W.H. Auden's Poetry*. London: Chatto and Windus, 1972.

Emig, Rainer, *W.H. Auden: Towards a Postmodern Poetics*. London: Macmillan, 1999.

Everett, Barbara, *Auden*. Edinburgh: Oliver and Boyd, 1964.

Greenberg, Herbert, *Quest for the Necessary: W.H. Auden and the Dilemma of*

Divided Consciousness. Cambridge, Massachusetts: Harvard University Press, 1968.

Hecht, Anthony, *The Hidden Law: The Poetry of W.H. Auden*. London and Cambridge, Massachusetts: Harvard University Press, 1993.

Hoggart, Richard, *Auden: An Introductory Essay*. London: Chatto and Windus; New Haven: Yale University Press, 1951.

Jacobs, Alan, *What Became of Wystan: Change and Continuity in Auden's Poetry*. Fayetteville: University of Arkansas Press, 1998.

Johnson, Richard, *Man's Place: An Essay on Auden*. Ithaca: Cornell University Press, 1973.

McDiarmid, Lucy, *Auden's Apologies for Poetry*. Princeton, N. J.: Princeton University Press, 1990.

Mendelson, Edward, *Early Auden*. London: Faber, 1981.

Mendelson, Edward, *Later Auden*. London: Faber, 1999.

Mitchell, Donald, *Britten and Auden in the Thirties: The Year 1936*. London: Faber and Faber, 1981.

Nelson, Gerald, *Changes of Heart: A Study of the Poetry of W.H. Auden*. Berkeley and Los Angeles: University of California Press, 1969.

Replogle, Justin, *Auden's Poetry*. London: Methuen, 1969.

Smith, Stan, *W.H. Auden*. Oxford: Blackwell, 1985.

Spears, Monroe K., *The Poetry of W.H. Auden: The Disenchanted Island*. New York: Oxford U.P., 1963.

Wright, George T., *W.H. Auden*. New York: Twayne, 1969.

Articles on Auden in Journals (cited in the main text)

Gingerich's Reference Guide is an invaluable resource up to 1976 as he gives a brief description of all articles, essays and books that he lists. After 1976 try searching on-line databases such as the MLA (Modern Language Association) and BIDS (Bath Information and Data Services) which are available at most University or College libraries. Also use the indexes and bibliographies of books on Auden as a resource.

Hynes, Samuel, 'The Voice of Exile: Auden in 1940', *Sewanee Review* XC.1, (Winter 1982): 31–52.

Megaw, Moira, 'Auden's First Poems', *Essays in Criticism* 25, iii, pp. 378–82.

Mendelson, Edward, 'Revision and Power: The Example of W.H. Auden', *Yale French Studies*, no.89, (1996), pp. 103–12.

Replogle, Justin, 'The Gang Myth in Auden's Early Poetry', *Journal of English and Germanic Philology*, 61 no. 3, (1962), pp. 481–95.

Collections of Essays, Criticism and Chapters from Books

Alvarez, A., *The Shaping Spirit*. London: Chatto and Windus, 1958.

Bayley, John, *The Romantic Survival*. London: Constable, 1957.

Bergonzi, Bernard, *Reading the Thirties*. London: Macmillan, 1978.

Bold, Alan, ed., *W.H. Auden: The Far Interior*. London: Vision Press, New Jersey: Barnes and Noble, 1985.

Brodsky, Joseph, *Less Than One: Selected Essays*. Harmondsworth: Penguin-Viking, 1986.

Brooks, Cleanth, *Modern Poetry and The Tradition*. Chapel Hill: University of North Carolina Press, 1939.

Davie, Donald, *Thomas Hardy and British Poetry*. London: Routledge and Kegan Paul, 1973.

Day-Lewis, C., *A Hope for Poetry*. Oxford: Basil Blackwell, 1934.

Ellis, Steve, *The English Eliot*. London: Routledge, 1991.

Everett, Barbara, *Poets in Their Time: Essays on English Poetry from Donne to Larkin*. London: Faber, 1986.

Fraser, G. S., *Vision and Rhetoric*. London: Faber and Faber, 1959.

Grigson, Geoffrey, ed., *Auden Double Number*, Spec. issue of *New Verse*, 26–27 (Nov. 1937): 1–47.

Jarrell, Randall, *Kipling, Auden & Co.: Essays and Reviews 1935–1964*. New York: Parrar, Straus and Giroux, 1980; Manchester: Carcanet Press, 1981.

Jarrell, Randall, *The Third Book of Criticism*. London: Faber, 1975. Includes 'Changes of Attitude and Rhetoric in Auden's Poetry', and 'Freud to Paul: The Stages of Auden's Ideology'.

Larkin, Philip, *Required Writing: Miscellaneous Pieces 1955–1982*. London: Faber, 1983.

Leavis, F. R., *New Bearings In English Poetry* (1932). 2nd edn., London: Chatto and Windus, 1950.

MacNeice, Louis, *Modern Poetry: A Personal Essay*. London: Oxford University Press, 1938.

Roberts, Michael, ed., *New Country: Prose and Poetry by the Authors of 'New Signatures'*. London: Hogarth, 1933.

——, ed., *New Signatures: Poems by Several Hands*. London: Hogarth, 1932.

Savage, D. S., 'The Strange Case of W.H. Auden' in *The Personal Principle*. London: Routledge, 1944.

Scarfe, Francis, *Auden and After: The Liberation of Poetry 1930–1941*. London: Routledge, 1942.

Sidnell, Michael, *Dances of Death: The Group Theatre of London in the Thirties*. London: Faber, 1984.

Spears, Monroe K., *Auden: A Collection of Critical Essays*. Englewood Cliffs, N.J.: Prentice-Hall, 1964.

Spender, Stephen, *The Destructive Element*. London: Jonathan Cape, 1935.

Trotter, David, *The Making of the Reader: Language and Subjectivity in Modern American, English and Irish Poetry*. London and Basingstoke: Macmillan, 1984.

Guides and Introductions

Fuller, John, *A Reader's Guide to W.H. Auden*. London: Thames and Hudson, 1970.

Fuller, John, *W.H. Auden: A Commentary*. London: Faber, 1998.

Rodway, Allan, *A Preface to Auden*. London: Longman, 1984.

Smith, Stan, *W.H. Auden*. 'Writers and their Work' series. Plymouth: Northcote House, 1997.

Books or Essays about the Thirties

Carter, Ronald, ed., *Thirties Poets: 'The Auden Group'*. Casebook Series, London and Basingstoke: Macmillan, 1984.

Caudwell, Christopher, *Illusion and Reality: A Study of the Sources of Poetry*. 1937. New. ed. London: Lawrence and Wishart, 1946.

Clark, Jon; Heinemann, Margot; Margolies, David; and Snee, Carole, eds., *Culture and Crisis in Britain in the 30s*. London: Lawrence and Wishart, 1979.

Connolly, Cyril, *Enemies of Promise*. 1938. Rev. ed. London: Andre Deutsch, 1988.

Cunningham, Valentine, *British Writers of the Thirties*. Oxford: Oxford U.P., 1989.

——, ed., *Spanish Front: Writers on the Civil War*. Oxford: O.U.P., 1986.

Gloversmith, Frank, ed., *Class, Culture and Social Change: A New View of the 1930s*. Sussex: Harvester, 1980.

Graves, R., and Hodge, A., *The Long Weekend: A Social History of Great Britain, 1918–1939*. London: Faber, 1940.

Grigson, Geoffrey, ed., *The Arts To-day*. London: Bodley Head, 1935.

Hoskins, Katherine, *Today the Struggle: Literature and Politics in England during the Spanish Civil War*. Austin: University of Texas Press, 1969.

Hynes, Samuel, *The Auden Generation: Literature and Politics in England in the 1930s*. London: Bodley Head, 1976; rpt. London: Faber and Faber, 1979.

Lucas, John, ed., *The 1930s: A Challenge to Orthodoxy*. Sussex: Harvester Press, 1978.

Maxwell, D.E.S., *Poets of the Thirties*. London: Routledge and Kegan Paul, 1969.

Montefiore, Janet, *Men and Women Writers of the 1930s*. London: Routledge, 1996.

Mulhern, Francis, *The Moment of 'Scrutiny'*. London: Verso, 1981.

O'Neill, Michael, and Reeves, Gareth, *Auden, MacNeice, Spender: The Thirties Poetry*. Basingstoke and London: Macmillan, 1992.

Orwell, George, 'Inside the Whale', *Collected Essays, Journalism, Letters. Vol 1. An Age Like This, 1920–1940*. London: Secker and Warburg, 1968.

Orwell, George, *The Road to Wigan Pier*. 1937. London: Secker and Warburg, 1973.

Skelton, Robin, ed., *Poetry of the Thirties*. Harmondsworth, Middlesex: Penguin, 1964.

Symons, Julian, *The Thirties: A Dream Revolved*. London: Cresset Press, 1960; rev. edn., London: Faber and Faber, 1975.

Tolley, A.T., *The Poetry of the Thirties*. London: Gollancz, 1975.

Williams, Keith, and Matthews, Steven, eds., *Rewriting the Thirties: Modernism and After*. London: Longman, 1997.

General

Ansen, Alan, *The Table Talk of W.H. Auden*. 1989. London: Faber, 1991.

Auden, W.H., and Garrett, John, *The Poet's Tongue*. London: Bell, 1935.

Barthes, Roland, *Image Music Text*. 1977. Trans. Stephen Heath. London: Fontana, 1984.

Clark, Thekla, *Wystan and Chester: A Personal Memoir of W.H. Auden and Chester Kallman*. London: Faber, 1995.

Day-Lewis, C., *A Hope for Poetry*. Oxford: Basil Blackwell, 1934.

Eliot, T.S., *After Strange Gods*. New York: Harcourt, Brace and Company, 1934.

——, 'Tradition and the Individual Talent', *The Sacred Wood*. 1920. London: Methuen, 1960.

Farnan, Dorothy J., *Auden in Love*. London: Faber, 1985.

Isherwood, Christopher, *Christopher and his Kind: 1929–1939*. London: Methuen, 1977.

Isherwood, Christopher, *Lions and Shadows: An Education in the Twenties*. London: Hogarth Press, 1938.

Kierkegaard, Søren, *Fear and Trembling: Repetition*. Kierkegaard's Writings. Ed. and trans. Howard V. Hong and Edna H. Hong. New Jersey: Princeton University Press, 1983.

Norse, Harold, *Memoirs of a Bastard Angel*. London: Bloomsbury, 1990.

Rowse, A.L., *The Poet Auden: A Personal Memoir*. London: Methuen, 1987.

Spender, Stephen, *World Within World*. London: Hamish Hamilton, 1951.

ACKNOWLEDGEMENTS

The editor and publisher wish to thank the following for their permission to reprint copyright material: Blackwell (for material from *W.H. Auden*); Faber (for material from 'Changes of Attitude and Rhetoric in Auden's Poetry', in *The Third Book of Criticism*; the 'Introduction' to *W.H. Auden: Juvenilia. Poems 1922–1928*; *The Auden Generation: Literature and Politics in the 1930s; Dances of Death: The Group Theatre of London in the Thirties*; 'What's Become of Wystan?', in *Required Writing* [Philip Larkin]: *Miscellaneous Pieces 1955–1982*; and 'Reading', in *The Dyer's Hand*); Cornell University Press (for material from *Reading Auden: The Returns of Caliban*); Princeton University Press (for material from *The Poetic Art of W.H. Auden* and *Auden's Apologies for Poetry*); Constable (for material from *The Romantic Survival*); Prentice-Hall (for material from the 'Introduction', 'Auden's *New Year Letter*: A New Style of Architecture', and 'The Career of W.H. Auden', in *Auden: A Collection of Critical Essays*); Routledge (for material from *W.H. Auden: The Critical Heritage; The English Eliot; Men and Women Writers of the 1930s*; and 'The Hawk's Eye', in *Thomas Hardy and British Poetry*); Jonathan Cape (for material from *The Destructive Element*); Macmillan (for material from the 'Introduction' to *Thirties Poets: 'The Auden Group'; Auden, MacNeice, Spender: The Thirties Poetry*; and *The Making of the Reader: Language and Subjectivity in Modern American, English and Irish Poetry*); Harvester Press (for material from 'Letters from Iceland: Going North', in *The 1930s: A Challenge to Orthodoxy*); Lawrence and Wishart (for material from 'W.H. Auden: Poetry and Politics in the Thirties', in *Culture and Crisis in Britain in the 30s*); Penguin-Viking (for material from 'On "September 1, 1939" by W.H. Auden', in *Less Than One: Selected Essays of Joseph Brodsky*); Vision Press (for material from 'Auden's Political Vision', in *W.H. Auden: The Far Interior*); *Sewanee Review* (for material from 'The Voice of Exile: Auden in 1940'); Oxford University Press (for material from 'The Shift in Perspective', in *The Poetry of W.H. Auden: The Disenchanted Island*; and *Auden: A Carnival of Intellect*); *Yale French Studies* (for material from 'Revision and Power: The Example of W.H. Auden'); University of Minnesota Press (for material from *The Making of the Auden Canon*); *London Review of Books* (for material from 'What Kind of Guy?').

There are instances where we have been unable to trace or contact copyright holders before our printing deadline. If notified, the publisher will be pleased to acknowledge the use of copyright material.

The editor would like to thank Min Wild for reading through a draft of the commentary and suggesting changes, and Sue Inskip for tracing some elusive references.

Paul Hendon has written on the painter Paul Nash and on the 1951 Festival of Britain. He is currently working on a book on W.H. Auden.

INDEX